THUNDER IN THE MOUNTAINS

THUNDER
in the Mountains

*The West Virginia
Mine War,
1920–21*

LON SAVAGE

UNIVERSITY OF PITTSBURGH PRESS

In memory of Ellen

Published 1990 by the University of Pittsburgh Press, Pittsburgh, Pa. 15261
Originally published 1985 by Jalamap Publications, Inc.
Copyright © 1986, 1990, Lon Savage
All rights reserved
Manufactured in the United States of America
Printed on acid-free paper
10   9   8   7   6

Library of Congress Cataloging-in-Publication Data

Savage, Lon, 1928–
      Thunder in the mountains : the West Virginia mine war, 1920–21 /
   Lon Savage.
            p.   cm. – (Pittsburgh series in social and labor history)
      Originally published: Jalamap Publications, 1985.
      Includes bibliographical references.
      ISBN 0-8229-3634-8. – ISBN 0-8229-5426-5 (pbk.)
      1. Coal Strike, W. Va., 1920–1921.   I. Title.   II. Series.
   HD 5325.M631920
   [.W47   1989]
   331.89'282334'097543–dc20   89-39087
                                                                        CIP

Contents

Foreword　　vii

Introduction　　ix

Acknowledgments　　xvii

1.　"On to Mingo"　　3

2.　Everyone called him "Sid"　　10

3.　The Battle of Matewan　　19

4.　"We have organized all the camps"　　25

5.　"The most complete deadlock of any industrial struggle"　　32

6.　"It's good to have friends"　　42

7.　"Our citizens are being shot down like rats"　　50

8.　". . . to clean up Mingo County"　　55

9.　"You saw nothing wrong in that?"　　64

10.　"Don't shoot him any more!"　　68

11.　"There can be no peace"　　72

12.　"We'll hang Don Chafin to a sour apple tree!"　　76

13.　"No armed mob will cross Logan County"　　81

14.　"It's your real Uncle Sam"　　86

15.　"By God, we're goin' through"　　90

16.　"We wouldn't revolt against the national guv'ment"　　98

CONTENTS

17. "The thugs are coming" 102
18. "There was a different feeling" 106
19. "I, Warren G. Harding . . . do hereby command" 111
20. "Bring your raincoats and machine guns" 114
21. "Bullets were hissing back and forth" 119
22. "Things slacked off after we ate" 130
23. "These strange new craft" 142
24. "The miners have withdrawn their lines" 147
25. "It was Uncle Sam did it" 160

Epilogue 165
Notes 169
Bibliography 183
Index 189

Foreword

John Sayles

HISTORY is a picture filtered through the lenses of time, language, and point of view. The history of the moment, of the daily headline, has immediacy and heat but can often lack the depth and accumulation of detail a later look can provide. Language can alter the perception of an incident without altering the "facts," can turn "striking workers" into "unemployed rioters" and back again with a brushstroke. As for point of view, accounts of an event vary not only with the witnesses' physical perception of the instant but also their political and philosophical perception of the world and of human nature itself. History is a tricky story that depends on who is telling it and where they're coming from.

I first heard stories of the coal wars of the twenties, of the Matewan Massacre and the Battle of Blair Mountain, by word of mouth from coal miners and their relatives as I hitchhiked through West Virginia. Some years later I wrote a screenplay for a movie called *Matewan* based on what I'd heard and what little I could find that was written about it. Most of this came from people on one side or the other of the union struggle, people who were there in the thick of the fight and chose their words as weapons in a battle still raging. But as history usually belongs to the winners, and the story of the coal wars is largely that of people who lost and continue to lose, it was a story more often told in ballads and folktales than in the pages of library books.

As we began shooting the movie, we discovered Lon Savage's *Thunder in the Mountains.* For the first time I felt there was someone with a feel for the people and place who had gone out and done the legwork, had tracked down the stray bits of story, poked and probed at what was already on the record, and dug up whatever new information was available. Savage recognizes that if history is a mirror it is a broken one, not one perception of the truth but hundreds of them, odd-shaped fragments of memory that must all be examined to form some kind of coherent story. The story Lon Savage tells is a dramatic and important one, as much a part of our heritage as that of the Alamo or Gettysburg or the winning of the West. It is the story of people who pulled a hard living from a hard land, people who lived under the heel of power and who finally could be pushed only so far.

One of the questions that led me to this story was that of political violence. Though the Battle of Blair Mountain ended in a tactical and political defeat for the miners who took up arms there, the psychological victory of those violent days may have been more important. When a colonized people learn they can fight back together, life can never again be so comfortable for their exploiters. And if people's deeds last beyond their lives, it is partly through the stories we tell about them. With *Thunder in the Mountains,* Lon Savage helps give shape to those lives, to those times, and brings us a story too long untold.

Introduction

John Williams

T HE W EST V IRGINIA mine wars—and particularly their cli-
mactic episode, the miners' march on Logan in August and September 1921—make for a rousing good story, and no one has
told it as well or as fully as Lon Savage does in *Thunder in the
Mountains*. Drawing on his years of experience as a professional
journalist, Savage has written a masterful narrative, full of apt
description and colorful characterizations, yet based solidly on
the historical record.

History is more than a story, however. Historians ask why
as well as how events happened. Approached from this angle,
the mine wars and the march on Logan appear as episodes in
larger narratives. They were episodes in American labor and
business history and in the social and cultural history of Appalachia and of West Virginia, the Appalachian region's prototypi-
cal state.

An essential first step toward understanding these episodes
is to understand the place of the West Virginia coal industry
in that American economy and in the nation's labor relations
during the first decades of the twentieth century. American industry ran on coal in 1921. So did the nation's railroads and
streetcars (the latter through coal-fired, steam-generated electri-
cal power). Most homes and businesses were heated by coal.
It was therefore always puzzling to observers that this essential
commodity did not confer wealth and stability on the people
and communities that drew their livelihood from coal. Far from
it. Coal communities were impoverished and disorderly, and coal

companies competed in a market which seemed to spiral end-lessly between boom and bust. In this age of emergent Big Business, there was no U.S. coal corporation of comparable scope to giants like Standard Oil, U.S. Steel, or General Motors. The four largest coal companies in the country controlled less than six percent of the market in 1920. West Virginia's four largest coal companies accounted for less than fourteen percent of the Mountain State's production.[1]

A simple fact accounted for the paradox of coal. It was an essential commodity, but it was also plentiful in the United States. The richest markets for coal were the Northeast and Midwest, in the growing industrial cities of the Atlantic seaboard and the Great Lakes. The "river trade" of coal barged to Cincinnati, St. Louis, and other Mississippi Valley cities provided a third market, although a much smaller one than the "seaboard" and "lake" trades. West Virginia industries consumed only a small proportion of the state's output, but many of the coal-consuming states — Pennsylvania, Maryland, Ohio, Indiana, and Illinois — also had mines of their own. In fact, of the major coal-consuming regions, only New England lacked local mines. And even New England could have imported coal more cheaply from Canadian mines in neighboring Nova Scotia were it not for tariff barriers that West Virginia politicians had worked hard to erect and maintain.[2]

Some southern West Virginia mines produced coal of superior steam-raising qualities, and so succeeded in capturing what today we would call a "niche" market, like the bunker coal market for large seagoing vessels. (The proximity of West Virginia coal was one of the factors that made Norfolk the country's greatest naval base during this era.)[3] But generally — except in boom times — West Virginia coal competed at a disadvantage in all three of the major coal trades, owing to the fact that the state's mines were more distant than competing mines from the biggest markets on the seaboard, lakes, and rivers. This meant that the transportation costs of West Virginia producers were higher. Since the only other significant factor in the wholesale price of coal was the cost of mining it, this geographic pattern led to consistent downward pressure on the wages of West Virginia miners. Only if their wage bill were smaller could West Virginia's coal producers gain and keep a share of the national coal market proportionate to the state's share of the nation's bituminous coal reserves.

Another factor that shaped the outlook of West Virginia coal producers was their dependence on the railroads. Prior to the canalization of the Ohio and Kanawha rivers, most West Virginia coal traveled all or part of the way to market over the rails. There was no rail competition at the mine mouth, and even those producers who had managed to take advantage of railroad competition once their coal cars reached places where competing lines crossed found their options limited after 1900 as northeastern and midwestern railroads consolidated into a few large corporations and the price of transportation came increasingly to be administered by federal regulators. Moreover, all but the largest producers were dependent upon the railroads for coal cars or gondolas. Nothing reduced producers and miners to feelings of angry frustration more than to have a mine shut down during the height of the fall stockpiling season because of a shortage of "gons."[4]

It is also important to note that the demand for coal was inelastic relative both to prices and the national economy. Lowering the price of coal did not increase demand during periods of sluggish national economic growth, and after 1910 coal began to lose ground in the national energy market to fuel oil, hydroelectric power, and natural gas. Only during periods of extraordinary economic boom did coal producers and workers enjoy the prosperity which had once seemed guaranteed to them. The era of World War I was one such period, but by 1921 the coal boom associated with the war was over. During the next two years, the number of days that the average miner could count on working each year fell to 142 days, compared with a 1918 peak of 249. During the next fifty years, total national demand for bituminous coal rose only one percent, compared with 662 percent for crude petroleum and 2,589 percent for natural gas.[5] Thus, the violence in West Virginia was symptomatic both of a sharp short-run downturn in the coal industry and the onset of long-term stagnation.

The outlook of union men was shaped by many of the same geographic and economic factors that influenced coal producers. The United Mine Workers of America had originated in the

Midwest in 1890, and the union's headquarters remained in Indianapolis until it moved to Washington in 1933. Wage contracts negotiated in the Central Competitive Field, consisting of the mining districts of Illinois, Indiana, Ohio, and western Pennsylvania, were the yardstick against which coal prices and wages of other regions were measured. The union's leaders were from Pennsylvania or the Midwest, and union contracts signed with Central Field coal producers pledged the union to organizing drives in West Virginia and eastern Kentucky so as to prevent low-priced coal from these states from undercutting the price of union-mined coal from the Central Field. Beginning in the mid-1890s, the UMWA mounted a sustained effort which fitfully but steadily pushed the frontier of union organization southward through West Virginia. Frequently this drive was accompanied by violence, notably in the Cabin Creek–Paint Creek Mine War in the Kanawha coal field east of Charleston in 1912–13. Patriotic fervor and government edict called a halt to further organizing during World War I, but the war also brought high wages and plenty of work. In the immediate postwar era, union leaders were determined to hold the line on wages and to push the boundary between union and nonunion mines further south, through the Logan, Mingo, and Pocahontas coalfields along West Virginia's southern border. Coal producers in these districts were equally determined to resist.[6]

It is easy to see now that neither union organizers nor coal producers were realistic in their postwar aims. The conditions spawned by World War I had indeed been extraordinary. Without the war, coal production might have entered into a prolonged but perhaps more peaceful period of stagnation owing to the inroads of competing fuels in the energy markets. Instead, the war induced a feverish export boom. With French, Belgian, and German coal mines in or near the path of the contending armies, European wartime demand for coal soared past the level of the remaining European mines and manpower to produce it. American exports soared and for once–thanks to the recently expanded coal handling ports of Norfolk and Newport News–the mines of southern West Virginia faced no geographic handicap in grabbing their share. U.S. bituminous coal production peaked at 579 million tons in 1918, of which some ninety million tons came from West Virginia.[7] Postwar dislocation in Europe sustained the boom for a few years after the war, but by 1921 the export boom was over and the domestic market was unable to absorb the excess productive capacity that the war had called into being. By 1923, the U.S. market for coal was down to less than half of what the nation was capable of producing. Prices fell accordingly and this increased the pressure on wages. West Virginia's characteristic position in the domestic coal market guaranteed that the effects of this change would be felt early and sharply in the Mountain State, particularly in southern West Virginia in precisely those counties along the union/nonunion frontier.

There was a nationwide recession—as we would now call it—in 1920 and 1921, and there were strikes in many other industries as workers and union leaders tried to hold on to the gains they had made during the war.[8] The West Virginia coal fields were therefore not exceptional in this regard. What *was* exceptional was the ferocity of the struggle and the character of the violence that ensued. Neutral and partisan observers alike compared the violence in West Virginia to civil war. The comparison was perhaps inevitable, but misleading.

The state of West Virginia was of course the product of civil war, and the stamp of irregular warfare and social violence is deep on its history and legend. Fifty years before the mine wars broke out, the coal fields of southern West Virginia had formed part of a rugged and thinly populated "interior" (as it was known to the residents of Ohio Valley towns). The interior had been a no-man's-land for the regular armies and a theater of guerrilla combat during the Civil War. A generation later, many of the same districts witnessed a determined and occasionally violent federal crusade against moonshining, as well as the celebrated outbreak of private warfare known as the Hatfield-McCoy feud.[9] Observers have tried to explain this pattern of violence in a number of ways, notably as some sort of outgrowth of regional character.[10] The presence of members of extended families such as the Hatfields in each of the episodes lends credence to such explanations, but accounting for the continuity does not require explanations grounded in personalities or the supposed psychological traits of mountain people. Notwithstanding the involvement of men such as Sid Hatfield or Don Chafin who bore time-honored local names, most of the participants in the mine wars were new men, and the communities over whose future they struggled were as raw and new as frontier outposts. The continuity of the mine wars with earlier violent episodes of West Virginia history lay not with individuals or character but with issues, particularly the fundamental issue of who would control West Virginia's interior and who would profit from the development of its natural resources.

The coal boom of World War I and the preceding booms which punctuated the opening of the West Virginia interior to industrial development had naturally been accompanied by population booms. Southern West Virginia's population as a whole quadrupled between 1890 and 1920; the growth rate in coalfield counties such as Logan, McDowell, and Mingo was twice as high.[11] It was in fact by just such statistics that the people who flocked into the coal fields to open banks and law offices or to teach school or to sell dry goods or insurances or hardware or dental services measured their hopes and success. Dozens of new towns and hundreds of coal "camps" sprang up in southern West Virginia between 1890 and 1920. Each town had its complement of union men among the railroad workers or carpenters and each had its representatives of old families (among whom it was not uncommon to find a disproportionate share of office holders) who looked askance at the changes taking place around them. But both of these groups were far outnumbered by ambitious and optimistic newcomers, "people who live in two-story houses," as one journalist put it, overlooking the new bottomland towns and creekside coal tipples and miners' shacks. This middle class had supported modest reforms designed to prevent the worst labor abuses and tax evasions during the progressive first decade of the century. But its members reacted with intense hostility to the surge of union militancy after the war and particularly to the socialist rhetoric which sometimes accompanied it. Don Chafin and the other antiunion sheriffs of southern West Virginia had no lack of middle-class volunteers to man their militias. Had the federal government not succeeded in quashing the violence, southern West Virginia would have seen an outbreak of class warfare that was eager and bitter on both sides.[12]

The marching miners were likewise new men. While many of the leaders indicted for treason in the aftermath of the Logan March bore the names of long-settled West Virginia families, the marchers also carried the Irish and Welsh immigrant names which had populated the coalfields for a generation, and there were representatives of the Italian, Greek, and Slavic immigrants who had surged into southern West Virginia after 1900 and of the blacks who had come to the coalfields from the Virginia and North Carolina Piedmont. It was one of the union's great achievements to have forged a degree of unity among a heterogenous working population thrown together only recently and under adverse circumstances. And though this unity was fragile and sporadic, its memory was fortified by the many tellings and re-tellings of the events of 1921 and helped to bring into existence the more militant and enduring miners' unity that emerged during the 1930s.[13]

The character of the Appalachian coalfield community was another factor in shaping the character of the mine wars. A federal study completed in 1924 showed that eighty percent of West Virginia miners lived in company-owned towns, compared with nine percent in Indiana and Illinois. In southern West Virginia this proportion was even higher. Like the population mix, this pattern was an outgrowth of industrialization in a previously thinly populated country. It had been necessary to provide housing and other services in order to attract workers to newly opened mines, and it was also profitable to do so in most cases. But this meant that mine owners and miners confronted one another not only as employers and workers, but as landlords and tenants and as the purveyors and consumers of goods and services. This compounded the social tensions arising out of economics and labor relations and helps to explain why the worst violence – like the worst housing and the worst working conditions in the industry – seemed always to be found in the Appalachian states.[14]

The events which Lon Savage relates with such verve and skill were thus the product both of local forces and of national and world events. World War I was important not only because of the collapse of the export boom that shaped the goals of both sides in the mine wars, but because of its effect on individual outlooks and actions. Military training taught the rudiments of military discipline to those who had previously shouldered a gun only for hunting. Savage's account, like the newspaper dispatches at the time, emphasizes the importance of veterans among the miners as well as among the middle-class volunteers. But, unlike the contemporary press, his account places this factor in perspective, pointing out that the miners' military experience was not enough to lend much order to their movements beyond the much-publicized drilling sessions and the operations of handfuls of men. There were no generals among the miners, notwithstanding the authorities' subsequent hunt for conspirators. There were only angry men, determined to do something, but unable—apart from commandeering trains and automobiles and digging trenches along the ridgetops—to figure out quite what to do.

The recent experience of war was a greater advantage to the other side. There were veterans among the state police and local vigilantes, and the war both directly occasioned and indirectly shaped the federal intervention that ended the march. The fact that West Virginia's National Guard had not been reorganized following its wartime federalization accounted for the frantic and eventually successful pleas of Governor Morgan for federal troops. The intervention of federal troops in labor confrontations was not in itself unprecedented, but the attempted use of Army Air Service planes was. Fresh from his triumphant demonstration that bombs could sink battleships, General Billy Mitchell saw in the West Virginia conflict an opportunity to demonstrate the value of air power in civil disturbances. Given the conservative mood in this first decade following the Bolshevik Revolution in Russia, and the aborted worker insurrections which followed in Central and Eastern Europe, Mitchell correctly gauged that this prospect would appeal to his superiors, and so off the bombers went, heading for disaster en route.[15] If it had not been for the comic execution, Mitchell's scheme would have been thrown into a much more sinister light by later events, for in its plan to use air power against civilians, it was nothing less than a foretaste of Guernica, Dresden, and Hiroshima in the West Virginia hills.

Acknowledgments

T HIS BOOK is the product of research done mostly in the 1970s, prior to its first appearance as a paperback, when I spent years combing through records and talking to persons who knew of, or had access to information about the West Virginia mine war of 1920–21. In 1989, preparing for its publication in this updated and more complete version, I was able to talk to several additional persons, to fill in a few gaps in the previous treatment.

The first person to help me was my late father, Joe Savage, who participated in the mine war (on the governor's side) and who told his children stories of it as we grew up. He actually did some research about the mine war himself and wrote a story of his involvement in it, a story that was not published until after this book made its first appearance and after he had died. A second person who also helped make this book possible, and who also did not live to see it published, was my first wife, Ellen, who gave much encouragement in her final years of life. My current wife, Ginny, has been of inestimable encouragement and assistance in the preparation of this second version.

While updating this book for its current appearance, I was fortunate to meet several persons whom I did not know in the earlier preparation and who helped in filling in a few holes in the narrative. They include Jack Testerman of Naugatuck, West Virginia, who was five years old when his father, Mayor C. C. Testerman, was shot to death in the Battle of Matewan; ten days later his mother married Sid Hatfield, who might be called the hero of this story. Another is Paul J. Lively of Tucker, Georgia, who, although born after these events took place, made available valuable records and photographs about his father, Charlie Lively, one of the men who killed Sid Hatfield. Both of these gentlemen spoke freely and without rancor of the events that carried so much bitterness for their parents.

Others who played an important part in helping me to fill gaps in the photographic and documented record of these events were Christy Venham of the West Virginia and Regional History Collection of the West Virginia University Library in Morgantown; C. Paul McAllister, Jr., Director of the Matewan Development Center – who rapidly is becoming a fount of information about these events, and Marat Moore of the *UMW Journal*.

Back in the 1970s, when most of this research was done, I received help from so many that I hesitate to cite names. One who helped me enormously was Marshall Fishwick, who provided advice, criticism, and encouragement. I must also express appreciation to John Duray, who was then with the *UMW Journal;* John A. Cuthbert and Mary Markey, then curators of the West Virginia and Regional History Collection at the West Virginia University Library; Frank M. Allara Sr., chairman of the board of the Matewan National Bank and a witness to some of the events described here; William C. Blizzard of Beckley, West Virginia, son of the man some said was the "general" of the miners' army; Jesse Boyd, one of the striking miners who stood trial with Sid Hatfield for participation in the Matewan battle; Lydia Hansbarger of Charleston, West Virginia, who was a child in Matewan at the time of the battle; and her mother, the late Mrs. H. Sol White, who was postmistress of Matewan at the time of the battle; Allen Hatfield of Beech Creek in Mingo County, who talked of coal mining life in the first two decades of this century; Don Hatfield of Freeburn, Kentucky, who knew Sid Hatfield; Emory Cornelius Lewis of Matewan, a mine foreman who was involved in many of the events which are related here; Willard Smith of Matewan, a striking coal miner who witnessed the Matewan battle and took part in many of the other events described in this book; Earl Stafford of Blackberry City, West Virginia, whose family was involved in the Mingo events; J. Hence Varney of Matewan, a former coal miner with a good memory about life in general during these events; and others who gave interviews in the early 1960s for my father's research: C. Frank Keeney, George Coyle, Francis Roller, Grant Hall, John Charnock, and James W. Martin, all of whom I believe lived in and around Charleston at that time. Finally, I want to say a special word of thanks to Harry Lynch and David Bice who brought this book out in its earliest form.

I must also express special appreciation to the professional staff of the Newman Library at Virginia Polytechnic Institute and State University in Blacksburg, who gave unselfishly of their time and professional knowledge in locating and securing books, records, documents, newspapers, and other sources from which this book was written. Special thanks go to Dorothy McCombs, who recently retired from that library, and Robert E. Molyneux, who has gone on to other challenges in the library field, both of whom went to extra efforts to help me. I also want to say thanks to the employees of the town of Matewan, the city of Williamson, and the counties of Mingo in West Virginia and Pike in Kentucky, who helped in locating records.

THUNDER IN THE MOUNTAINS

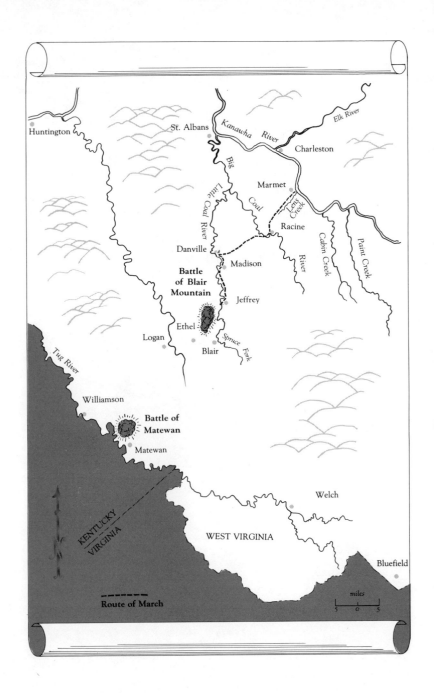

1

"On to Mingo"

IN AUGUST of 1921, West Virginia's miners began pouring into Lens Creek Valley near Charleston. They came first in hundreds and then in thousands. They overflowed the seats, aisles, vestibules, and even engine tenders of incoming trains. Nearly a thousand miners arrived on a single train at Cabin Creek Junction, and formed an armed mob that moved forward like a swarm of angry bees.

All day men walked along mountain roads, carrying guns and packs. Others rode in big spoke-wheeled cars that bumped over rocky roads or through creeks, hub deep in water. In some places the creek was the road. Some few came on horses or in wagons pulled by mules. All converged on Lens Creek, the starting place for their march.

Guns bristled everywhere. Men carried revolvers in their belts, Winchesters in their arms, bandoliers across their chests, old army Springfields slung over their shoulders, some with bayonets attached. Many wore their army uniforms, jackets and breeches and wrap-around leggings, and some buckled on their old World War I steel helmets. As their numbers grew, they showed up increasingly in a uniform for a miners' army: blue bib overalls with red neckerchiefs.

They were muscular, grizzled men, natives of West Virginia hollows who had joined the miners' union, emotional men who spoke their hearts in robust Appalachian dialect: men like Bill Blizzard, a square-jawed young Irishman who had led the miners at Paint Creek nearly a decade before; Savoy Holt, a fiery

3

young militant from Ward who had been to see the governor; and Walter Allen of Dry Branch who led his union local to Lens Creek. Many were black, the children of former slaves who had come to the coalfields from worn-out tobacco farms and cotton fields, and they marched, as they had worked in the mines, alongside the whites. Though most were young, veterans of decades in West Virginia's mines also came, their gray-stubbled faces appearing older than their years.

Along Lens Creek they pitched camp beneath the oak trees and talked of Baldwin-Felts thugs and martial law, of miners jailed without charge, and of Sid Hatfield's death.

"They gunned him down in cold blood," a miner said. "Shot him down like a dog."

Sid's best friend, Ed Chambers, also had been killed.

"They killed 'em in front of their wives," the miners said.

For three weeks the story of the brutal slayings had spread through the mining camps and union halls, and miners flocked to mass meetings.

They came from Kelly's Creek, where Savoy Holt had told them they must "gather across the river. The time for action has arrived."

They came from Longacre on the Kanawha River, where a young miner shouted his speech in the rain: "Now it is up to us. If you are men, you will be there, prepared and instructed."

At Laurel City, they read a message from Frank Keeney, district president of the miners' union: "Every drop of blood and every dollar of the union will be spent in the attempt to lift martial law in Mingo County," and the miners cheered.

"On to Mingo!"

At scores of gritty mining camps in West Virginia's southern mountains, miners streamed from their board-and-battened cabins and headed down the hollows. From Glen Jean and Marfork and Boomer some five hundred set out on foot to join the miners' army. At Montcoal and Ameagle they came with fifteen hundred dollars in union funds.

At the mining camp of Dry Branch, where Walter Allen was in charge, the men were orderly. They took a vote; the motion carried, and they set out, guns in hand.

But at Edwight, things got out of hand. Miners cheered and

yelled and shot their guns into the night sky, and they robbed five hundred dollars from the local union's burial fund. When a state policeman came to investigate, they shot him in the chest and left the officer critically wounded.

On Saturday, August 20, miners milled through the encampment along Lens Creek, publicly proclaiming their march on Mingo, and roads to Lens Creek were clogged with more.

They organized themselves. Blizzard, the subdistrict president of the UMWA, was only twenty-eight, but he had been leading the miners since their uprising in 1912–13, and they obeyed when he directed them to resting spots on Lens Creek. Ed Reynolds, who arrived from Monmouth with two hundred dollars in union funds, found himself leading a force of three hundred men. Savoy Holt presided from a buggy in appointing a finance committee. Men yelled names from the crowd: "Walter Allen," "U. S. Cantley," "Dee Munsey."

"You couldn't get three better men," Holt shouted back, and they, plus Holt, were elected by acclamation.

Still, there weren't enough. Miners went back home to get more. At Leevale two men went through camp yelling, "If you fellows don't turn out, there's enough down there and we will come and get you!" At the railroad depot at Whitesville, twenty armed miners, calling themselves "the Coal River Hellcats," jumped off a train, answered roll call, and marched off to spread the word: if union men didn't show up at Lens Creek, they had better not be home when the marchers returned.

And the drumfire continued, orchestrated by the miners' union.

"MEN HAVE BEEN AND ARE BEING JAILED WITHOUT DUE PROCESS OF LAW," screamed a union leaflet.

"Miners have been murdered by the Baldwin-Felts detectives and gunmen of the corporations!"

"They shot Sid down like a dog on the courthouse steps at Welch!"

"Strikers' leaders have been indicted, jailed, and murdered!"

"Down with the hired murderers!"

"Stand by the miners of Mingo!"

"On to Mingo!"

A mob of miners marched down the track along the Kanawha,

swarming aboard every trolley until the drivers pulled away, leaving men running and shouting behind.

Three hundred miners with train tickets, finding passenger trains swamped, commandeered a freight train at gunpoint and rode it into Cabin Creek Junction, carefully giving their tickets to the yardmaster.

Men chartered trucks and wagons, loaded them with provisions, and headed for Lens Creek. They hailed taxis, pointed revolvers at the drivers, and gave their destination: Lens Creek. When a teamster refused to carry supplies with his horse and wagon, a black miner displayed a gun. "Throw the harness on and come on," the miner said, and the teamster obeyed.

The number of miners on Lens Creek reached two thousand by Monday, four thousand Tuesday, and by Wednesday estimates ranged from five to thirteen thousand men spread for eight miles along the creek, ready for the word from where no one knew to march on Mingo and avenge Sid Hatfield's death.

No one seemed in charge. They were held together loosely by their union organizations, solidly by their anger. They were unsophisticated men, thin-skinned, thick-headed, emotional, gullible, fierce in loyalty, dangerous in hatred. They were so straightforward that they might kill a man rather than dissemble. Although many were churchgoing Christians, they included a few exconvicts and still others who would be in prison except for good luck. Some were ignorant; most were unlearned; but many, too, were bright, alert, and perceptive.

They felt, rather than knew, their history. Their grandfathers had stood by—even helped—as outsiders stripped the timber from their mountains and floated it off on streams. Their fathers had stood by—even signed papers—as outsiders took the minerals from beneath their mountains and carried it off on trains. They had gone into the mines to do the work few outsiders wanted. As coal prospered, they lived on company land in company cabins, shopped in company stores, worshipped in company churches, died in company hospitals, were buried in company cemeteries. Their lore was bloody: they had been crushed and killed on their jobs and fired from them when they tried to organize a union that could articulate their needs. They had been evicted from their company homes and machine-gunned in their union tents. Periodically they had risen in fury.

Now it was Sid Hatfield's death that had set them off again. It was time to take charge by force. They would march to Mingo County, overrun the entire southern quarter of the state, drive out the thugs, free the miners, install their union. Or something like that. No one was sure, but they knew enough to act.

Kanawha County Sheriff Henry Walker entered the Lens Creek encampment and summoned the courage to order the miners to disband. They ignored him. Back in Charleston, ten miles away, the sheriff told the governor the situation was beyond his control. With no National Guard and with only one hundred state policemen in the entire state, the governor told frantic callers it was beyond his, too.

All over southern West Virginia mines closed. The rows of cabins in the mining camps were deserted except for women, children, and a few lame old men, and they talked only of Sid Hatfield's death and the vengeance that was beginning.

Two Charleston newspapermen got into the encampment and found it strangely peaceful, as in the eye of a hurricane. Men with rifles walked about, talking of everyday affairs. Cars were scattered through the woods; horses were tied to trees. Men threw dice, calling "Baby needs shoes," and "Come Sweet Phoebe." Some ate watermelon by the creek. Some cooked beans over open fires. Then, three armed men hustled the reporters away, and one of them, a whiskered miner with a .44 six-shooter, explained: "We are a committee which has been told to ask you to get off the grounds. We don't want nothin' about this in the papers. There's no hard feelings." He extended his hand and smiled.

Leaders spoke from the backs of trucks and wagons and told how Sid and Ed were defenseless when they were killed, how Mingo's miners were herded into jail like animals, how their families were forced from their homes at gunpoint. Some had been to the funeral and had seen the anguish of the two young widows.

Blacks among the miners recruited men and raised money. A black miner had been among those who stood with Sid against the coal operators in Mingo County, and blacks, like whites, were in Mingo County's jail. A leader made speeches along the creek to the black miners: If the white people got guns, he said, blacks had better get them too.

Miners formed military-like companies, organized around their union locals, and put out armed guards to halt traffic. A passing farmer was stopped so often it took him hours to get through. A motorist described the miners: "They mean business. They are the meanest looking gang I ever saw. Not two out of ten but have the Winchester rifle over their shoulders and big calibered revolvers stuck in their waistbands or slung in their holsters." Miners marched and countermarched under direction of men in uniform, and wagon after wagon hauled supplies into the camp. One miner stroked a .45 revolver in his shoulder holster and said he would put "forty nicks in this baby" before he got back from Mingo.

In neighborhoods around the encampment, squawking chickens disappeared from coops, and vegetables silently vanished from gardens. A salesmen from Baltimore stepped from a train at Marmet and was ordered at gunpoint to leave town. A deputy constable was robbed on the encampment's outskirts. Several Marmet residents praised the men's behavior, but they spoke too soon.

A twin cockpit plane flew low over the encampment to take pictures, and scores of miners opened fire on it. Several bullets struck the aircraft, one only inches from the pilot.

Marauders robbed company stores at nearby mines. A knock late in the night brought Josiah Keeley, a mine company executive, to his door, and masked men marched him at gunpoint down the road to his company store where they helped themselves to guns, ammunition, and supplies. Others broke into homes of coal company officials and made off with guns and ammunition.

A group of miners returned to the encampment with a Gatling gun and five thousand rounds of ammunition, and machine guns were reported stolen from a Cabin Creek company store. Other miners reported bringing in a machine gun stolen from Baldwin-Felts detectives the year before. They would be ready for heavy fighting.

A half dozen nurses, the wives of union miners, appeared in camp on Tuesday, outfitted in white uniforms and caps, their local union numbers on their caps in place of red crosses. They would tend the wounded, and they brought bandages, iodine and thermometers.

National newspapers front-paged the story, and Charleston's printed little else. A report that the men would march on Charleston set off a near panic, and police rushed to the east end of town before the report proved false.

In the Charleston headquarters of the United Mine Workers, District President Frank Keeney watched approvingly as the uprising developed. Although he and his staff unquestionably had helped to organize the rebellion, he acted as if he had nothing to do with it: "I wash my hands of the whole affair," Keeney said. "I've interfered time and again. . . . This time they can march to Mingo as far as I'm concerned."

Heber Blankenhorn, veteran labor writer for *The Nation*, made his way into the encampment and talked to miners.

"You heard of Sid Hatfield and Ed Chambers?" a miner asked him. "The governor gives them safe conduct; they leave their guns behind and get killed in front of their wives."

"Then they let the murderer, that Baldwin-Felts, Lively, out on bond—free!—with a hundred miners in jail in Mingo on no charge at all."

"Them Baldwin-Feltses has got to go! They gotta stop shooting miners down there. . . . If nobody else can budge them thugs, we're the boys that can."

"We're going through to Mingo."

2

Everyone called him "Sid"

I

HE CAME from the head of Blackberry Creek in the wilderness of the West Virginia–Kentucky border. Everyone called him Sid: farmers, coal loaders, shot firers, trap boys, and the legless beggars who had been crushed in the mines. He knew them all, liked them all, was one of them.

He was born in 1893 in the Hatfield-McCoy feuding country of the Tug River, where a few years earlier the Hatfields had tied three McCoys to a pawpaw bush and shot them dead, and he grew up with that meanness in him. They say he was the bastard son of a man named Crabtree who took up with Jake Hatfield's wife, but it didn't matter. Jake raised Sid with the rest of his brood and with the Hatfield name.

It was wild, rugged, brutal country, isolated from a growing nation by miles and miles of mountains, twisting creeks, and narrow hollows. To get there from West Virginia's capital at Charleston – seventy miles away as the crow flies – was a long day's journey even after the railroads came, and before that people seldom went. Even the mountain dialect was different in this wilderness pocket between the Ohio River and Cumberland Gap, where it seemed every third person was a Hatfield and another tenth were McCoys.

The coal industry and Sid Hatfield grew up together along the Tug. A few years before Sid's birth, five thousand workers had laid the Norfolk and Western trunk line through the area, building more than sixty bridges and blasting eight tunnels through the mountains to lay a hundred and ninety miles of track. The first mine opened about the time Sid was born. As a boy, he watched as tracks pushed up the hollows, cabins spread along the tracks and perched on mountainsides, huge tipples and company stores appeared in hollows, and slag heaps covered mountainsides. The mountain men donned miners' caps and ventured into the tunnels, following the coal seams into the earth, and mules pulled their day's work out. Investors came in from Ohio and Pennsylvania and New York to tour the valley and inspect the lands, and long coal trains rumbled along the river.

As Sid grew older, he learned of miners' dissatisfactions. Periodically, men were killed in this most dangerous of all vocations, and Sid saw the anguish of families when shrouded bodies were carried from the drift mouths. He had been only a boy during the Spanish-American War, when the nation lost some three hundred men in battle, but he became aware in the ensuing years that West Virginia had lost more men than that in a single year of coal mining accidents. After one of his family's friends was crushed to death, the widow and children were evicted without compensation from their company home to make room for a replacement miner. Sid saw new men arrive from Pennsylvania and Tennessee and the West; exslaves from southern cottonfields; Italians and Hungarians, speaking little English, shipped from the docks like imported cargo. He watched all this happen and was as much a part of it as the river and the coal.

Sid attended a one-room school, nearly half-filled with Hatfields, and he learned to read. County school records carried his name for twelve years, although it is doubtful he attended school that length of time. When he came of age, like all around him, he went into the mines. He started in a small operation on Blackberry Creek, on the Kentucky side, and moved from there to the Allburn mine across the river from the West Virginia town of Matewan. Daily, miners like Sid rode prone on coal cars deep into the earth, crawled through blackness in three-foot shafts, drilled holes with long breast augurs into walls of coal, and brought them down in massive dynamite explosions. Sweating on their knees, they shoveled coal into waiting rail cars, ate lunch in dark headings, tapped ceiling posts into place, laid rail on cross ties, watched mules pull their payloads toward the surface, and emerged black-faced with the sun behind the mountains.

Sid had been a boy when the United Mine Workers union began moving into West Virginia at the turn of the century, and he followed news of the union's development after he had become a miner. In the Kanawha coalfield around Charleston, the miners struck for greater union recognition in 1912, and hell broke loose; armed detectives of the infamous Baldwin-Felts Detective Agency of Bluefield forced striking miners from their homes, dumped their meager belongings along the railroad, and drove the families at gunpoint from the hollows. Gunfire and death followed; a heavily armored train, the Bullmoose Special, moved at night through a tent colony of evicted strikers and sprayed the tents with machine-gun fire, killing one person and injuring others. It ended with increased union recognition.

Along the Tug, though, there was no prospect of union. Coal operators refused even to meet with union representatives or discuss the subject. If they wished to work, miners had to sign "yaller dog" contracts swearing they would not "affiliate with or assist or give aid to any labor organization," under penalty of immediate loss of jobs and company homes. Even talk of unions would end in discharge as Baldwin-Felts spies circulated secretly among the miners, reporting those who favored union.

In this situation, the miners prospered. When Sid was twenty-five, ninety mines employed six thousand men along the Tug.

Sid developed into a small, wiry, but rather handsome, young man, slender, no more than 150 pounds in weight and five feet six in height, light brown hair, high cheekbones, jug ears, a dimple in his chin, an engaging smile that showed gold in his teeth. He made friends and kept them. As miners could, he prospered. He was promoted to blacksmith and worked in the fresh air outside. Still later, he became a skilled worker who moved coal cars down steep tracks to the tipple at the bottom of the mountain. But he never forgot the underground miners or that he was one of them.

From high on the Kentucky mountain top, Sid could look across the Tug to Matewan on the West Virginia side. Matewan was eight hundred people, a block of businesses, a main street lined by maples with whitewashed trunks, big wooden houses behind the maples, miners' cabins along Mate Creek and the railroad, and a high rock cliff behind it all. There were a depot, a bank, a company store, a hotel, a hardware, two drugstores, and the Do-Drop Inn. There was also Testerman's jewelry, run by the town's nattily dressed mayor and his attractive young wife, offering musical instruments, tobacco, patent medicines, eyeglasses, and ice cream from a marble-topped soda fountain, as well as jewelry. Pool rooms, saloons, and prostitutes prospered from the miners' trade; moonshine, shooting, and fighting abounded; corruption was expected, and votes were bought and sold. Coal operators in the area paid deputy sheriffs and private detectives to enforce the laws they liked; company spies circulated secretly among the miners to learn of any union activity, and most people believed public officials took graft from gamblers and prostitutes. It was a frontier town as wild as the West. Matewan, some of the town's leading citizens once said, was "the worst governed town in the state."

Sid liked it. He played pool, poker, and slot machines, chewed, smoked, drank at the Blue Goose Saloon, and chased the women. He fought often, and he beat one opponent so badly they had to hospitalize the man. He shot guns along the river bank, and they still say in Mingo that Sid could throw a potato in the air, draw his pistol, and split it open. After he became famous, he told a group of congressmen he once had "a little shooting match with a fellow by the name of Wilson" in the Allburn mines. Wilson was the mine foreman. Sid didn't finish the story except to say he, Sid, was arrested, tried, and "found clear."

These were qualities that won respect in Matewan, and they caught the eye not only of Mingo's miners. C. C. Testerman, the mayor, appointed Sid Hatfield as the town's first chief of police.

II

John L. Lewis, the bushy-browed new president of the United Mine Workers of America, came to southern West Virginia to make the announcement: the union would launch a campaign to organize coal miners of the southern Appalachians. Miners throughout the region, Lewis said, had expressed a wish to join the union, and the union wanted them. The union had considered such a campaign for years. "Now is the logical time for this work," he said, speaking in the coal town of Bluefield on the West Virginia–Virginia border, "and the campaign will be pushed through to a finish." It was January 30, 1920.

The campaign was essential for Lewis. All during November and December organized miners across the nation had been on strike. The operators finally had yielded. As Lewis spoke, negotiators worked on what promised to be a comfortable wage increase for union miners all over the country. One major fault appeared in the union's position: as union mines sat idle, long coal trains rumbled every day from the southern Appalachians, filled with fuel to heat America's homes. Union miners everywhere, including those in central West Virginia around Charleston, demanded action in the southern part of the state and eastern Kentucky. Even Midwestern coal operators, hurt by the competition, urged the union to push forward. Lewis had been president of the big miners' union less than a year; this strike was his first major effort; the southern Appalachians had to be organized.

Lewis understood that opposition would be encountered. "Every agency within the power of the coal operators is expected to be invoked to thwart the movement," he said in Bluefield. But it would go forward.

In Mingo County, West Virginia, Sid Hatfield, too, understood how tough the campaign would be. Coal operators considered it a basic freedom to hire nonunion men exclusively, and they intended to stand on that right, one of them said later, "as long as there is any respect whatever for the laws of this land." Every mine around Matewan rigidly enforced "yaller dog" contracts, and the state's supreme court had held them legal. It was Sid's job as police chief to enforce them.

The national strike was settled during the winter, and union miners across the country received a twenty-seven percent pay increase. Nonunion miners did not.

Along the Tug, miners began to stir. For more than twenty years, coal operators had controlled their very being; had arranged for their homes and towns, churches, schools, and recreation centers; had provided doctors and teachers and preachers; had employed many of their law officers; had even selected the silent motion picture shows that were beginning to appear in theaters; had told them, finally, where and how they were to live and discharged those who did not conform. In this context, the union's organizing campaign gave the miners a new vision: not only better pay and working conditions but independence, power, freedom, justice, and prestige for people who felt they had lost them all.

The miners at Burnwell, three miles from Matewan, were first to organize. "We want this twenty-seven percent increase," they said, and a delegation returned from Charleston with a union charter. The campaign had begun.

Sid was delighted. Night after night that spring, miners filled Matewan's little Baptist church to learn about the union, while Sid stood by to assure that the meetings went undisturbed. Three hundred miners signed in a single night. Among them was boyish Ed Chambers, newly married and Sid's best friend.

Sid had gained popularity among the miners as Matewan's police chief, for he understood them. Sid worked well with Mayor Testerman, 37, a pudgy, short-haired man who dressed nattily in suit and bow tie and tended to favor the miners. Sid wore his badge and guns but no uniform and enforced the law in a way that could only please the miners. When miners fought, he pulled them apart; when they got drunk, he took them home; when they became obstreperous, he calmed them down or looked the other way. Rarely did a miner occupy Sid's little jail. Once, however, he saw a man known to be against the miners' union carrying a weapon in violation of Matewan law, and he arrested the man, knocked him to the ground, and slapped him in the lockup. To the delight of Matewan's miners, Sid even got in trouble with the law himself in the winter of 1919–20, once for possessing illegal whiskey and once for fighting. Both times Mayor Testerman posted bond and kept Sid in his job. By spring, as the union drive began, Sid's popularity was such that he announced as a candidate for the Democratic nomination for constable of the Matewan district.

The organizing campaign quickly became bitter. Miners who joined the union were summarily fired from their jobs, and idle men loitered around the train stations urging others to join the union. Coal operators brought in Baldwin-Felts detectives, the professional strong-arm men who had fought the miners' strikes at Paint Creek, Cripple Creek, and Ludlow, and, carrying guns, they evicted union families from their company homes. At the Burnwell mine, they piled furniture, bedding, dishes, and clothing out on the road as the evicted miners and their families looked on. Several days later they repeated the scene in Matewan while Sid stood by in rage.

Al Felts, field manager of the hated detective agency, let it be known he would break the organizing drive "if it puts one hundred men in jail and costs a million dollars." He came to Sid and Mayor Testerman and offered five hundred dollars for permission to place machine guns in Matewan, in case there might be trouble. Sid indignantly refused and ordered Felts out of town.

Evictions continued. Union miners boiled with rage. Professional union organizers came in. Frank Keeney, president of District 17 of the UMW covering most of West Virginia, came down from Charleston, carrying a gun, to supervise. Billy Blizzard, fiery president of the union subdistrict, spoke to miners in a downpour of rain. Five hundred miners prayed and sang at a union meeting in Matewan, and a black miner clowned and made everyone laugh when he said, "If I wouldn't be a union man I'd go home and ask my wife to chain me in the yard with the dog."

Mother Jones, ninety-year-old patron saint of miners and self-proclaimed hell-raiser, arrived, her long black dress trailing in the dusty street, and spoke beside the railroad underpass. Sid met her, talked with her, established a lasting friendship. Mary Harris Jones, her real name, was a native of Ireland, emigrated to America as a child after the potato famine, lived during the presidencies of Jackson, Lincoln, and now Woodrow Wilson. She lost her four children and husband in a yellow fever epidemic in 1867 and her seamstress shop in the Chicago fire, and she gave the rest of her life to labor. Wherever there was labor strife, she was there leading workers: copper strikes in Michigan, streetcar strikes in New York, a chemical workers' strike in New Jersey. She organized women bottlers in Milwaukee's breweries and shirtwaist makers in Philadelphia. She addressed Finnish iron ore miners in Minnesota and Polish steelworkers at Gary. She led an "army" of little children from Philadelphia to New York and on to Teddy Roosevelt's home at Oyster Bay to protest child labor. She walked the halls of Congress and conferred with presidents and millionaires.

But coal miners were her "boys." No one could match her in bringing America's attention to the horrors of the coal digger's life. She gazed down into the Black Hole of Ludlow where miners' wives and children were burned to death; she stood defiantly in front of a machine gun in Cabin Creek and challenged the gunman to shoot. She led miners' wives, carrying mops and beating tin pans like cymbals, through Pennsylvania's mountains to dramatize their husbands' grievances. Colorado coal operators feared her so much they held her under military confinement for nine weeks without charge or hearing.

But "Medieval West Virginia," as she called it, was her favorite operating ground. For twenty years she had exhorted her "boys" in the Mountain State to do something about the "damnable infamous conditions" in West Virginia. Her words on the capitol steps in Charleston during the Cabin Creek strike of 1912, before a crowd of excited, yelling miners, typify her style:

> If there is no one else in the State of West Virginia to protest, I will protest. [Loud applause, and cries of "Yes, she will; Mother will."]
>
> . . . .
>
> They wouldn't keep their dog where they keep you fellows. You know that. They have a good place for their dogs and a slave to take care of them. The mine owners' wives will take the dogs up, and say, I love you, "dea-h."
>
> Now, my friends, the day for petting dogs is gone; the day for raising children to a nobler manhood and better womanhood is here. [Applause and cries of "Amen! Amen!"]
>
> . . . .
>
> Do you wonder at this uprising? And, you fellows have stood it entirely too long. It is time now to put a stop to it. We will give the governor until tomorrow night to take them guards out of Cabin Creek.
>
> [Very loud applause, and cries of: "And no longer."]
>
> Here on the steps of the capitol of West Virginia, I say that if the governor won't make them go, then we will make them go.

[Loud applause, and cries of: "That we will," "Only one more day," "the guards have got to go."]

If you are too cowardly to fight, I will fight. You ought to be ashamed of yourselves, actually to the Lord you ought, just to see one old woman who is not afraid of all the bloodhounds.

. . . .

It is freedom or death, and your children will be free. We are not going to leave a slave class to the coming generation, and I want to say to you the next generation will not charge us for what we have done; they will charge and condemn us for what we have left undone. [Cries of "That is right."]

In Matewan, as elsewhere, her words galvanized her "boys." Every miner of the Stone Mountain mine joined the union and was fired, and the mine closed. At Red Jacket, four miles away, some five hundred men were fired. The drive spread down the river to Williamson, Mingo County seat, where a hundred miners took the obligation in a black cafe, and 150 union miners paraded through town and heard speeches on the courthouse lawn. Two hundred miners joined from below Williamson and from the Kentucky mines across the river. So many were made homeless that the union rented land and opened tent colonies that quickly were filled.

By May 15, Sid's twenty-seventh birthday, three thousand miners along the Tug belonged to the United Mine Workers. Hundreds lived in tent colonies, where women and children circulated among the canvasses and clothes flapped on lines along the river.

The drive was so successful that the Baldwin-Felts detectives made new plans. They would "buy" Sid Hatfield's cooperation, said Tom Felts, president of the agency, and he instructed his brother Al to pay Sid up to three hundred dollars per month to turn against the union miners.

3

The Battle of Matewan

THIRTEEN BALDWIN-FELTS detectives, tall, heavy men in dark suits, arrived in Matewan on the noon train. The group was headed by two of the three Felts brothers who ran the company, Albert, the field manager, and his younger brother Lee. Miners watched sullenly as the men—"thugs" as the miners called them—stepped down from the train car. The detectives made their way on foot to the Urias Hotel on Mate Street, a block away.

It was Wednesday, May 19, 1920. Gray clouds blotted out the sun, and a light rain fell intermittently. Idle miners, men who had lost their jobs because they had joined the union, knew that the detectives' arrival meant some of them also would lose their homes.

The Baldwin-Felts men assembled at the Urias Hotel, where Anse Hatfield, the proprietor, fed them lunch. They came out on the main street again, carrying rifles, and climbed into three waiting cars. The vehicles chugged out of town along the road up Mate Creek toward the Stone Mountain Coal Company, a quarter mile away, where several striking miners still lived in company-owned homes.

Word spread quickly. The hated thugs were back to throw more miners out of their homes. Soon, word came back to the miners waiting in Matewan that the so-called detectives, by force of arms, were evicting the first family from a home, throwing their furniture out onto the county road. Men hurried into town, fearful and angry, talked briefly, then headed back home for their guns.

Sid was furious. He had warned Felts not to do this. He talked to Mayor Testerman, and they decided to talk to Felts. They walked up the railroad track as it forked up Mate creek to where the evictions were taking place. Angry miners fell in behind them. When they arrived at the Stone Mountain camp, a small crowd was with them.

The Baldwin-Felts men were in the process of evicting the family of Charley Kelly when Sid and the mayor arrived. Kelly and his wife stood outside their weatherboarded home. Mrs. Kelly had been washing clothes on the back porch when the detectives had arrived, guns in hand. She asked them to wait until her husband came home. "We haven't got time," a detective answered. Four of them went inside and reappeared moments later carrying furniture. They dumped it unceremoniously in the unpaved road. Kelly arrived home in the midst of the process, and Sid, the mayor, and the miners arrived shortly afterward.

Sid approached Al Felts. Al wore a revolver in his holster but had given his rifle to another detective. Sid asked if the detectives had proper authority to make the evictions. Yes, Al responded, he had checked with the court and had gotten authority to make the evictions. Sid asked to see the authority. Al told Sid if he didn't believe it, he could go back to Matewan to find out if they had proper authority. There was a minor argument. Finally, Sid and the mayor returned to town, the crowd of miners still behind them.

Sid called the sheriff's office in Williamson ten miles away. There, a deputy told him the detectives had no authority to evict families from their homes. Then, Sid said with some pleasure, he could arrest the detectives. He asked the deputy to send county warrants on the next train for the arrest of the detectives. Somewhere in the conversation, he said, "We'll kill the God damned sons of bitches before they get out of Matewan."

A block away, two teenaged telephone operators looked at each other wide eyed. They had listened in to the conversation.

To make certain that he could arrest the Baldwin-Felts men, Sid asked Mayor Testerman to prepare town warrants charging the detectives with illegally carrying weapons. One way or another, he would get them.

By then, everyone talked of violence. Union miners hurried

from their homes with guns. The report circulated that a family with several children had been forced at gunpoint from their home, their furniture set out in the rain, the children left to stand in the drizzle. The stories grew worse: the detectives had thrown out a pregnant woman, a sick child, a tiny baby in its crib, all with nowhere to go. The miners' fury rose.

Sid, waiting for the warrants on the five o'clock train, was livid. If the warrants didn't work to stop the detectives, he commented, they would "kill every God damned one of them without any God damned warrants." Testerman, alarmed at the mood, asked a miner who called himself a gospel minister to find some "sober-sided men" to act as policemen; the self-proclaimed minister later commented he planned to kill a few detectives himself.

Finally, shortly before four o'clock, the detectives returned. They had forced six families from their homes. The drizzle continued. The detectives ate an early dinner at the Urias Hotel under Anse Hatfield's care, put their rifles in cases, and left to walk toward the depot. At least four of them still carried their pistols in pockets or holsters. They planned to catch the five o'clock train to Bluefield, the same train bringing in the warrants.

Sid, his guns holstered, approached them as they passed Chambers Hardware on the square between the block of buildings and the railroad track. Armed miners looked on intently from the square, from the hardware store, and from the doors and windows of nearby buildings. Ed Chambers and several others crowded around as Sid spoke.

He had warrants, he told Al, to arrest all of the Baldwin-Felts detectives.

Felts was not bothered. "I'll return the compliment," he said. "I've got a warrant for you, too." With that, he produced a paper and told Sid he was under arrest and would have to go with the detectives as they returned to Bluefield.

This was a new one. Miners looked surprised. One ran off shouting, "They've got Sid under arrest!"

Someone ran into Testerman's Jewelry Store and said sharply, "Sid needs you!" Mayor Testerman dropped everything and hurried out, leaving his five-year-old son behind.

Testerman arrived at the altercation as miners grumbled and began shifting weapons. Someone commented that the warrant for Sid's arrest might as well have been "written on gingerbread."

Testerman asked to see the warrant, and Felts produced a piece of paper. Testerman inspected it and announced, "This is a bogus warrant."

They stood by the door of Chambers Hardware. Inside the store, a half dozen armed miners watched, guns ready; scores of others stood around outside. As Testerman, Al Felts, and Sid glared at each other, the first shot was fired.

Mingo County folks still argue who fired it. Sid said Al Felts shot Mayor Testerman and he, Sid, then pulled a gun and shot Felts. Others say miners in the hardware store shot first, killing Testerman. The Felts family always claimed Sid shot first. Whoever fired it, Al Felts and Testerman fell to the ground, Felts with a bullet in his head, Testerman shot through the stomach. Sid pulled both of his guns and began firing. Then all joined in, miners and detectives, shooting from the street, from the hardware store, from windows upstairs.

The detectives, realizing they were ambushed, tried to flee. John McDowell, a former policeman, jumped behind a telephone pole as shots zipped past him. He pulled his pistol and fired three times at a miner without hitting him, then ran toward the river.

Diving into the water, he waded and swam across, climbed the opposite bank and disappeared into the Kentucky woods.

Other detectives were less fortunate. One—Troy Higgins, a former Virginia police chief—broke out running when the firing started; the movement attracted the attention of William Bowman, a miner, who took aim with his rifle and shot, and the detective fell into the dirt.

Two detectives were brothers, Walter and Tim Anderson, and they jumped a fence and scurried into a house; inside, they ran into armed miners and a bullet slammed into Walter's shoulder. Still on his feet, he and his brother ran into the house next door. Outside, the battle raged so fiercely they were not missed. When their train pulled in minutes later, the brothers sneaked to it and boarded the last car as the train pulled out.

Lee Felts, Al's younger brother, drew two pistols when his brother fell. Art Williams, a miner, emptied his .32 pistol in a futile attempt to bring down the youngest of the Felts brothers.

Unharmed, Lee emptied his pistol at Art without hitting him. Reece Chambers, Ed Chambers's father, then took aim at Lee with his rifle and fired. Lee dropped to the ground and died.

Art Williams was not through. He kicked one of Lee's pistols from the dying man's hand and ran with it to the nearby bank in time to see a detective lurching, apparently from a blow or bullet wound. Williams shot the detective from such close range that blood spurted back on the pistol. The detective was A. J. Booher, former Bristol, Virginia, police chief.

Another former policeman among the Baldwin-Felts men, E. O. Powell of Marion, Virginia, was shot to death. Powell's body was found among the others after the battle, but no one seemed to know who had shot him. Booher, himself, had drawn blood before he died, and the victim was one of the day's most unfortunate. Bob Mullins, 53, a miner, had been fired that morning for joining the union, and he arrived in Matewan in time to witness the beginning of the battle. When the shooting started, Mullins ran toward the bank building. Booher shot Mullins as he ran. "Oh, Lord, I'm shot," Mullins screamed as he fell, and those were his last words.

Lee Felts, too, may have killed a bystander before he went down. A witness said Lee shot in the direction of Tot Tinsley, an unarmed miner whose body was found afterward, a bullet hole in his head.

Oscar Bennett, another of the detectives, escaped because of a lucky choice. Just before the first shot was fired, he went in search of a pack of cigarettes. When the shooting began, he quickly grasped its meaning and calmly walked to the railroad station. There, in the waiting room, he quietly stood at a window and watched the battle, while silently tearing up his identification papers. When the train pulled in, he walked to the Pullman loading area and waited, still silent. When the train pulled away, Bennett was safely inside.

C. B. Cunningham, detective next in command behind the Felts brothers, stood beside Al Felts when the battle began. As Al went down, Cunningham drew a gun and fired into the hardware store. Sid and several miners all claimed to have brought Cunningham down, and perhaps all did. His body was found riddled, half of his head blown off.

Isaac Brewer, a friend of Sid's, was inside the hardware store and saw Cunningham draw his gun. A shot, probably Cunningham's, smashed into Brewer's right chest. Still on his feet, Brewer pulled his own gun, only to have it shot from his hand. Gravely wounded he retreated to the back of the hardware store to stop the blood.

Detective J. W. Ferguson, a former police chief, was wounded in the initial firing, and he lurched down the street crying, "I'm shot to pieces." A town employee helped him into a nearby home, and the lady who lived there eased him into a wicker chair. Suddenly, several armed men crashed through the house from the front, and the town employee ran in fright. Moments later, Ferguson lay dead in the alley beside the house, nine bullet wounds in his body. He was shot as he tried to climb a fence beside the alley, witnesses said.

C. B. Hildebrand had come with the detectives to carry furniture from the homes. Unarmed, he ran down the street when the first shot was fired. A bullet neatly lifted his hat from his head. He ran behind a home, ducked into a shed, and climbed inside an empty barrel. Several hours later, a woman and child entered the shed, noticed the barrel moving, and fled in terror. At 11:30 P.M., six hours after he had climbed inside, Hildebrand left the shed. Out on the now quiet street, he lit a cigarette and walked briskly through town, whistling, to safety.

When the battle ended, the streets were lined with dead and dying. Men hid beneath railroad boxcars, behind walls and trees and in ditches. Both Felts brothers, five other detectives, and two miners had been killed, and Mayor Testerman lay dying on a cot, ministered to by his wife. Five others had been wounded.

Moments later, the five o'clock train, No. 16, pulled into Matewan, and the engineer and passengers looked out, wide eyed, at the bodies lying in a row on the street before them. Sid, his guns back in their holsters, walked among them, searching the bodies. As he stood over the remains of Al Felts, he brandished the warrant for the detective's arrest and said, "Now, you son of a bitch, I'll serve it on you."

4

"We have organized all the camps"

I

SID WAS A MINER'S HERO. Someone at long last had stood up to the hated Baldwin-Felts detectives. For twenty years these extra legal strike-breaking guns-for-hire had harassed union miners all over the country. Stories of their atrocities were told in every miner's cabin: it was Baldwin-Feltses who burned the women and children at Ludlow in Colorado; Baldwin-Feltses tracked down miners with bloodhounds and throwed 'em in jail; "Baldwins" forced little children from their home at gunpoint; Baldwins machine-gunned sleeping miners at Holly Grove; even a buddy might turn out to be a Baldwin-Felts in disguise. These were the thugs of West Virginia mining lore, hired by out-of-state money to keep the miner down. But Sid Hatfield had refused to yield.

As the story of the Matewan battle spread, coal miners everywhere grinned. When word of the battle was telephoned to the UMW office in Charleston, a union official shook hands with himself and danced around the room.

"Them sons of bitches had it comin'," a miner said.

Tom Felts, surviving brother of the Felts family, learned of the battle while in Virginia and stormed into Mingo County on the night train with a posse of his detectives. Learning of the rapid approaching of Felts, Sid and Mingo sheriff Blankenship deputized a hundred miners to keep order in Matewan. As Felts's train raced toward Matewan, it appeared another gun battle was in the making, but the engineer averted it by highballing his train through its scheduled stop at Matewan, taking Felts and his men, protesting all the way, to Williamson. There, Tom viewed the riddled bodies of his brothers and detectives the next day and commented that the battle wasn't fair; if they'd had a fair chance, he said, "our boys would have dropped twice as many as the miners did."

Around the country, reaction was short lived. The national press front paged the battle and concluded the Hatfield-McCoy feud had erupted again. A senator from Maryland suggested President Wilson send federal troops into West Virginia. Sam Gompers, president of the American Federation of Labor, called for a congressional investigation. John L. Lewis urged West Virginia's governor to act to prevent further outrages by "murderers, hirelings of the coal operators." Such evils, he said, had gone on for years, but "nothing has been done to ensure to peaceful citizens the right to live." The governor only deplored the unfavorable publicity.

West Virginia's entire state police force, fifty strong, converged on Matewan, and Sid met the first contingent at the depot. "Disarm and dismiss your men," a lieutenant commanded, and Sid obliged; his deputy miners stacked their arms in Chambers Hardware and the state police took over.

Mayor Testerman, Mullins, and Tinsley were buried high on the mountaintop across the river from Matewan in Kentucky, while state police stood guard. At Galax, Virginia, more than three thousand came for the funerals of Al and Lee Felts.

Sid took satisfaction in turning over to the county prosecuting attorney papers he had found on Al Felts's body revealing the detectives' plan to pay him a monthly salary to "stand squarely behind us" in breaking up the strike.

Sid's popularity was demonstrated six days after the battle in the statewide Democratic primary elections. When the votes were counted, Sid carried all six precincts of Magnolia District and became the Democratic nominee for constable. It was his first try at popular election.

II

For the rest of his life, until his untimely death, Sid was the target of Tom Felts and his detectives. Immediately after the Matewan battle, Sid made himself extraordinarily vulnerable to the agency's campaign by courting and marrying the widow of Mayor Testerman.

Jessie Testerman, 26, had creamy skin, dimples, shiny brown hair, a well-shaped figure, and, since her marriage to Mayor Testerman some nine years earlier, an inexhaustible supply of jewelry, hats, and fashionable clothing. She had attracted more than one admiring glance from Matewan's miners as she clerked in her husband's store and strolled through town with their cute, blond, five-year-old son. When Sid became her husband's police chief, he spent many hours with the mayor and his bride. In fact, his enemies later claimed Sid had been seen quietly strolling along the Tug with Jessie in the months before her husband's death.

Sid's name was already something of a household word in West Virginia on the night of June 1, eleven days after the Matewan battle, when he and Jessie were arrested together in a hotel room in Huntington. The state's newspapers pulled out their biggest headline type.

It was at 10:30 P.M. when two city policemen knocked at the door of their room at the Florentine Hotel, apprehended the pair, and took them off to jail, charged with "improper relations." Almost as quickly, the reason for the arrests became clear. Tom Felts called a press conference in another part of Huntington to trumpet the news. Sid and Jessie were having an affair, he announced. That was the reason for the Matewan battle. "Hatfield shot Testerman to get him out the way," he said. "The charge that Albert Felts killed Testerman is a dirty vicious lie."

The reporters stampeded to the jail to see Sid and Jessie. Sid was unrepentant. He first said he and Jessie were married. He had known Jessie "as long as I have been chief of police of Matewan," and there was nothing improper in their relations. Told of Tom Felts's allegation that he had killed Testerman, Sid said the mayor "was killed by Albert Felts. Felts shot from the hip. He carried two guns. Any other statement is foolish."

The reporters found Jessie in the women's section of the jail, reading a magazine, modestly dressed in a blue suit. She handled them with grace and charm. "No," she said, "we are not married." She and Sid had come to Huntington to get married, "but it was late when we got the marriage license, and we had some difficulty in locating a minister." They finally located one and returned to the hotel, she said, but they were arrested before the ceremony could be performed.

Sid, she said, "always has been a perfect gentleman." Mayor Testerman had considered Sid a good friend and had told her that if anything ever happened to him she should marry Sid. They would be married, she said, "as soon as this trouble is over."

Next morning, Sid and Jessie, dressed in their finest, appeared in a packed courtroom in Huntington, presented their marriage license, which was dated the day before, and walked away free. The judge said a ten dollar fine would be remitted if they were married that day.

A crowd of reporters and onlookers followed them to a nearby church. There, as a nephew and niece of the late Mayor Testerman looked on approvingly, Sid and Jessie were married.

III

Nightly through the month of June, miners met in villages along the Tug and joined the union with new confidence. An organizer reported to John L. Lewis: "We have organized all the camps going east to the McDowell County line with the exception of two," and those two were in the plans.

Coal operators, refusing even to talk with union representatives, increased their evictions. All along the Tug, miners left their company homes willingly, moving into tents or empty shacks. The union rented lands and shipped in more tents, and tent cities grew along the tracks and bottomlands; miners' wives cooked on open fires; children played among the guy ropes, and families bathed in the river.

Mother Jones stormed into Mingo again on June 21, spitting expletives, wearing a white dickey and her long black dress, and fifteen hundred delighted miners gathered to hear her on the courthouse steps in Williamson. The coal operators were "robbers and rascals," she told them, but the miners were even worse. Criticizing her "boys" was one of her favorite tactics to goad them into action: "You," she yelled at the gallused, grizzled men, "have stood and seen yourselves robbed." Of every ton of coal they mined so much was taken out, and professional murderers were hired to keep you in subjection, and you paid for it! Damn you, you are not fit to live under the flag. You paid professional murderers with that money you were robbed of, and then you never said a word. You stood there like a lot of cowards, robbed by the mine owners. And you let him do it, and then you go about shaking your rotten head – not a thing inside. You call yourselves Americans. Let me tell you, America need not feel proud of you.

The miners loved it. They cheered, and she went on: "We cleaned them in Kanawha, didn't we? When I went into the Kanawha River in 1900, miners were working fourteen hours a day, they got forty cents for every ton of coal. . . . The children were in the mines. They saw no school."

Responding to a local clergyman who had said her "vile, rough talk gave the lie to the sacred name of Mother," she said Mingo's clergymen were "afraid of the high class burglars coal operators and their dollars." The county's judges, too, were owned by the operators, "but bye and bye we will be the judges, and we will put them on the scrap pile.

"It is the new era, the new manhood and womanhood coming into life, my friends."

In a region where even dancing was considered immoral, such talk from this white-haired old woman was tonic, and the miners hung on every word.

Mother Jones went on to Matewan where Sid, smoking his pipe, greeted her in suit and vest and posed with her for photographs. That evening, she spoke again to Matewan's miners.

Two days later, she was with four thousand miners who swarmed into Williamson for a union convention and celebration of victory in breaking the Tug coalfield. There were speeches, resolutions, and great smiles by union officials, and they unanimously voted to go on strike July 1, unless the operators agreed to negotiate. That question was quickly answered: "We have nothing to discuss with you," the operators responded, and Keeney, district president of the UMW, called the strike. On July 1, mines all along the Tug closed down. By mid-July, coal production had come almost to a halt.

Scattered violence broke out immediately and continued all summer. In neighboring McDowell County, three men were wounded in a July 4 gun battle between union miners and deputy sheriffs; a hundred men reenforced the deputies, and dozens of miners were arrested. One of the deputies had been a Mingo County miner who had turned against the union; he mysteriously lost his home in a fire, and a few days later, as he walked along a railroad track, was shot and killed from ambush.

In Mingo County, guerilla warfare began. Bullets peppered down on working nonunion miners at the Borderland mine near Williamson. One hundred union miners opened fire on nonunion miners at Freeburn, Kentucky, shooting from the West Virginia mountains across the Tug Valley. An operator of the mine's cable cars fell wounded, and women and children ran screaming through the camp.

Kentucky's governor dispatched two hundred National Guardsmen to the Kentucky side of the river, and West Virginia's ordered state police back to Mingo. Violence only increased. On August 4, riflemen shot down from the West Virginia mountains at Kentucky guardsmen opposite Matewan; a horse was shot out from under one guardsman, and a bullet ripped through another's campaign hat. When strikers attacked at Freeburn again, Kentucky guardsmen drove them back with machine-gun fire. Freeburn was attacked a third time. A gun battle broke out at Mohawk. A railcar was torpedoed. A power house was dynamited. Deputies beat a black striker with clubs and dumped him, semiconscious, from an automobile. A baseball game turned into a free-for-all between union and nonunion sympathizers. Everyone bought guns. Coal operators ordered rifles and machine guns as part of their mine equipment. State police rushed from one outbreak to another, and Captain J. R. Brockus, their tall, rangy commander, hurried along the river by train, riding in a special caboose.

In the midst of all this, a grand jury indicted Sid and twenty-two of his friends for the murders of the seven Baldwin-Felts detectives. Ed Chambers and his father, Reece, were among them. All became instant celebrities, and more than five hundred persons gathered simply to watch them being arraigned in the courthouse at Williamson. Matewan townspeople happily posted ten thousand dollars bond for each. Jessie posted Sid's bond, using the mayor's estate as surety.

Sid tried to remain aloof from the violence. Wearing his guns, he walked the block of businesses in Matewan, met incoming trains, smiled and chatted with townspeople, and helped Jessie operate Testerman's store. In the warm summer evenings he sat on the bench outside the store, chatting with Ed Chambers and other friends about the strike.

It was such an evening August 14 when he found himself again involved in murder. The victim was Anse Hatfield, the hated hotel operator who had assisted the Baldwin-Felts detectives before the Matewan battle. Intensifying the union miners' hatred, Anse had testified against Sid at the grand jury investigation. He would be a key prosecution witness at the trial.

Anse sat that evening outside his hotel on Main Street as darkness set in, talking with a local dentist. The shot came without warning from the railroad track, and the bullet ripped through Anse's chest, came out his back and struck the dentist in the jaw. Both fell, Anse mortally wounded.

Sid said later he and Ed were sitting on the other side of Testerman's store, a hundred feet away, when they heard the shot. They ran to the hotel and searched for the assailant. A state trooper found Fred Burgraff, one of the twenty-three defendants in the Matewan battle case, holding a rifle near the railroad. The trooper arrested Burgraff and asked Sid to jail him. Sid demurred. The trooper flared; he would arrest Sid, too, if he did not cooperate, and unhappily Sid put his friend in jail.

Things got worse for Sid. The family revealed Anse Hatfield had received a note threatening his life because he had testified to the grand jury against union miners. As public horror increased, other witnesses came forth saying they, too, had received threatening notes. George Gunnoe, Matewan school principal, was so frightened by a note that he resigned his job and moved to Huntington. Rumor spread that Sid was both author of the notes and killer of Anse Hatfield. "I never heard of those letters," Sid told the local press, but it did no good. Another murder charge was filed against him, the eighth.

In Charleston, Governor John J. Cornwell had had enough. He called Washington and asked for federal troops.

5

"The most complete deadlock of any industrial struggle"

I

As John L. Lewis had predicted, Mingo County's coal operators applied all of their considerable power during the fall and winter of 1920 to break the strike and to bring Sid Hatfield to bay. But Sid and the union miners found they had power too.

At Governor Cornwell's request, federal troops occupied Mingo in late August. In a flood of leggings, Sam Browne belts, and campaign hats, they arrived by train, nearly five hundred strong, with machine guns, a cannon, motor trucks, motorcycles, and pack mules. One of their largest detachments camped at Matewan, where little children watched in awe as soldiers cooked potatoes and beans in huge pots.

They went into action almost immediately. The day after the soldiers arrived, two hundred strikers opened a crossfire from the mountains at Howard Colliery. With classic infantry tactics, a squad of soldiers returned the fire and worked their way up the mountainside, shooting as they moved, until the attackers fled over the ridge. Next day, other soldiers drove back a larger force at Thacker. Newspapers delightedly reported these events like military battles.

Sid may have helped plan one attack, with singular lack of success, at Mohawk in neighboring McDowell County, where there were no soldiers. When the attacking miners opened fire, a line of deputies, dug in for defense, returned a withering fire with rifles and Browning automatic machine guns. The attackers fled in panic, bullets whizzing over them. One, a black, fell as a bullet struck his leg, and other miners helped him run limping away.

Someone had tipped off the deputies. Months later, Sid and his friends learned who it was.

A Baldwin-Felts detective was in their midst, working as a spy. He was Charlie E. Lively, 33, a small, wiry exminer who had come to Matewan with his wife and four children in the spring as the union drive began. Lively had immediately joined the union and became one of its most active members, organizing meetings, swearing in new recruits, planning strategies. He had participated enthusiastically in the strike convention, posing with Mother Jones and the convention leaders for a photograph. During the summer, he opened a little restaurant next to Testerman's store, where Sid spent his time, and he rented the second floor of the building to the United Mine Workers for their Matewan office. There, in the heart of the strike activity, while his wife ran their restaurant, Lively engaged Sid and the union miners in long discussions of the Matewan battle and helped plan attacks on nonunion mines. The restaurant prospered as a union hangout, and Lively made money while he spied. Then at night he secretly wrote his reports to the Baldwin-Felts Detective Agency, signing them "Number Nine," and sending them off to fake addresses for ultimate delivery to the detective agency in Bluefield. There, in the agency's inner sanctum, he had been known for years as one of their best spies.

II

As the soldiers brought Mingo County's violence under control, the mine war shifted to Charleston and the West Virginia legislature. Because the Nineteenth Amendment had just been ratified, Governor John J. Cornwell called a special session of the legislature to pass laws for initial registration of women voters. When the legislators convened, however, Cornwell introduced surprise legislation to allow counties to import juries from other counties. The purpose was clear: to provide the necessary jurymen in Mingo County to try the twenty-three men indicted for seven murders apiece in the Matewan battle case.

West Virginia's miners set up an immediate howl. They well knew a jury of Mingo citizens would be reluctant to convict Sid and his friends because of the general hatred of the Baldwin-Felts detectives. A Kanawha County local union angrily called for a statewide strike "as a protest to our legislators and governor against the passing of any laws to assist in railroading workers to the penitentiary or gallows at the behest of the capitalist-controlled governor." They demanded "for Sid Hatfield a fair and impartial trial by his peers." Petitions against the bill were read to the legislators from labor groups throughout the state.

The governor recognized that he could not win, and the bill quietly died. Sid had won another fight.

Back in Matewan, Sid politicked for his cause in the November 2 general election. As a leader of coal miners, police chief and the Democratic nominee for constable in his district, Sid had some little political influence in Mingo County. There is evidence he used it well.

Early in the campaign, a banner appeared across Matewan's main street urging votes for James M. Cox for president, Samuel B. Montgomery for governor, and the "entire Democratic County and District tickets." These were precisely Sid's choices, including the endorsement of Montgomery, the labor candidate, rather than the Democratic nominee, one Arthur Koontz, whom Sid considered as "Cornwell's candidate." Montgomery came by Matewan during the campaign to speak and to cement his friendship with the controversial young police chief.

Sid's selective enforcement of the law continued. Although he was courteous to Democratic candidates, Republicans charged that, as police chief, he stood by idly while teenaged boys continuously catcalled and interrupted speeches by Republican campaigners. It was certainly in character for Sid.

The election results gratified Sid. Matewan and Mingo both went for Cox. Montgomery was defeated, but so was Koontz; the gubernatorial election went to Ephraim F. Morgan, 52, a Republican lawyer-farmer who parted his white hair in the middle. The election of Warren G. Harding as president of the United States was of little concern to Sid.

In his own race, Sid was elected constable by a narrow plurality over three opponents. With this success, he named Ed Chambers as a special officer to assist him.

III

Late at night, sixteen men stepped from a train at Williamson and quietly walked across the bridge into Kentucky to work the Pond Creek mines. They were the first miners imported to the Tug River since the strike began.

It was September 16. Thereafter, "transportations," as the local miners called them, arrived regularly, wives, children, and bags in hand, to dig Tug River coal. Employment agencies, promising "for immediate shipment any number of experienced miners, with or without families, of any nationality desired," recruited them in Akron, Louisville, Pittsburgh, Memphis, and on New York's wharves.

Immediately, crowds of angry strikers gathered to meet every train, shouting and demonstrating as the "scabs" stepped to the platform. The miners hung a sign at the Williamson depot proclaiming: "Be Advised That There Is a Strike in Progress."

More than a hundred strikers met one train; fights broke out as the newcomers tried to push through; several were knocked down. A call went out, and soldiers arrived on the run. As strikers ran down the streets, threw rocks and cursed and yelled in frustration, armed soldiers escorted the newcomers to safety. Ben Page, the lone black among the defendants in the Matewan battle case, was jailed.

In ensuing weeks, soldiers escorted hundreds of strikebreakers to the mines. Coal production, only fifty thousand tons in August, rose rapidly throughout the fall, reaching normal production of 176,000 tons in December. Mines that had closed in July reopened in the fall and winter with nonunion miners. Desertions began in union ranks. Four mines reopened under union contracts, but it was devastating to the union when three of them closed for lack of orders.

Mother Jones came back to rebuild strikers' spirits, and miners filled the Circuit Courtroom to hear her proclaim "a new day is dawning for labor." Despite the setbacks, hundreds of the original strikers, like mustached Martin Justice, the "mayor" of Lick Creek tent colony, held firm. "I have been in a tent ever since July 1," he wrote to the UMW Journal, "and if it takes that to make the coal company come over to their milk, I am willing to stay there five years."

IV

The mine war was fought not only with gunfire in the mountains; it was also fought with lawsuits and injunctions, and here again Sid found himself in the middle of the battle.

In the fall of 1920, the Red Jacket Coal Company near Matewan filed suit in the Federal Court of the Southern District of West Virginia against Sid and other leaders of the strike: John L. Lewis, Mother Jones, Keeney, Fred Burgraff, Ben Page, and more than twenty others. The suit asked that union representatives be prohibited from virtually any contact with nonunion miners about the strike.

There was precedent for the request. It was based on the famous "yaller dog" contracts which working miners were forced to sign in Mingo County, promising they would not join the miners' union. These contracts became even more demanding as the Mingo strike continued. In the neighboring Pocahontas coalfield around Bluefield and in Virginia, the miner agreed not only that he would not join the UMWA, the IWW "or any other mine labor organization" but also that, should he be fired for joining such an organization (as assuredly he would be), he thereafter would not "in any manner molest, annoy or interfere with the business, customers or employees of the employer."

Thousands of miners in southern West Virginia signed such contracts in 1920, and once in existence they provided the basis of injunctions that completed the operators' iron grip on union organizing activity.

The legal battle against the union took new life in August, when forty-seven of the largest coal companies in the Pocahontas field sought an injunction from a circuit court to prohibit the UMWA "from the interfering with contracts now in force between operators and miners." The case quickly found its way before three justices of the West Virginia Supreme Court of Appeals, who, on September 16, less than three weeks after the case was filed, granted the requested injunction. When made permanent later, the injunction forbade the United Mine Workers:

from in anywise molesting or interfering with or attempting to molest or interfere with the employees of the plaintiffs in the performance and fulfillment of their contracts . . . and from compelling or inducing, by violence, threats, intimidation, abusive or violent language or *persuasion* the employees of the plaintiff, or either of them, to break their contracts of service. (emphasis added)

Further, the court prohibited union leaders from "entering upon the ground and premises of the plaintiffs, or their mines to persuade them [the workers] to join the United Mine Workers of America, in violation of their contracts."

To make the victory complete for the operators, the court required the union to pay the costs of the suit.

It was with this precedent that the Red Jacket Coal Company on September 30 filed its suit against Sid and the UMWA leadership. A month later, Federal District Judge Edmund Waddill, Jr., granted a preliminary injunction giving the company virtually all it sought. The union leaders were prohibited from "willfully inducing plaintiffs' employees, present or future, to leave plaintiffs' service on the ground that plaintiff does not recognize the United Mine Workers of America." They were forbidden to trespass on the coal company's property for the purpose of persuading the employees "to refuse or fail to perform their duties."

Even this, however, did not complete the legal noose around the miners' union. Reacting to the efforts to dissuade imported laborers from working in the strike zone as they arrived at the Williamson train station, the Pond Creek Coal Company sought an injunction in federal district court to restrain union representatives even from approaching newcomers at the depot to tell them about the strike. Judge Waddill again granted the company virtually all it asked. In what appears today to be an incredible order, the judge restrained the union from

advertising, representing, stating by word, by posted notices, or by placards displayed at any point in the State of West Virginia or elsewhere, that a strike exists in the Pond Creek field, or at plaintiff's mines, and from warning or notifying persons to remain away from said Pond Creek field or from plaintiff's mines.

Harold Houston, attorney for the UMWA in West Virginia, commented about the Pond Creek case, "If a union cannot make the simple statement that a strike exists in a field covered by an official strike order, what can it do?"

The miners along the Tug had an answer, and one gave it to a reporter:

"We'll go to jail."

V

The fall of 1920 seemed peaceful in Mingo County, compared to the preceding summer, largely because of the presence of federal troops. In mid-October, striking miners fired on a truck loaded with nonunion miners and wounded two of them, while others fired down from the hills on workers at two mines, causing no harm. A week later, union and nonunion miners shot it out at a newly opened mine, and John Yates, the mine blacksmith, a nonunion worker, was killed. But the incidents were scattered, and most were of little consequence.

Noting that fact, Governor Cornwell requested withdrawal of the federal troops, promising that if there were further violence he would recall them, "and if I have to recall them it will be followed by drastic steps." The soldiers left November 4, and Captain Brockus and his state police returned to maintain order.

The troops hardly had left when major violence resumed.

On November 7, tent colonists fired on working miners at Nolan, two men were wounded in a gun battle at Rawl, and a huge tipple fell in a dynamite explosion at Thacker. After a single quiet day, another dynamite explosion sent a railroad trestle tumbling down onto the county road, and two mine company buildings went up in flames. In the days following, a state trooper was shot and killed in an altercation with moonshiners, strikers shot from the mountains on nonunion workers at two mines and beat up other workers as they emerged from a third, and two union men were shot, one of them fatally, in a gunfight with nonunion miners on a moving railway train.

The two murders, especially the trooper's, sent West Virginia's leadership into an uproar again. More than a hundred businessmen in Mingo County appealed to Cornwell to recall the troops, and he needed little persuasion. On November 27, he proclaimed Mingo County "to be in a state of insurrection" and, until further notice, would "be under the direct charge of the commanding general of the Fifth Corps Area." Mingo had endured twenty-four days without federal troops.

VI

Five hundred men of the Nineteenth Infantry Regiment gave Mingo County a much heavier dose of martial law. Colonel Herman Hall, their white-thatched commander, took over the county courthouse, posted guards outside, and banned public assemblies, parades, and demonstrations. He sent strong detachments of troops to Matewan, Borderland, and Kermit, where they patroled the roads with fixed bayonets. When several of his soldiers were robbed by prostitutes, he ordered the Williamson Town Council to clean up vice. Responding enthusiastically, town police arrested prostitutes and bootleggers who had been around for years, while other unsavory people nervously left town. County deputies caught the spirit and went from door to door asking citizens to disarm; hundreds voluntarily gave up their guns. When a fire broke out in Williamson, a bugle sounded "Assembly" and soldiers ran to help put it out. Violence dropped almost to zero. Mingo citizens, growing fond of the troops, gathered appreciatively to watch every guard mount.

Disregarding the legal tangle of injunctions and lawsuits, Hall set up firm rules to govern the arrival of nonunion miners. He permitted union pickets to approach the newcomers and to try to persuade them to work elsewhere; if the persuasion failed, however, they were allowed to go to work without intimidation. Both union and company officials commented on his fairness.

The strike was now a major news event. Reporters from national newspapers and newsreel cameramen flocked in to photograph the tent colonies and army camps and to write heartrending accounts of the miners' plight. *Coal Age* called it "the most complete deadlock of any industrial struggle in the country," and the *New York World* editorialized that "political bankruptcy cannot reach more degrading levels."

Rain, snow, and wind swept across the Appalachian range,

tearing the last leaves from the hardwoods and exposing the rocks and brown compost of the mountains. In the tent colonies, miners built fireplaces of rock and mortar, and many floored their tents. Families of five lived on ten dollars a week; barefoot children played in snow; women gave birth in tents, children died in tents. In a widely published story, one reporter told of following a barefoot child through snow to a tent near Matewan:

Inside, on a "cot" improvised of bricks and sand, a woman was writhing in pain. By her side sat a skeleton-like man, coughing desperately. On the bare frozen ground these barefoot children sat huddled together holding hands over a miserable little wood fire. The tent sagged and strained under the whipping of the wind.

At the tent colony at Lick Creek near Williamson, a tattered American flag flew over some forty tents arranged in rows around a "public square." Several tents lay flat and abandoned on the ground. Cows, horses, and chickens occupied others. Children, black and white, played along the "streets." None attended school.

A *New York Times* reporter sloshed by car along a muddy road around hairpin bends to get to the colony. He stopped at a tent where he found an open fireplace, table, chairs, sewing machine, four beds, and a crib. The mother said they had been there since June, and her family's clothing appeared clean.

The reporter distributed several pounds of candy to the colony's children but noted "no screams of delight." They talked of Santa Claus. One child said his brother was too sick to come for candy, and they all went to the sick child's tent. There, a pale, blue-eyed little boy held up his hands and was nearly buried with candy.

The tent colonies grew larger as winter advanced. More than eighty strikers were evicted from their homes in December, at least one family on Christmas Eve. Some coal operators were sympathetic, however; one invited tent colonists to occupy his empty houses, rent free, until the cold weather ended.

State health inspectors came through the tent colonies and reported "none is suited for habitation." They found 365 persons, 205 of them children, living in more than a hundred tents, all of them risking sickness or death in an epidemic.

As Christmas approached, strikers, miners, operators, and

soldiers combined to alleviate the misery. An army truck labored into the mountains and brought back a large Christmas tree for the courthouse yard in Williamson, where it was strung with electric bulbs. All over the country, people who had seen the publicity sent money and food; a train carload of two thousand hams arrived; cars came with candy, nuts, fruit, and toys. Volunteers, including the visiting wives of army officers, distributed them. The union sent out a Christmas circular urging strikers to "keep within the law."

On Christmas day, stockings hung in tents, and union leaders said not a child was forgotten. The army served turkey to the troops, and the soldiers put up Christmas trees at each outpost. On Christmas night, the first public assembly in the occupation was permitted about the community Christmas tree in the courthouse yard at Williamson. Strikers, nonunion miners, soldiers and local citizens gathered about the tree and sang carols.

6

"It's good to have friends"

FINALLY CAME THE TRIAL: Sid and twenty-two defendants charged with a single murder, that of Albert Felts. It was the biggest in West Virginia's history, and people crowded into Williamson days beforehand in anticipation. Hotel rooms were booked, and townspeople pointed out the defendants, lawyers, prosecutors, and newspaper reporters like celebrities. The lawyers drew special admiration as they strode through town: Harold W. Houston, tall, handsome, literary, white-haired, "brains" and general counsel of the UMWA in West Virginia; John J. Conniff of Wheeling, one of the state's foremost attorneys, employed by the union in his first murder case in years; Joseph M. Sanders of Bluefield, former justice of the West Virginia Supreme Court now working for the coal operators; James Damron, who had resigned in August from the circuit court, where the case was to be tried, in order to work for the coal operators; John S. Marcum of Williamson, raconteur of mountain lore and veteran of five hundred murder trials.

As the trial opened, hundreds tramped through slush and snow to get seats and to watch the twenty-three defendants troop into the barnlike courtroom with its wooden benches and railings. Sid came in a natty brown suit which he admitted with a grin he had bought for the occasion, and all eyes were on him. Jessie held his arm, looking pretty with a rope of pearls around her neck, jewels on her fingers, and brooches on her dress. The other defendants wore overalls, riding breeches, or corduroys, further distinguishing Sid as their leader. Behind the bench, Judge

R. D. Bailey, thick-set, with red hair, red face, and blue eyes, sat next to Colonel Hall, and the two gave an air of commanding dignity.

Sid caused a sensation the first day when court officers learned he had brought his two guns in his pockets to the trial. Judge Bailey had difficulty containing his emotions in announcing that firearms no longer would be allowed. Next morning, deputies searched everyone who entered, and Sid obligingly checked his guns at the door.

Reporters were there from a dozen newspapers, and Sid talked freely with them. "I reckon you thought I had horns," he told one reporter with a grin. "It's the limit what I read about myself." He smiled for everyone, and the press promptly called him "Smiling Sid" and "Boy Leader of the Mountains."

He and Jessie told the full story of the Matewan battle to a reporter from the *Philadelphia Public Ledger*. "It was a question of life or death for me," Sid said.

I did no more than other men would do. I was backed against the wall. The detectives surrounded me . . . Mayor Testerman was in the rear. The detectives had a warrant for my arrest. Testerman said it was bogus. Felts drew his gun and shot Testerman, then swung his gun over his shoulder and shot Brewer. I drew two guns. One was shot out of my hand. A second later a bullet tore through my hat. I started firing as rapidly as I could. It was all over within two minutes.

Judge Bailey surprised the defendants by terminating their bonds. All were led off that evening to the little jail behind the courthouse, where they remained, except during sessions, for the remainder of the trial. Jail life was far from unpleasant. The jailer's wife took Jessie into her home so she could stay with Sid, and the jailer brought in new mattresses and left the cell doors unlocked so the Matewan boys could visit each other. The food was good, and they listened pensively as two black prisoners sang hymns in a nearby cell.

On Sunday, their wives, mothers, and girlfriends came from Matewan with candy, cakes, and cigars, and inside the jail they danced to whistled tunes, played dominoes, smoked, and ate. Reporters gathered outside, and Sid came to a window in overalls to greet them, still smiling. "This ain't a jail," he cracked, "this is the Matewan Hotel."

Getting a jury was even more difficult than predicted. Finding jurymen unrelated to any of the defendants' families – including both Hatfields and McCoys – appeared impossible. When the name "Anse Hatfield" was called, a lawyer responded, "He's dead, your honor," as two men named Anse Hatfield stepped forward. The jury wheel turned again and again, and deputies fanned out across the county to bring in men. Veniremen arrived by car, horseback, and hobo-style on trains. Their simplicity and honesty impressed reporters, as did their almost uniform hatred of Baldwin-Felts detectives. One thought he was showing impartiality when he announced he was neither "a union man nor a Baldwin-Felts thug." Nearly a thousand veniremen were summoned and more than four hundred examined. There was even talk of allowing women to serve in view of their newly won right to vote, but West Virginia's attorney general, in a hasty decision, ruled women could not serve on juries. Someone suggested taking blacks as jurymen, but Judge Bailey refused to countenance it. Finally, on February 9, twelve men sat in the jury box: two school teachers, four farmers, five laborers and an illiterate old backwoodsman who had ridden to town on horseback.

As the trial opened, charges were dropped against Ben Page, the black, and Nathan H. Atwood, Sid's friend. Atwood was furious. "I want to be tried with the rest of these boys," he said. When the judge held firm, Atwood stormed out. "I don't like this a damn bit. I want to be tried and acquitted with the rest of these boys."

John McDowell, the detective who escaped from the battle by plunging into the Tug River, was the first witness and methodically reviewed the events of May 19. Conniff, in his cross-examination, played for the jury's sympathy: "How many sick persons were evicted? Wasn't it true that a sick woman was evicted?"

The two young telephone operators told of overhearing Sid's statement to the sheriff's office: "We'll kill the blank blank blank blank blank before they get out of Matewan," the five blanks representing "five unprintable oaths." Pressed to say the words, one of the girls blushed and squirmed before whispering, "God damn sons of bitches." No newspaper printed them.

One after another, prosecution witnesses identified the defendants and their parts in the slayings: Reece Chambers, Ed Chambers, Bill Bowman, Fred Burgraff, and above all, Sid. The audience filled every seat, and time and again the judge ordered spectators back from the railing.

A school teacher visibly affected the audience when she went down on her knees on the witness stand and aimed a curtain rod at the jury box, demonstrating how a miner shot a detective. Witnesses described the gruesome details of Ferguson's death. A dentist testified Al Felts could not possibly have shot Testerman.

Charges against Isaac Brewer were dropped, and the reason became apparent: he had turned state's evidence. Taking the stand as the defendants glowered at him, Brewer told a hushed audience that Sid, seconds before the shooting began, had cupped his hands over Brewer's ear and whispered, "Let's kill every God damned one of them." Testerman objected to killing the detectives, Brewer said, and Sid told Brewer he could "cut him in two with a bullet." Sid listened but did not lose his poise.

Two feet of snow fell, but the trial went on. An automobile backfired, and spectators stampeded from the courtroom in fright.

The big shock came when Lively took the stand to reveal his true identity. Spectators had begun to leave for the day when Lively took the stand, and his testimony brought them hurrying back to their seats. Sid, the other defendants, the audience, and jury listened entranced as Lively told all: he had come to Matewan to spy, had befriended Sid and the others only for that reason, had joined the union, had opened the restaurant, all in his role as spy. Then, one by one, Lively told what he said the defendants had told him: Sid said he shot Al Felts; Reece Chambers said he shot Lee Felts; Fred Burgraff said he shot Ferguson; Art Williams said he shot Al Felts in the head after the detective had fallen, and on and on.

Lively's main attack was at Sid. "Did Sid Hatfield make any statement to you at any time as to who killed Testerman?" the prosecution asked.

"Yes, sir he did."

"Who did he say killed Mayor Testerman?"

"He said he did."

"State to the jury in what way he made that statement."

"We were talking about the killing. He said after Albert Felts was shot he shot Mayor Testerman. Testerman was getting too well lined up with those Baldwin men."

Lively talked of Sid's marriage: "Well, at one time before this [battle], Sid and I were talking. I asked him if he was married, and he said, 'No, and a poor chance to get married,' that another man had the woman he wanted . . . I took it more as a joke than anything else. I said, 'You must be crazy about that little blonde.' He said. 'She is not a blonde; she is a brunette. I will have her if I have to go through hell to get her.'"

In cross-examination, Conniff forced Lively to tell of his ten years of spying on others, in Colorado, Illinois, Missouri, and elsewhere. "So you used your membership to practice falsehood and deceit?" "With your union card in your pocket, you worked against the union?" Conniff struck paydirt when he asked Lively if Sid had told him about being offered money to take a machine gun into Matewan.

"He said something about an offer," Lively responded, visibly distressed.

"He turned the offer down, didn't he?"

"That was the substance of it."

"Was anything else said about the subject?"

"Well, he said something about being offered one thousand dollars and a monthly salary."

As the defense began, charges were dropped against two more defendants, reducing the number to eighteen. Then Conniff began, putting forth witnesses who raised new doubts about the charge, who emphasized the self-defensive nature of the killings, the horror of the evictions and the affinity between jurymen and defendants. A barber testified Al Felts shot into the hardware store with one gun while shooting Testerman with the other. A miner said he heard Al Felts promise to kill Sid and Testerman. An uncle of Isaac Brewer testified Brewer originally told friends Felts fired first at Testerman.

The trial continued all day March 4 while in Washington Warren G. Harding stood bareheaded in a brilliant sun and took the oath of office as president and in Charleston Ephraim Morgan became West Virginia's governor. Piece by piece, the defense painted a picture of highly armed private detectives employed by big out-of-state coal corporations to prey on helpless miners and their families. Witnesses heaped praise on Sid, and one woman pushed her way down from the witness stand saying, "I never met Sid Hatfield in my life. I don't know him now, but I want to meet him," and she thrust her hand at Sid and said, "I am mighty glad to meet you, Mr. Hatfield," as the crowd reacted noisily.

After forty-three days, the judge began night sessions. Tension mounted. Sallie Chambers, Ed's wife, snapped at Isaac Brewer as he passed, and a deputy escorted her from the room. On March 18, as final arguments began, the crowd overflowed the courtroom.

Harold Houston, presenting the defense, gratified them fully: "It is time," he said with clear oratorical effect, "that Mingo County should be governed by the taxpayers, and not by a private detective agency."

He played upon the labor issue. "What crime had these men committed? . . . The crime they committed, calling down the power of the coal operators upon them, was joining the miners union."

The detectives tried to bribe Sid, he said. "They wanted to buy him, like they did Isaac Brewer and C. E. Lively. If Hatfield could have been bought he would have been in the place of Brewer and Lively today. But he could not be bought, and he stands trial for his life. I am proud to know that Matewan elected such unimpeachable men to office. Poor, perhaps, but men who will not sell their manhood. They tried not only to buy Sid Hatfield but offered to pay one thousand dollars to permit them to bring a machine gun into Matewan. And what for? To shoot down that little band of union men." He pictured the little children who had fled to the hills on that fatal day, "kneeling beside their beds in prayer at night for the return of their daddies." Women in the audience cried, and a tear flowed down Sid's cheek.

Marcum responded: "No doubt there were women and children waiting and longing for their husbands and fathers, but they were in the homes of Ferguson, Booher and Powell, Higgins and the other detectives killed at Matewan."

Marcum concentrated his attack on Sid, who he said had been "played as a hero."

"I really don't think he appreciates the enormity of his crime, for he sat smiling through the trial, and he is smiling now." Sid's smile diminished slightly.

"Sid may smile and smile and smile and offend John Marcum," Conniff responded, "but he will offend no man who believes in the performance of duty." The detectives had "struck at a vital point in the miner's life by striking at what he works and slaves for, his home." He condemned the prosecution for the "dragging of Mrs. Sid Hatfield's name into the case. . . . It is ridiculous to believe that Sid killed Testerman because he married the mayor's widow two weeks after his death. Would Sid have gone out alone and precipitated a fight with thirteen men, armed to the teeth, merely to gain his prize? Thank God there's one place the Baldwin-Felts Detective Agency cannot get in, and that's the jury box."

Judge Sanders summed up the state's case in four hours of oratory. Judge Bailey instructed the jury, and it retired. As it did, charges were dropped against another defendant, J. C. McCoy. The number charged now stood at seventeen.

It was Saturday evening. While the jury was out, the defendants, counsel, and reporters scattered around the courtroom in little clusters. All seemed strangely in good humor. Sid smiled and talked amiably with his attorneys. Outside, crowds waited in the streets. At 9:15 P.M., with no verdict, Judge Bailey ordered the court adjourned until Monday.

The weekend passed quietly, the only disturbance coming when unknown assailants shot at nonunion miners at Merrimac, near Matewan. It seemed routine.

Monday was hot. The jury deliberated from 8:00 until 11:00 A.M. as miners and mountaineers assembled around the courthouse and relatives of the prisoners gathered on the jailhouse porch. Shortly after eleven o'clock the jury returned. Reporters scribbled to record every detail: Sid continued to smile but gripped his chair.

They still tell how the jury reached its verdict. One of the jurors, a farmer from the little town of Gilbert far back in the mountain wilderness, had looked at the other jurymen and then looked out the window at the mountains. When the trial started, he said, the mountains were brown and bare. Now the trial was ending, and the mountains were turning green and the dogwood and laurel were about to bloom. He was ready to sit there, he said, until the mountains turned brown again and the dogwoods bloomed again before he'd vote to convict a single Matewan boy.

And the old man's argument prevailed. The jury acquitted all seventeen Matewan boys. As the jury gave its verdict, onlookers signaled the word to the crowd outside, who cheered. The overjoyed defendants congratulated Conniff.

Late that afternoon, Sid and the sixteen other defendants emerged from the jail and into the arms of their wives and families, who wept and laughed with joy. A heavy guard of state police escorted them through the streets to the depot, where they boarded a special railroad car, surrounded by well-wishers, shaking hands with all. It was the famous "No. 16," the five o'clock train that had been a byword in the trial, the one that had come upon the battle scene in Matewan. The defendants waved and smiled as the train pulled out.

At Matewan, the entire population was at the depot to welcome home the heroes of the battle trial. State troopers and deputies escorted the men from the train into the arms of the crowd. There were hand shakings and back slappings, hilarity and weeping. "It's the happiest day Matewan ever knew," someone said. "At least for me," Sid said.

It took more than an hour for Sid and Jessie to make their way through the crowd to their home above the jewelry store two hundred feet away, shaking hands and embracing people all the way. When they finally got there, Sid looked at his right hand, swollen from the grasps of his neighbors, and remarked, "It's good to know you have so many friends."

7

"Our citizens are being shot down like rats"

Spring came to the Tug with breathtaking beauty. Birds sang along the river. The vast mountainsides turned from brown to many delicate shades of green, dotted with pink blossoms of mountain laurel and white of dogwood. Climbing roses bloomed on miners' cabins.

To America's miners, Sid was now a greater hero than ever. The *UMW Journal* headlined the Matewan trial every issue and praised the verdict: "It is believed that it will really result in the complete elimination of the brutal gang of gunmen" in West Virginia. The union hired a small moving picture company which made a silent movie called *Smilin' Sid,* showing the tent colonies, mining camps, and Sid brandishing guns and leading the miners, and the picture was shown in union mining camps.

Sid took up duties as constable of Magnolia District and helped Jessie run the store. To the horror of the coal operators, he converted it to a weapons business and sold guns and ammunition to his miner friends. Much of his time he passed sitting on the bench outside the store with Ed Chambers and his other friends, talking and kibitzing the continuous checkers game that went on there. At other times, he and Jessie and her little boy enjoyed life in their attractive five-room apartment with bath that Jessie had inherited from the mayor.

Lively, knowing that to remain in Matewan would mean his death, moved his family to Bluefield the very evening he gave his testimony, his wife packing their bags as he testified. The

United Mine Workers expelled him from its membership for ninety-nine years, and Sid allowed he would give every tooth in his head to have known about Lively before the trial.

Sid's friends openly expressed fear for his life, as Tom Felts and his Baldwin-Felts detectives made disparaging remarks about the trial. Sid, himself, told friends he was a "marked man. They will get me sooner or later."

Strongest reaction to the trial came in the West Virginia legislature. The lawmakers, convening in Charleston, rushed through a bill, sponsored by State Senator Joseph Sanders, chief counsel for the prosecution in the Matewan trial, to make it possible to draw a county court jury from another county, the same legislation the miners had defeated the preceding fall. They also doubled the size of the state police and authorized re-establishing the state's National Guard.

Peace reigned only briefly. The soldiers pulled out, and the embattled Captain Brockus and his state police returned, only to learn that the striking miners planned an all-out assault on nonunion mines in early May. This time, nonunion miners made it clear they would shoot back, and they formed their own firing groups.

As if on schedule, fighting erupted in the rainy morning hours of Thursday, May 12, when bullets peppered down from the West Virginia mountains on a half dozen mining towns near Matewan. Immediately, nonunion miners returned the fire from the Kentucky mountains. By mid-morning, fighting was general, and shots rang out from every mountain. No one could tell who was shooting at whom. Nonunion miners in the valley shot blindly back, and deputies opened fire with machine guns. Hundreds, then thousands of shots boomed and echoed until in places they became a continuous roar. Bullets cut telephone wires and tore through houses and buildings in the miners' camps. Women and children hid in closets and cellars and ran from their homes. Bullets ripped through the walls of houses, and at the state police headquarters near Matewan a bullet came through a wall and smashed a mirror as four troopers looked on. Two men were wounded by stray bullets as they huddled in their homes. Harry C. Staton, who had testified against Sid at the trial, was shot and killed as he stepped from his home, and before the day ended police arrested J. C. McCoy, one of Sid's fellow defendants in the trial, for murder.

In the midst of all this, a passenger train snaked up the river, and sharpshooters opened fire from mountains on both sides. Screaming passengers threw themselves on the floor as bullets hit around them. The train roared full speed through a scheduled stop and halted outside the Hatfield Tunnel. There, five state troopers jumped off and ran, dodging bullets, for the protection of nearby woods.

Captain Brockus and his men rushed through the valley in automobiles, bogging down in mud until they put chains on their wheels and finally abandoned the vehicles. Brockus led his men on foot over the mountains to outflank a group of attackers west of Matewan and returned, discouraged and unsuccessful, after dark.

That night, families slept on floors, under beds, in cellars, and the shooting continued. Lighted windows drew gunfire until, one by one, they blinked out. At Matewan, street lights were extinguished. The battle resumed full fury at dawn Friday and raged all day. A woman walking across a clearing with her baby drew fire near Matewan; she ran for safety, clutching her child, as bullets kicked up dust around her. A teamster jumped from his wagon and fled amid a hail of bullets as his mule stampeded aimlessly, the wagon bouncing behind him. Two more persons were killed. Ambrose Gooslin, 16, was hit in the stomach on a railroad bridge near Matewan and lay there all day, alive, as bullets hit around him; he died two days later. Dan Whitt of Matewan was killed the same morning when he left his family to go for water.

Forty miners were hemmed in at a mine by heavy fire. Stray bullets killed a half dozen cattle and a mule. At one mine, a bookkeeper was driven back by gunfire each time he left his building to retrieve a pile of groceries that were spoiling by the railroad. Like running a gauntlet, passenger trains roared through the valley at full speed, their passengers lying on the floors. In Matewan, businesses closed, school was canceled, and nonunion miners abandoned their cabins and fled. Sid walked through the largely deserted town with his friends, heavily armed, and found the superintendent of the Stone Mountain Coal Company supervising a group of men unloading a railcar. They quarreled, and Sid hit the superintendent; some said Sid struck him with his rifle; Sid admitted only that he "slapped him down." The superintendent was hospitalized nine days, and another criminal charge, the tenth, was filed against the young constable of Magnolia District.

On Friday, a deputy sheriff waving a piece of white muslin made contact with union riflemen in the mountains behind Matewan, and they promised to stop shooting if their opponents would do so, too. Acting on that promise, Brockus sent a prominent physician into the Kentucky mountains to negotiate with the nonunion fighters there. The physician crawled a half mile under fire and, standing among bullet-riddled buildings, obtained a promise that the nonunion miners would cease firing. The doctor returned triumphantly Saturday night to Matewan where an elated Brockus welcomed him. As word spread, the "Three Days Battle" slowed and stopped.

In Charleston, a panic-stricken Governor Morgan, experiencing the first major outbreak of Mingo County warfare in his administration, fired off telegram after telegram to President Harding calling for federal troops. "Nothing short of 100 per cent martial law" could restore order, he pleaded. Five hundred troops would be needed "to prevent wanton slaughter of innocent citizens." Mingo was a "smoldering volcano." A Huntington man wired Secretary of War John W. Weeks: "In the name of GOD, please hurry Federal aid to Matewan. Our citizens are being shot down like rats."

Adding to the alarm, union miners in central West Virginia near Charleston held mass meetings and talked angrily of mobilizing to march on Mingo. Bill Blizzard, subdistrict union president, worked "to cool off the hotheads."

In Washington, Weeks dispatched Major C. F. Thompson, destined to play an increasing role in West Virginia's future, to investigate the mine war. Convinced initially that federal intervention was necessary, Weeks prepared a declaration of martial law for President Harding's signature. Before it was issued, however, the signals changed. Governor Morrow of Kentucky sent 150 guardsmen to the Tug and reported the situation improving. Major Thompson wired after a quick investigation: "Do not see justification for use of Federal troops." After a little more investigation, Thompson reported the delay in sending troops "has had a beneficial effect in arousing the community and officials to a sense of obligation." General George W. Reade, commander of the Fifth Corps Area, wired Weeks that danger on the Tug did not seem imminent. That conclusion began to prevail. Weeks conferred with a delegation from West Virginia and talked to Morgan by telephone, then discussed the situation with the president at a Cabinet meeting. It was clear, he said, the West Virginians had not done all they could to halt the fighting but simply had cried for federal troops. The martial law proclamation was discarded, and Presidential Secretary George Christian wired Governor Morgan the troops would not be forthcoming: "The President is not convinced," the message stated, "that West Virginia has exhausted all its own resources, and he awaits more definite assurances."

8

"... to clean up Mingo County"

I

CAPTAIN BROCKUS called them the "better people" of Mingo County: lawyers, physicians, clergymen, insurance men, merchants, leaders of the American Legion and YMCA. It was with a sense of crisis that they were called together in Williamson following the "Three Days Battle" along the Tug. They filled every seat in the great courtroom of the county courthouse where Sid had been tried. They sang "My Country, 'Tis of Thee," and a legionnaire explained the purpose of their gathering:

It was "a call for men who will stand up for law and order in Mingo County."

It was time for them to enforce the law themselves.

Dr. J. W. Carpenter, minister of Williamson's First Presbyterian Church, elaborated: President Harding had told them they must use their own resources before calling for federal help; clergy had seized on the idea with patriotic fervor and had called community leaders together. They must form their own military organization in Mingo County. "It is just as much a patriotic duty to clean up Mingo County as it was France," he said, and added, "I don't know a thing about a rifle, but I am sure I can wield one, or a baseball bat, if necessary."

Lant Slavin, an attorney, also spoke. "Who knows how soon they will be firing on Williamson?" he asked, adding, "I am here to offer my service as deputy and will gladly do my part to maintain order."

"There may be a few losses among us," another said, "but

who would not be willing to make a sacrifice for the sake of patriotism and law and order in Mingo County?"

Major Ike Wilder, commander of the Kentucky militia in the area, strode forward in uniform and spurs and read a supporting telegram from his governor.

Then Mingo's new sheriff, A. C. Pinson, disclosed he had been in lengthy contact with Governor Morgan, who strongly endorsed the meeting and committed his support. Pinson read a telegram from Morgan: "No time should be lost in placing under arrest every person in the county who has engaged, aided or abetted in the recent murders, attempted murders and destruction of property. Sufficient force should be deputized, cooperating with state police, to ensure the apprehension and disarming of all violators and those suspected of participation in the insurrection."

Brockus arrived late from a hasty trip to Matewan. He walked down the aisle like a hero returned from the front, and he thrilled his listeners: "It is clearly up to you," he said, and the men listened silently, soberly. "It is for you to decide whether you will have lawlessness, order or disorder. . . . It is for you the citizens of Mingo County, through full cooperation with the constituted authorities, to clean it up quickly and effectively. Will you do it?"

They nodded emphatically.

"Unless you have a rifle on your shoulder and are ready to do your duty, then we will have no order in Mingo County. Unless you show up to take your place, then there is no hope."

They nodded more emphatically.

Like an evangelist beckoning sinners, he called for every man to stand "who is willing to shoulder a rifle tomorrow and go out and do his bit!"

In unison, all sprang to their feet and waved their hands high. "It seems to be unanimous," Brockus said dramatically, and the meeting ended.

Next day, Governor Morgan placed Mingo County under martial law. It was the governor's own brand, far more oppressive than anything the army had visited on the county the previous winter. Issued on May 19, the anniversary of the Matewan battle, the martial law proclamation cited a "state of war, insurrection and riot" in Mingo County, banned processions, parades, public assemblies, and the carrying of firearms except by special authority, and it directed that "no publication, either newspaper, pamphlet, handbill, or otherwise, reflecting in any way upon the United States or the State of West Virginia . . . may be published, distributed, displayed, or circulated." Violators would be "arrested, disarmed, detained and imprisoned." Major Thomas B. Davis, acting state adjutant general, was named militia commander, and he came to Williamson to post the proclamation personally.

Volunteers flocked to enlist: clerks, lawyers, automobile salesmen, merchants, bookkeepers, real estate men, engineers, contractors. Mine superintendents recommended nonunion miners, excluding foreign-born and blacks. A "Law and Order Committee" of leading citizens approved enlistments, and police issued badges, rifles, and striped arm bands for identification. Four quick blasts of the Williamson fire siren, repeated three times, became the call to arms. By June 1, eight hundred men had signed up.

From its inception, the citizens' militia enforced martial law exclusively against the striking miners. Church services and motion pictures continued before large crowds. Those enforcing martial law, themselves, held regular meetings to enlist more militia. The Salvation Army conducted processions. On May 30, Williamson held a Memorial Day parade, and Brockus and his state police, members of the local American Legion post, and the Law and Order Committee marched through the main streets as townspeople applauded from the sidewalks. But in Matewan, if as many as three striking miners gathered, state policemen or volunteer militiamen ordered them to move on or be arrested.

Major Davis decided what would be offenses against martial law and how those offenses would be punished, unencumbered by warrants, charges, hearings, evidence, or trials. A large man with heavy jaws, he became an instant villain to striking miners, who called him "the bulldog."

Arrests began immediately. On May 23, A. D. Lavinder, union organizer, refused to turn over his pistol to state police because he had a permit; the troopers seized Lavinder roughly and marched him off to the county jail. When several union men gathered outside the jail to protest, Brockus drove them away saying they were violating the mandate against public assemblies.

Almost daily thereafter, police and militiamen brought in union miners, handcuffed together in groups of five and ten, all jailed without bond or hearing. Brockus acknowledged miners were jailed for carrying union literature. Many were held also for carrying arms, resisting officers, speaking against martial law, or "agitating." Police forced a union official to remove a placard from his wall because of the wording that described a strike. When the family of a jailed black miner asked if he would be granted bond or trial, Major Davis told them they would be jailed, too, if they continued asking questions.

Within ten days, the county jail overflowed. Davis sent prisoners to jails in surrounding counties.

In Charleston, Fred Mooney, secretary of District 17 of the UMW, called the governor's martial law "a declaration of military dictatorship." The union challenged the constitutionality of his martial law proclamation in the state supreme court, and for a short time the challenge succeeded; the court held the proclamation unconstitutional because Mingo was not under state military occupation. The governor quickly issued a new proclamation, reaffirming the earlier one but mustering the militia "into the service of the State." That rectified the legal problem and martial law continued.

Even jails in neighboring counties overflowed, and Davis released some of his prisoners simply to relieve congestion. Miners found themselves arrested, jailed, and released without a hearing at either end.

The striking miners responded as they knew how. A dynamite explosion destroyed the head house of the War Eagle Coal Company. The head house of the Stone Mountain Coal Company burned. The company store at Lynn, near Matewan, was looted and burned. On the night of May 25, Kentucky militia and West Virginia state police collided in pitch darkness with strikers at Nolan; there were angry words; someone struck a match; a gun went off, then several guns. West Virginia State Trooper Charles M. Kackley and Kentucky Militiaman Manley Vaughan fell dead, both shot through the head. George A. Crum, a striker, was shot through the lungs and died the next day.

In June, another state trooper, William McMillion, was shot

and killed as he passed a tent colony near Matewan. Striking miners were arrested for the murder.

In July, eighty-five policemen and militiamen raided a tent colony near Matewan and arrested twenty-six men on charges of burning the Lynn company store. The jails couldn't hold them. They were held prisoners on the courthouse lawn in Williamson, surrounded by militiamen, who told them to stand. In response, the miners lay down and "told 'em to kiss our asses," one of them said years later.

II

Major Davis and Brockus gave increasing attention to the tent colony at Lick Creek near Williamson, largest of the tent cities along the Tug and center of much of the violence.

On June 3, Lick Creek colonists shot at a passing state trooper, and the reaction was immediate. Brockus and forty troopers moved through the tents arresting every man they could catch; they bagged forty-two, the rest fleeing into the woods. All were jailed.

Ten days later, Major Davis, himself, passed the tent colony, and the miners opened fire at him. Davis declared war. Under his order, a trooper sprayed submachine-gun bullets into the tents, and Davis raced back to Williamson. The fire siren screamed four quick blasts, repeated three times, and within minutes seventy militiamen were there, rifles in hand. Reinforced with state police, they sped back to Lick Creek in a caravan of cars and deployed on foot around the tents. Some moved in from the rear, others from the front, walking abreast, rifles ready, like hunters. Davis ordered them to arrest everyone they saw and to take armed miners dead or alive.

A squad of militia spotted a group of armed tent colonists in a wooded valley to the rear of the tents. Both sides began shooting. State Trooper James A. Bowles shot a miner in the pit of the stomach, and the man crumpled forward and died. Bowles was hit by a bullet that ripped through his shoulder and lower neck, and he fell seriously wounded; miners said later he was shot by his own men.

Four militiamen with Bowles—a bank clerk, insurance man,

post office employee and nonunion miner – had thrown themselves to the ground, and they kept up a steady fire. Martin Justice, colorful "mayor" of Lick Creek tent colony, bolted from the
rear of the colony and ran along a hillside trying to escape. All
opened fire on him. Two bullets hit him, but he kept on running
and disappeared into the woods, bleeding from wounds in his
cheek and leg.

At the other end of the tent colony, Brockus and the major
force of his militia spread through the tents, knocking them
down, slashing canvas with knives, kicking over furniture, flush-
ing out miners and their families, and collaring prisoners. Several families were bathing in the river, and the militiamen herded
them out of the water and took them prisoners. Other families
ran from the tents and hid beneath a concrete bridge over Lick
Creek; Brockus and his men ordered them out at gunpoint,
formed them on the road, freed the women and children and
marched the men off to jail, forty-seven in all. They carried
Bowles to a hospital, where he survived. The miner who was
killed was identified as Alexander Breedlove, one of the first to
have been evicted from his home the preceding spring and one
of the most popular of Mingo's union miners. His body was
taken to Williamson and turned over to his widow. Police later
captured Justice, not seriously hurt despite his two bullet wounds,
and added him to their bag of prisoners. All were placed in a
single jail cell.

III

The United Mine Workers operated an office at a hotel in Williamson, until Major Davis decided that, too, violated martial
law. On July 8, after several warnings, he and Brockus personally led a raid on the office, arrested everyone present, handcuffed them, and shipped them off to jail in McDowell County.
The prisoners, twelve in all, included four miners who had come
to the office to ask for relief.

The incident quickly became national in its implications.
John L. Lewis wired Governor Morgan protesting: the union men
were doing only union business. Morgan offered no help. Lewis
appealed to President Harding with no better success. Philip Mur-

ray, UMWA vice president, hurried to West Virginia and conferred with Major Davis; they worked out a compromise in which the four union organizers who had been arrested would be freed only if they left the state. In a helpless rage, Murray agreed.

IV

Sid tried to stay out of the public eye following the Three Days Battle, but he was not successful. The battle brought newsmen hurrying back to the Tug, and several came by to see him. One had persuaded him to pose for a photo outside his store; he did, with a pistol in each hand and a huge smile across his face. The picture appeared in publications everywhere along with references to him as "Smilin' Sid," "Two-Gun Sid," and "the Terror of the Tug." After that, Sid stopped being so friendly to the press. "Every newspaper correspondent who has visited Matewan has been run out of town by Hatfield," a *New York Times* correspondent reported.

That tactic didn't work either. On May 24, Sid caught the noon train to Williamson to talk with Sheriff Pinson about one of the charges against him, and word of his impending arrival spread through the county seat. When his train pulled in, the Williamson depot was crowded with people waiting to see the famous constable, including Major Davis, Captain Brockus, a score of state troopers, more than a hundred militiamen, news correspondents, and a motion picture cameraman. They were all disappointed; Sid did not appear. Minutes later, the crowd learned why: Sid had slipped off the far side of the train to avoid the crowd and had sneaked into town alone. People ran to the courthouse, and there stood Sid on the steps, wearing his famous grin.

Sid finished his business with the sheriff and then walked around Williamson awaiting his return train. Newsmen followed him. Scores of passers-by waved and shouted, "Hello, Sid," and Sid exchanged friendly greetings with them all. There was "no trace or inkling of the 'bad man' about him," a newsman observed. Sid used the occasion to make a few comments for the press: Matewan was quiet, he said, and there would be no trouble "if they leave us alone."

"We have as peaceful and law-abiding a town as there is in this part of the country, and never had any trouble until the operators began bringing in their gunmen."

Sid hated the martial law edict and gave it minimum cooperation. His attitude became clear when state police arrested a union miner in Matewan on a martial law charge and asked him to place the prisoner in Matewan's jail. Sid said he did not have a key. The state officers found Matewan's new mayor who insisted the jail key was in Sid's custody. They came back to Sid.

"Search me," Sid said with a grin.

The troopers took their prisoner to the county jail in Williamson, and Matewan's jail stayed empty.

Major Davis was furious when he heard about it. He fired off a letter to the mayor saying he understood "some of the officials in your city could not locate the key to the jail."

"I want to state as plainly as I can that must never happen again," Davis wrote, and he threatened to put Sid, himself, in jail. As for the key, Matewan officials "had better have one located the next time we want to put prisoners in that jail."

Sid shrugged it off. He was "a law unto himself," the *New York Times* observed. This was further evidenced a few days later, at the height of martial law, when police confiscated ten thousand rounds of Krag ammunition being shipped to Matewan. Sid freely acknowledged he had ordered it to sell in his store.

V

Following the Three Days Battle and the raid on Lick Creek tent colony, pressure for a Congressional investigation of the Mingo situation mounted rapidly. Senator Hiram Johnson of California had introduced a resolution calling for such an investigation, and it drew increasing support as the violence continued. The Lick Creek raid and the killing of Breedlove brought the issue to a head.

Exaggerated stories of the raid reached the floor of Congress. Breedlove was trying to surrender when he was killed, the story went. A union miner signed an affidavit describing the killing: "Breedlove had his hands up above his head at the time he was shot; Bowles said to Breedlove, 'Hold up your hands, God damn you, and if you have anything to say, say it fast,' and Breedlove said, 'Lord, have mercy,' and instantly the gun fired and Breedlove fell."

Photos appeared in the press of the desolation caused by the Lick Creek raid; miners' wives and children stood in their shredded tents, their heads protruding through holes slashed by the invading militia. The stories grew: the militiamen had knocked down women, beaten babies, poured groceries onto the ground, burned clothing, poured kerosene in baby's milk, broken dishes, and torn down the colony's American flag and stamped it in the dirt.

Hundreds had attended Breedlove's funeral and repeated the stories of his death. Miners along the Kanawha River were so enraged that they began mobilizing to march on Mingo, and telephone wires were cut. Rumors spread that Keeney was killed at Lick Creek, and Keeney himself traveled along the river to calm the men down.

In Washington, Senator Johnson took the Senate floor and told of Breedlove's death. Breedlove, he said, was trying to surrender and was praying for mercy when "a soft-nosed bullet penetrated his body and killed him at once." Within days, the Senate adopted a resolution calling for an investigation by the Senate Committee on Labor and Education into the violence of West Virginia's coalfields.

9

"You saw nothing wrong in that?"

WHEN SID WALKED into the Senate hearing room in Washington, it created a little stir. Harold Houston, his union attorney, introduced him, and Senator William S. Kenyon of Iowa, chairman of the Senate Committee on Education and Labor, which had called the hearing, noted his presence: "There are a few questions that the committee will ask Mr. Hatfield." Kenyon mentioned the criminal indictments against Sid and emphasized to Houston, "We do not want to try Mr. Hatfield's case. . . . If you want to object to any questions you are at liberty to do so."

Sid was duly sworn. Under questioning, before a room full of senators, lawyers, news reporters and spectators, Sid quietly told the story of the Matewan battle as he saw it. The Baldwin-Felts detectives had come to Matewan to throw miners out of their homes, he said. "Well, me and the mayor of the town went up and asked did they have a right to do that, and Mr. Felts, the superintendent of the agency, said that he had. . . . They went ahead and throwed the people out, and about 3:30 they came back to Matewan—"

"I cannot understand you," Senator Kenyon said. "You must speak louder."

"About 3:30 they came back to Matewan and they had guns on their shoulders," and on and on until, in Sid's words, Al Felts "shot the mayor. Then the shooting started in general."

It was July 16, Saturday, the third day of a hearing which had opened with union charges that Mingo county was under virtual dictatorship. "A condition obtains in Mingo County that has no parallel, even in Soviet Russia or any land in the world," said Neil Burkinshaw, union attorney. "All civil processes are abolished, and the entire government is in the hands of a single man."

Z. T. Vinson, attorney for the coal operators, quickly responded: "All the trouble, violence and murder that have occurred in Mingo and Pike Counties for the past year have been directly caused by the activities and criminal practices of the United Mine Workers."

For eight days witnesses paraded before the committee: Keeney, Mooney, Captain Brockus, miners and operators, in a torrent of words that eventually filled a thousand pages of small print. Sid's testimony was one of the highlights. In short responses to senators' questions, he told how coal operators sought to enforce the law in Mingo County. On the day of the battle, he said, the Baldwin-Felts detectives tried to arrest him in his own town, where he served as police chief, and carry him one hundred miles away without bond to their private headquarters in Bluefield, in answer to a charge that clearly was manufactured. Even a senator looked at the warrant and commented, "Void on its face."

The coal operators' attorneys tried to argue that Sid had killed Mayor Testerman, but Sid responded vigorously: one man, Isaac Brewer, had testified to that effect, and he was "a Baldwin-Felts man that they paid to turn state's evidence against the rest of us . . . they taken him out and got him to swear to anything."

Lively too was called to the stand, and the astonished senators listened as he described his life as a labor spy. Under questioning by his own attorneys, Lively freely told how he had gone to work as a spy for the Baldwin-Felts agency nearly ten years earlier while retaining membership in the United Mine Workers; he represented his local union at district conventions. Senator McKellar of Tennessee was incredulous: "You felt," the senator asked, "in the way you were working, you were doing entirely what was right and proper?"

"Yes, sir."

"You saw nothing wrong in that?"

"I saw nothing wrong about it."

Lively acknowledged he was at times paid expenses for his

work by both the union and the detective agency. In Colorado, he said, he was elected vice president of a miners' union local while spying on its members. Senator McKellar interrupted: "Do you mean to say you were vice president of the local lodge of the union while you were acting in the employ of the detective agency?"

"Yes, sir. I was there working on a murder case."

Seeing that the questioning had taken an unfavorable turn, Lively's attorney broke in: Lively had a "right" to do that. "That is the method practiced by the Department of Justice." In fact, the attorney said, "I think that it is practiced in every department in Washington."

McKellar was astounded. "I do not believe it . . . I will say that it violates every idea of right that I ever had. I never would have believed that such a thing like this would happen, and I am not surprised that you are having trouble down there in Mingo County."

It was while testifying that Sid received word he had been indicted in McDowell County. He was charged with taking part in a raid on the mining camp at Mohawk nearly a year earlier. An attorney for the operators, cross-examining him, seemed to let the information slip out accidentally as he tried to demonstrate to the senators that Sid was a criminal character: "Are you not under indictment in McDowell County, an indictment returning this week, charging you with a conspiracy, in connection with others, to blow up the coal tipple at Mohawk?"

Sid looked at the attorney, surprised. "This is the first I heard of it."

The cat was out of the bag. Returning to his hotel in Washington, Sid got the word officially: a grand jury had just indicted him and about thirty-five other Mingo miners on charges of attacking nonunion miners at Mohawk in August of 1920; Sid was to report to Welch for trial.

It had signs of a frame-up. Sid's friends immediately warned him not to go. Sid told Sam Montgomery, who had come with him to the hearing, he was afraid he would be killed if he went to Welch. Montgomery counseled him to go. If he conducted himself peaceably and as a law-abiding man, Montgomery said, he would be safe in McDowell County. To make sure, Montgomery wrote directly to Judge James French Strother in Welch, who would try the case, expressing concern about Sid's safety.

Two weeks later, back in Matewan, McDowell Sheriff William Hatfield and Welch Police Chief Harry Chafin appeared at Sid's store and arrested the famous constable. Sid surrendered peacefully. He and Jessie traveled by train to Welch with the sheriff and police chief. Sid spent the night in McDowell jail, and next morning Jessie posted two thousand dollars bond. They returned together by train.

The McDowell sheriff promised Jessie her husband would be safe. "There isn't going to be any trouble," he told reporters who called. "We'll see to that."

Sid's friends still were concerned. Keeney asked Governor Morgan to give Sid special protection at Welch. The Governor refused. Montgomery called the *Wheeling Intelligencer* to get his concern on public record: "I am very anxious regarding Sid Hatfield's case," he said. Sid's friends, he told the newspaper, were afraid "if he submitted himself to be taken into McDowell County that he would be killed."

Like a premonition, Montgomery's statement was published two days before Sid left for Welch.

10

"Don't shoot him any more!"

SID AND JESSIE got up before daylight to catch the early train for Welch. Ed and Sallie Chambers went with them; Ed planned to testify in Sid's defense. Jim Kirkpatrick, a Mingo deputy sheriff and good friend, went, too, to provide protection. They met at the depot. "Uncle Eb" Chambers, Ed's uncle and founder of the Matewan bank, was there, and he begged Sid not to go. Sid was firm, and they boarded a coach when the train steamed in.

The train wound slowly eastward, puffing around bends, gliding alongside the river, as the sun's first rays found their way to the valley bottom. To their right, the water of the Tug splashed and glistened. The train passed coal camps every few minutes: Thacker, Edgarton, Vulcan, Wharncliffe, Panther, Roderfield. It passed through Mohawk, scene of the attack for which Sid was to stand trial.

Seventeen miles from Welch, at the little town of Iaeger, Lively boarded. He spoke to them and sat down with Kirkpatrick. They remained calm.

When the train pulled in at Welch, it was too early for the trial. Sid and his group went to the Carter Hotel, across from the depot and the courthouse in the tiny mountain town. There were no rooms. They went around the corner and had breakfast in a restaurant. As they ate, Lively entered, nodded to them, and ordered breakfast too.

Breakfast eaten, the five—Sid, Jessie, Ed, Sallie, and Kirkpatrick—returned to the hotel, where they met C. J. Van Fleet, the union attorney who would defend Sid. Van Fleet had come

68

in the night before, and he invited them to his room to rest before the trial.

Sid strolled to the barber shop and got a shave. He then returned to the hotel, and the Matewan contingent assembled in Van Fleet's room.

Idly, to pass time in the hotel room, Sid opened Jessie's traveling case. He had put two revolvers in it when they left home that morning, and he got them out to show Kirkpatrick. "As men will do," Jessie said later.

Jessie was worried. "You better take the guns," she said.

'No," Sid replied. He might be searched in court. He did not want to create embarrassment as he had done at his trial in Williamson.

Kirkpatrick admired Sid's large army revolver. He thought he might need a large gun like that, he said. Sid offered to let him use it, and they exchanged guns.

Van Fleet left to go to the courthouse.

Sid stretched out on the bed, while Kirkpatrick paced the floor. Kirkpatrick looked out the window to the courthouse across the street and stopped. Lively stood on the courthouse lawn, near the top of the steps. "He's keeping pretty close track on us this morning, isn't he?" Kirkpatrick said.

Sid got up and looked out at his old enemy. He said nothing. A train whistle blew down at the depot. They went downstairs.

The street was busy. Men flocked from the depot toward the courthouse. Most were involved in the forthcoming trial: witnesses, defendants, spectators. Sid knew many of them.

The McDowell Courthouse stood tall, ivy covered, Victorian, with a high clock tower atop a hill and back from the narrow street. A heavy stone wall eight feet high held back the hillside from the sidewalk, and above the wall the lawn sloped upward to the courthouse. Two sets of stone steps, running toward each other parallel to the street, led up to a common landing at the top of the wall. The steps there turned perpendicular to the street and led up another flight to the front entrance to the building.

Standing athwart the sidewalk and along the grass at the top of the steps were Lively and a half dozen other Baldwin-Felts detectives, all armed. They watched as the Matewan group crossed the street.

Sid, Jessie, Ed, and Sallie, with Kirkpatrick following behind, started up the steps. People were ahead of them, behind them, and on the street. It was a bright day. Sallie carried a parasol.

Ed, blond, innocent in appearance despite his experience, led the party, one hand on the stone balustrade, the other holding his wife's arm. They reached the first landing and started up the next flight toward the courthouse. Behind them, Sid and Jessie mounted to the first landing as a group of Sid's friends reached it from the opposite direction. Sid raised his hand in friendly greeting, smiled, and said, "Hello, boys."

When Sid's hand moved, as if by signal, the Baldwin-Felts detectives opened fire. Lively shot with two pistols. The others followed his lead.

It was over in ten seconds. One shot hit Sid in the arm. Another struck him in the lower breast. He spun around, as three more bullets slammed into him, and he pitched backward down the steps, rolling and sliding, coming to rest with his head on the third step from the street, his feet stretched back up toward the landing.

By then, Ed, too, was dead. A bullet struck him in the neck; another in the chest. Two more bullets ripped through an arm and penetrated his chest, and still two more hit him in the back. His body lurched backward, and he fell to the landing, blood gushing. He had hardly fallen when Lively ran to the body, put a gun to the ear and fired the coup de grace, as Sallie beat him with her parasol and screamed, "Don't shoot him any more!"

People ran screaming in every direction. Jessie, in disbelief, ran hysterically up the steps and into the courthouse to the sheriff's office, where only three days earlier Sheriff Bill Hatfield had promised Sid's safety. The sheriff wasn't there. He had gone to Virginia to be with friends at a spa.

Kirkpatrick had ducked behind the stone wall, and before he could act it was too late. He ran. Several friends tried to reach Sid, but the detectives stopped them. "Stay back," they said. "We'll take care of this."

Sallie had thrown herself on Ed's body, rubbing his hands and face and wailing, "Oh, no!" The detectives tried to move her into the courthouse. Seeing Lively, she broke loose in fury and attacked him again with her parasol. He yanked it from her and threw it away.

Police and detectives restrained Sallie as she screamed and spat at her husband's killers. They dragged her into the court-house.

"There can be no peace"

Two thousand persons walked in the procession. Still more lined the street. The pallbearers were Knights of Pythias, Oddfellows, and Redmen. They started from the Chambers's home with Ed's massive, metal casket and moved up Mate Street. The procession stopped in front of Sid's store, where Sid's even larger casket was borne to the street. Again the procession moved down the muddy street, Sid's casket at the head, Ed's a short distance behind. It had rained sporadically all morning. The procession moved across the railroad trestle over the rain-swollen Mate Creek and onto the swinging wire footbridge across the Tug River. Some in the crowd hurried in front of the caskets across the bridge, causing it to sway and bounce beneath their feet, and it sagged further as the caskets were carried across one at a time. On the Kentucky side of the river, the procession labored up the steep mountainside toward the graveyard at the top.

Jessie and Sallie had brought their husbands' bodies home to Matewan Monday night. It was midnight when the train arrived, but the station was filled with friends and neighbors. The two young widows descended sadly into the crowd, and all watched silently as the two caskets were lowered from the train. State police and vigilantes patroled the streets, their guns visible, alert for threatened reprisals. The caskets were carried to the two homes, and the crowd quietly disbanded.

All day Tuesday, coal miners came by with their wives and children to look into the caskets of Matewan's most famous citizens. Floral tributes and telegrams of condolence arrived from throughout the country. Police and armed militiamen continued to patrol the streets. Martial law was enforced cautiously, and people walked in pairs.

Jessie and Sallie were near collapse. At one point in the procession Sallie had to be placed in a chair for a rest, while Jessie sobbed. As her husband's casket was carried up the mountainside, Jessie cried loudly enough for some to hear, "I'll never forget you, my sweetheart."

At the cemetery, the Reverend J. C. Holbrook of the Methodist-Episcopal Church allowed the people to pass between the caskets. Rain began falling again, and the caskets were hastily closed. Then the rain poured down in sheets. Few had umbrellas or raincoats; some retreated down the mountain, but hundreds waited dumbly, drenched. The rain finally stopped, and the service began.

"And now abideth faith, hope, charity, these three: but the greatest of these is charity," Mr. Holbrook read.

The eulogy by Samuel Montgomery was more like a political speech: "There can be no peace in West Virginia," he told the mourners in the mountaintop cemetery, "until the enforcement of the law is removed from the hands of private detective agencies, and from those of deputy sheriffs who are paid, not by the state, but by great corporations, most of them owned by nonresidents who have no interest in West Virginia's tomorrow."

"Amen," the mourners said.

The absence of McDowell County's sheriff when Sid and Ed were killed was a circumstance for which the sheriff must "answer to his own conscience," Montgomery said, for Sid's and Ed's deaths "were cold blooded, premeditated murder."

"Amen," the mourners said.

"Even the heavens weep with the grief-stricken relatives and the bereaved friends of these two boys," he concluded.

Across West Virginia, the story swept from mining camp to mining camp: Sid Hatfield and Ed Chambers "was shot down like dogs on the courthouse steps at Welch . . . in front of their wives." The killers were free on bond, paid by leading citizens of southern West Virginia. And while the killers went free, hundreds of Mingo County miners, the miners Sid had defended all his life, remained in jail without formal charge or bond.

Newspapers screamed the news in headlines all over the country, and the United Mine Workers of America closed its district office in Charleston, posting a placard on the door: "Closed in memory of Sid Hatfield and Ed Chambers, murdered by Baldwin-Felts detectives while submitting themselves to a court of law."

When Montgomery returned to Charleston, hundreds of angry miners urged him to call a meeting. Mother Jones hurried into Charleston and urged union leaders to call a mass meeting where she would speak; when they demurred she cursed them roundly. A UMW attorney issued a statement that Sid had been lured to Welch "purposely to be murdered." Montgomery pointed to the newspaper clippings, published before Sid's death, predicting that he might be killed. Sheriff William Hatfield, the man who nevertheless was not there when the shots were fired, explained he had a "previous engagement" in Virginia, but had he stayed in Welch, "I do not think it would have made any difference." Even Lively issued a statement: he had shot in self-defense, he said, when Sid and Ed pulled guns. Governor Morgan promised "a most rigid investigation" and said he was "indeed, very sorry about this affair."

Sallie and Jessie granted a single interview. Sallie did most of the talking, and her words were published coast to coast: "All the time they were shooting Ed, I was begging for him. I was begging Lively to stop. . . . I would say, 'Oh, please, Mr. Lively, don't shoot Ed any more.' He was already dead then. With me begging like that he just walked down to where Ed was lying with his right cheek resting on the stone landing, and put his gun behind his left ear and fired twice."

The *Wheeling Intelligencer* called it "the most glaring and outrageous expression of contempt for law that has ever stained the history of West Virginia." The *UMW Journal* said, "Probably never in the history of the country did a cold-blooded murder ever create as much indignation," and lauded Sid as a "quiet, unassuming man, good natured and always wearing a smile," a man who "never hunted trouble, but he never backed away from danger."

Labor groups passed resolutions of grief and outrage. Sid had been "murdered by the hired gunmen and assassins of the coal barons," said an Illinois miners' union, and an Ohio local suggested a memorial.

In Charleston, miners held a mass meeting on the capitol lawn and passed a resolution of purple prose about Sid and Ed: "the bullets which pierced their bodies forever stained the escutcheons of our state. . . . Innocent blood stains official hands that should be white with purity." Keeney, Mooney, Blizzard, Dee Munsey, Walter Allen, and others spoke to express their outrage. Mother Jones alone was conciliatory; she urged the miners to calm down; nothing would bring Sid back. She went with others to the governor to present demands for an eight-hour day, elected check weighmen at the mines, and appointment of a committee of miners and operators to adjust wages and disputes. The governor, who had watched the rally apprehensively from his windows all day, denied them all.

Miners along Little Coal River, halfway across the wild mountain land between Charleston and Matewan, were the first to begin arming themselves. Patrols of miners with rifles appeared along the roads, and men yelled for revenge. The situation was so tense that Logan County Sheriff Don Chafin requested aid of state police. That made it worse.

On August 12, at Chafin's urging, five state troopers, in campaign hats and carrying guns, rode horseback into the area, and they pranced and ran their horses along a dirt street in the little mining town of Clothier as miners looked on sullenly. A trooper galloped his horse full speed into a parked car; the horse reared and fell, throwing the trooper. The troopers pulled a hapless miner from the car, arrested him, abused him, and sent him running for his mining cabin. The word spread: it was another example of the same West Virginia justice that had caused Sid Hatfield's death.

A mob of armed miners formed to retaliate. They mistook an innocent railroad man, riding several friends in his car, for a policeman, and they opened fire as he drove by; the motorist barreled through the shooting mob and later counted six bullet holes in his car and two in his straw hat. As evening fell, the mob stopped another car, filled this time with real state troopers who were hurrying to investigate the previous shooting, pulled the officers from their vehicle, disarmed them, shoved them, cursed them, and sent them fleeing back to safety in Logan Town.

The incident was to have a far-reaching effect on the rebellion that immediately began to form.

12

"We'll hang Don Chafin to a sour apple tree!"

L ENS C REEK springs from the mountain just below the Boone County line and tumbles and falls among beeches and oaks. Dropping four hundred feet in its eight-mile run, it gathers strength and widens as it passes Six Mile Branch and Four Mile Run, a cluster of buildings called Hernshaw, and an intermittent line of miners' cabins. As it nears the bottom, it flattens; its hollow grows wider; its pools grow deeper. Then, suddenly, it debouches from the mountains, sluices beneath a railroad track, flows out through the bottomland and the town of Marmet and empties into the broad Kanawha. In August 1921, a primitive road – nothing more than two ruts – ran down the hollow, squeezed between creek and mountain, running first on one side, then on the other, often in the creek itself. Though barely passable, it was an arterial road in West Virginia, the passageway from the state capital at Charleston to the wilderness of the state's southwestern coalfields.

On August 24, a guard of two hundred miners with rifles and revolvers stood across the mouth of Lens Creek, sentinels at the edge of the miners' army, checking all who came and went. Behind them, a line of men stretched all the way to the creek's source, and the mountains on either side were dotted with more, nearly all armed. They moved in groups – "companies," some called them – in military fashion, shifting restlessly, awaiting the word to start the march to avenge Sid Hatfield's death.

The word never came, but they started anyway. Shouting and yelling, the men moved, leaderless, in increasing numbers up the creek, groups leapfrogging each other, ever higher, until they reached the headwaters of Lens Creek. Then someone – no one knows who – went over the top of the ridge and down into Boone County, and others fell in behind. They were headed south toward Logan and Mingo Counties. Thus the march began.

In Logan, Sheriff Chafin announced dramatically: "No armed mob will cross Logan County," and the miners knew they would have to fight before they reached Mingo. The prospect excited them. They sang a song to the tune of John Browns Body:

"We'll hang Don Chafin to a sour apple tree,"
and took bets on who would shoot Chafin first. Along Lens Creek, their boasts echoed through the hollow: "Gonna go clean through to Mingo and kill Don Chafin on the way." "Gonna get our people out of jail." "Gonna blow up the Mingo Courthouse." "Gonna drive out the mine guards."

And always: "They shot Sid down like a dog."

The march started as a trickle of men going over the mountain, while others arrived in greater numbers at the creek's lower end, and the army kept growing. Men "are pouring into Marmet on trains, trolley cars and feet," the town's mayor said, even while miners poured out the other end, and in the surrounding mining camps the drum fire continued. At Boomer on the Kanawha, two blacks gathered a crowd on the river bank and told them they had a "yellow streak down their backs" if they didn't join the march, and they passed a hat for money beneath the sycamore trees. At the Mordue Colliery at Whitesville, there wasn't a miner – not a one. Men arrived from the northern part of West Virginia and from other states, and one of them, wearing an army uniform, compared the country to the Argonne, "only them hills wasn't so steep." In the encampment, Walter Allen, Savoy Holt, U. S. Cantley, and Billy Blizzard registered in truckloads of provisions and handed out rations and guns, answered questions, and sent men forward. Ed Reynolds led his company of three hundred men, most wearing blue bib overalls and red neckerchiefs, up the creek and over the mountain.

Some miners were reluctant to join the march. Chris Petry, 20, of Edwight was one. Sent to get guns at a company store, he returned empty-handed; miners cursed him; there was a burst of gunfire, and Petry fell with five bullets in him. Late in the night, someone dumped his riddled body on the front porch of an East Bank funeral home. "Take this damn scab," a male voice said, and a car drove off.

Before daylight, the undertaker had more business. Miners brought in the body of William Guinn, shot from ambush on the march, they said mysteriously, and they left.

Word swept through the miners' army that two other men had been killed. One, identified only as McGuire, was shot twelve times after he protested going on the march. A teamster told of carrying a black miner's bloody body away; he didn't know the man's name, only that "he knew too much." Both deaths were widely reported.

All four were killed within hours as the army began to move. Reports were sketchy, and police, soon caught up in larger events, never investigated them thoroughly. A coroner hurrying to East Bank to examine the two bodies at the funeral home was robbed by miners on the way.

Wednesday morning, Mother Jones arrived on Lens Creek. In the preceding days she had met with Governor Morgan and on his advice had gone to Mingo, where she visited the prisoners in jail, talked to them of Sid's death, and witnessed martial law. When the miners' army began to gather on Lens Creek she hurried back.

A crowd gathered near the creek mouth beneath the trees, and Mother Jones spoke. She surprised them all by urging moderation. The march would do no good, she said; they couldn't win. Go home, she said. She had a telegram from President Harding asking that the march on Mingo be abandoned, she said, and she pretended to read from it: "I request," she quoted the telegram, "that you abandon your purpose and return to your homes, and I assure you that my good offices will be used to forever eliminate the gunman system from the state of West Virginia."

It didn't sound like a president. Keeney, Mooney, Blizzard, and Holt were in the audience, and they couldn't believe it. They asked to see the telegram, and Mother Jones refused.

"It's a damn lie," Mooney shouted to the audience.

"Go to hell," Mother Jones shouted back.

Keeney, standing in an open car, got the crowd's attention. The old lady had turned against her boys, he said. The telegram was fake. It was too late to turn back. Pay no attention to Mother Jones.

But her words had had effect; the men visibly were faltering.

Blizzard followed with stronger words: "What in hell is the matter with you?" he shouted at the men. "Do you want some old woman to take you by the hand and lead you across the hill? Straighten up and be men!"

The matter wasn't resolved until Keeney and Mooney returned to Charleston, contacted the White House by telegram, and received assurance that President Harding had sent no telegram to Mother Jones. The old lady, indeed, had lied – for reasons she alone could explain, and she never did. With the discovery of her lie, her argument collapsed, and the march went on.

The incident actually made little difference. By then, miners marched across the ridge toward Mingo by the hundreds. Excitement of moving out swept down the hollow. By evening a steady stream of armed miners descended into Boone County, and all night they moved through darkened hollows. In the hours after midnight, the advance guard passed through Racine, first town on the route of march, where they crossed the Big Coal River. There they made camp along Indian Creek, and the army now stretched for some twenty miles.

By daylight, hundreds of men moved along the dirt street of Racine, past the several stores and houses, and joined the camp on Indian Creek. The army rested there as the rear caught up. As men arrived, a camp stretched out along Indian Creek, much as it had stretched along Lens Creek. Men prepared meals; others ate at little stores along the way.

More than a hundred crowded into P. D. Gillespie's general store in Racine, demanding service, roughly pawing through merchandise and, Gillespie was sure, stealing overalls and trousers. He was unnerved when he saw one miner holding a hand grenade.

Gillespie's telephone rang constantly, and he talked freely with callers, describing the men, their numbers, arms and movements, until a large miner with a rifle appeared at his counter. He was not to give out information, the miner told Gillespie. Gillespie argued, and the miner left. Minutes later, Gillespie's phone stopped ringing. Outside, Gillespie found the wire was cut.

Ed Reynolds, still leading his overalled company, reached

Racine where he noticed a switch engine and three flatcars on the C&O track. It was just what his men needed. At gunpoint, they ordered the crew to fire the engine, and it pulled out with Reynolds and his men riding on the flatcars. At Sproul, an alarmed railroad official refused to throw a switch to turn the kidnapped train south toward Logan, and Reynolds sent two men forward with orders to "put their guns on his ribs." The switch was thrown, and the train headed south toward Mingo.

On Indian Creek, miners rested Thursday afternoon in their new encampment. Men gathered in groups to listen to speeches again, just as on Lens Creek. Speakers told again of the murders of Sid and Ed, outlined and reoutlined their plans for the march, and tried to teach their men how to wage war: when fighting machine guns, "lie down, watch where the bullets cut the trees, outflank 'em, and get the snipers."

Evening came, and a night chill settled in. Men lit small fires for cooking and built them into bonfires in the darkness. Sentinels were posted, and for the first time the miners' army used a password: "On to Mingo."

The men went to bed, huddled in blankets. By midnight, most were asleep, but some bantered on into the night.

Sid Hatfield, Matewan police chief. His murder set off the miners' armed march.
West Virginia University Library / West Virginia and Regional History Collection

The town of Matewan, West Virginia, in 1920. The battle took place between the railroad tracks and the building at right. *Frank M. Allara, Sr.*

Site of the battle of Matewan. Railroad depot at far left, Chambers Hardware at far right. *Frank M. Allara, Sr.*

Downtown Matewan in spring of 1920, about the time of the Matewan battle. *Frank M. Allara, Sr.*

Left: Screen door and window of Chambers Hardware show bullet holes after battle. *Frank M. Allara, Sr.* Right: Bullet hole marred front window of the Matewan National Bank following the shoot-out. *Paul J. Lively*

Above: Matewan mayor, C. C. Testerman, killed in Matewan battle, May 19,
1920. *Jack Testerman*

Above right: Mayor Testerman and his
wife, Jessie, in happier days. *Jack
Testerman*

Right: "Two-Gun" Sid Hatfield. *West
Virginia University Library / West Virginia and Regional History Collection*

Sid Hatfield—a portrait as it appeared in the *United Mine Workers Journal*, August 15, 1921. *United Mine Workers Journal*

Sid Hatfield and his bride, the former Jessie Testerman, after their wedding. *West Virginia Hillbilly*

Sid and Jessie (center) enjoy life in their apartment with Jessie's step-niece, Blanche Testerman. Jessie's son by Mayor Testerman is partially visible at right. *Jack Testerman*

Mother Jones. *West Virginia University Library / West Virginia and Regional History Collection*

Sid Hatfield and Mother Jones surrounded by organizers in front of newly opened UMWA headquarters in Matewan, spring of 1920. Standing left to right: James Doyle of UMWA, W. H. Hutchinson of Matewan, Andrew Wilson of UMWA, W. Philips of Matewan. Seated left to right: C. H. Workman of UMWA, Mother Jones, Sid Hatfield, and I. E. Fry of Matewan. *West Virginia University Library / West Virginia and Regional History Collection*

Officers of the United Mine Workers' District 17, which covered most of West Virginia. From left: Billy Blizzard, subdistrict president and so-called general of the miners' army; Fred Mooney, secretary of the district; William Petry, district vice president, and Frank Keeney, district president. *West Virginia University Library / West Virginia and Regional History Collection*

Cartoon in *UMW Journal*, August 15, 1921. *United Mine Workers Journal*

Defendants in Matewan trial. From left, standing: Jim Maggard, foreman of jury; Reece Chambers, Charley Kiser, Fred Burgraff, Sid Hatfield, N. H. Atwood, Ed Chambers, Lee Toler, and Clare Overstreet. Kneeling, from left: William B. Coleman, Ben Mounts, Jesse Boyd, William Bowman, Van Clay, Art Williams, and Hallie Chambers. *West Virginia University Library / West Virginia and Regional History Collection*

Judge R. D. Bailey presided at the trial of twenty-three Matewan men. *Paul J. Lively*

Model of town of Matewan was displayed during trial. *Mrs. Carl Collett*

The jury that acquitted Sid Hatfield and the Matewan miners. Back row, from left: James Robinett, day laborer, of Williamson; Belcher, telephone company employee, of Gilbert; Evert Musick, farmer, of Pigeon Creek; Thomas Chapman, schoolteacher, of Pigeon Creek; Frank Ford, lumber company employee, of Gilbert; and Milt Trout of Dingess. Front row, from left: Julius Hall, schoolteacher and farmer, of Lenore; Wyatt Belcher, farmer, of Gilbert; J. B. Massie, railroad brakeman (and the only union member in the jury), of Williamson; John Farley, farmer, of Bias; Thomas Maggard, farmer, of Kermit; and Clarence Ireson, railroad shop foreman, of Williamson. *Paul J. Lively*

The Lick Creek tent colony near Williamson, site of gun-fights in June 1921. *United Mine Workers Journal*

Children's heads show rips in Lick Creek tent following raid. *United Mine Workers Journal*

Sid Hatfield (left) and Charlie Lively pose in friendlier days with unidentified women. *Paul J. Lively*

Charlie Lively, the Baldwin-Felts spy and leader of the men who shot Sid Hatfield. Photo taken in 1918. *Paul J. Lively*

The MacDowell County Courthouse at Welch, where Sid Hatfield and Ed Chambers were shot to death as they climbed the steps at left. *Paul J. Lively*

Sid Hatfield's funeral. Two thousand walked in the procession. Knights of Pythias, Odd-fellows, and Redmen carried the coffins of Sid Hatfield and Ed Chambers. *Jack Testerman*

Governor Ephraim F. Morgan. *West Virginia University Library / West Virginia and Regional History Collection*

Don Chafin, sheriff of Logan County. He organized an army to stop the miners. *West Virginia University Library / West Virginia and Regional History Collection*

Freight train loaded with miners on their way to the front, passing through Ramage in Boone County. *West Virginia University Library / West Virginia and Regional History Collection*

One of the homemade bombs dropped on miners' positions from Chafin's planes. *United Mine Workers Journal*

State troopers and volunteer militia man defensive position. *West Virginia University Library / West Virginia and Regional History Collection*

Brigadier General W. H. Bandholz commanded U.S. troops in West Virginia. *Underwood & Underwood*

General Billy Mitchell. He brought planes to stop the miners' rebellion. *United States Air Force*

Charleston girls sit in cockpit of Martin bomber military aircraft. It attracted hundreds of sightseers. *Richard A. André, from B. E. André Collection*

Wreckage of the Martin bomber that crashed in Nicholas County. *Richard A. André, from B. E. André Collection*

U.S. troops under General Bandholz on Hewitt Creek near Jeffrey. *West Virginia University Library / West Virginia and Regional History Collection*

Armed coal miners surrender their guns to U.S. soldiers. *WPBY-TV, Charleston, West Virginia*

13

"No armed mob will cross Logan County"

AT 2:00 A.M. THURSDAY, a fire siren wailed in the mining town of Logan. Men jumped from their beds, dressed, and hurried out into the night: bankers, clerks, lawyers, merchants, mine officials, a few nonunion miners.

It was the army of Don Chafin, fabled sheriff of Logan County, hastily organized to stop the miners' march. Chafin's county lay fifty miles south of Lens Creek, directly across the miners' road to Mingo, and West Virginians knew that if anyone in their state could halt the miners, Chafin could.

By car and on foot they rushed to the county courthouse, where men handed out guns and ammunition. Outside, under pale glowing streetlights, Model T's streamed from town, carrying armed men to mountain passes along the ridgetop of Blair Mountain, where they looked down from breastworks and trenches into the wooded Spruce Fork Valley, ready to shoot at advancing "rednecks." They had practiced such alerts for more than a week.

This was the moment for which Chafin had prepared. Don Chafin was decisive, resolute, laconic, and a little crooked. He had never known Sid Hatfield, but he had followed Sid's life and death, and he knew what to expect after Sid's murder. When armed union miners began assembling on Lens Creek, Chafin was ready. His ringing pronouncement, "No armed mob will cross Logan County," became a rallying cry.

Chafin ruled Logan County like a king. At 34, he had been in public office more than twelve years: four as county assessor, four as sheriff, four as county clerk (a necessary interregnum when his brother-in-law was sheriff), and then as sheriff again. His father before him had been Logan County's sheriff. With an announced salary never exceeding $3,500 per year, Chafin admitted to assets of a third of a million dollars. Logan's coal operators supported him well and paid the salaries of more than forty of his deputies to guard their property and to keep the union out. The deputies did their job well. Regularly they checked incoming trains for union organizers and ran off any who might intrude. Two years earlier, when fifty UMWA organizers had arrived in Logan, Chafin and his deputies met them with guns at the depot and simply forbade them from getting off the train; the organizers, under guard by deputies, rode back out of the county again. Occasionally, organizers managed to get into the county, only to land in jail. In 1919, Chafin pursued a black union man all the way into the District 17 union headquarters in Charleston; there, in a scuffle, District Vice-President Bill Petry shot Chafin in the chest. It sidelined him only temporarily.

When union miners mobilized on Lens Creek in mid-August, Chafin began organizing immediately to stop their march. He called for volunteers; hundreds came forth, and from them he shaped an army. He established a commissary in his courthouse, assembling rifles, machine guns, ammunition, and military equipment from the county arsenal and local hardware stores. He established the same defensive line he had planned two years earlier when union miners threatened a similar march, along the ridge separating the Guyan Valley from Spruce Fork of Little Coal River, and along that line, with special concentration in the passes, the volunteers and deputies dug trenches, felled trees, blocked roads, and built breastworks of boulders, dirt, and logs, for ten miles from Crooked Creek to Blair Mountain. He organized a fleet of privately owned cars to carry men and equipment to the front and even mobilized an air force of three biplanes that were parked on Logan's baseball field. The fire siren was the call to arms.

Throughout his planning, Chafin stayed in touch with Governor Morgan, who imposed only one restraint: the sheriff could take every step to defend his county, but under no condition was he to attack the miners' army.

All was done in secrecy, as Chafin also controlled his county's press. While newspapers across the nation carried front page stories on the miners' march, The *Logan Banner* published perfunctory articles and concealed any important information it might obtain. "The *Banner* regrets," a front page article stated, "not being able to give its readers full accounts of preparations being made but feels that in so doing it would defeat the sheriff's attitude of secrecy, and we know citizens of Logan agree with us."

After several alerts, the call to arms came Thursday morning, and Logan's darkened streets filled with cars and armed men hurrying to the front.

Deputy sheriffs rushed through the county's mining camps rousing nonunion miners, who went forth to fight their union brothers with varying degrees of enthusiasm. At one camp, a deputy yelled to the sleeping miners: "Anyone who doesn't come fight is fired!" At another, "It was just fight or go to jail," a miner said. ("I didn't care about being fired," the miner at the first camp recalled later, "and I didn't care about fighting either, so I figured I'd go along and see what I could think up.")

Within an hour of the fire siren, five hundred men streamed through the courthouse and toward the front, and by daylight seven hundred men manned breastworks along the ridge. More were on the way.

Women of Logan opened a food distribution center in the Aracoma Hotel in downtown Logan, where they talked excitedly and prepared bags of food that were carried to the front in motor trucks.

Later that day, an airplane took off from the Logan baseball park and soared out across Boone and Kanawha counties. The pilot looked down on the long column of armed miners advancing from Lens Creek toward Big Coal River. Several miners shot at the plane. After a thorough reconnaissance the plane returned to Logan, and the pilot reported his observations to Chafin.

At the same moment the fire siren wailed in Logan Town, a telephone rang in the governor's mansion in Charleston. It was the night city editor of the *Charleston Gazette,* and he needed the governor's comment. Armed miners were pouring from Lens Creek over the mountain into Boone County, headed toward Logan and Mingo Counties, to free the jailed miners, Sid Hatfield's friends, and to avenge Sid's murder. Already they had reached Big Coal River. What did the governor have to say?

Morgan had plenty to say but saved it. All day he had received reports, of Mother Jones's speech, of the advance of the miners from Lens Creek, of miners still arriving at Lens Creek from all directions, of mines closing throughout southern West Virginia. He had talked to Chafin several times. He had received a report that a train had been commandeered at Racine.

West Virginia's National Guard had been called to war in World War I and had never been reestablished. The legislature had approved rebuilding the guard earlier that year, following Sid's trial and the Three Days Battle, but there had not been time to implement the legislation. The governor had only one hundred state policemen — and that number had been doubled because of the Mingo warfare — to stop a moving miners' army estimated at seven thousand men.

Although Chafin might be able to slow the miners' army, Morgan felt he had only one real hope to stop it: the United States Army. He long since had made contact with the army. The secretary of war had dispatched an officer to Charleston to keep in touch with affairs, the same Major Thompson who had done similar duty in May in Mingo County.

By Thursday, southern West Virginia was in open rebellion, and Morgan began to pressure the White House. He sent an urgent appeal to President Harding for one thousand troops and military aircraft armed with machine guns. The miners had been "inflamed and infuriated by speeches of radical officers and leaders," he said in a public statement.

The War Department reacted half-heartedly. Fifth Corps in Indianapolis reinforced the Nineteenth Infantry Regiment to one thousand men, "ready to move on moment's notice," but it didn't move.

The air service was alerted. A makeshift landing field was found in Kanawha City, just east of Charleston. That afternoon, a Dehaviland 4B biplane with open cockpits made the 250-mile trip from Bolling Field near Washington to Charleston in only three and a half hours and one stop. Charlestonians buzzed with excitement as the aircraft flew low over the city and landed. The pilot reported to the capitol.

Major Thompson was not convinced. His first report questioned the immediate need of federal troops.

Secretary of War Weeks reviewed Thompson's report and the governor's repeated pleas for help. To resolve the conflict, he ordered Brigadier General Harry H. Bandholz, former provost marshal general with the American Expeditionary Force, to go to Charleston. Bandholz, known for his ability to handle tasks requiring a diplomat's tact and a soldier's firm hand, left at once by train.

14

"It's your real Uncle Sam"

THE MINERS' ARMY began moving again in the early hours of Friday, again without control or direction, but inexorably southward toward Logan and Mingo counties. Their route was the crude dirt road that led along the Big Coal River to Peytona, up Drawdy Creek and over the mountain, then down Rock Creek to Little Coal River, and they would follow the Little Coal into Danville and Madison. From there, the road turned up Spruce Fork to Sharples and Blair, then wound over Blair Mountain to Ethyl and Logan. By then they knew they would be in battle.

General Harry Hill Bandholz arrived in Charleston at 3:00 A.M. Friday to assess whether federal troops should intercede to stop the march. A friendly, balding man of fifty-six, he was dapper in mustache, Sam Browne belt, billed cap, riding breeches, and puttees as he arrived with an aide, Colonel Stanley H. Ford. They drove across the bridge over the Kanawha and down into the darkened city to the so-called "cardboard capital," a makeshift state capitol since the real one had burned in January. There, Major Thompson, who fast was becoming a veteran of West Virginia campaigns, met them and quickly briefed them.

Governor Mogan was called from his bed. He appeared at 4:00 A.M. and repeated to the general his oft-told story: it was full-fledged insurrection; Sid Hatfield's death had maddened the state's miners; they were killing and looting; he had no soldiers, little power. He had to have federal troops.

Keeney and Mooney, summoned from their beds, appeared as the governor finished. To them, the general was emphatic.

If martial law were declared, he said, they and other union officials would be held responsible for the acts committed by law-
breaking members of their organization. The miners' march had
gone out of all proportion to any probable intent and might soon
get entirely out of control. It had to be stopped, and the two
union officers were the men to stop it.

Keeney and Mooney accepted the assessment. The general
awed them. As outraged as they were, West Virginia's miners
were patriotic Americans, and they did not relish taking on the
U.S. Army.

At 5:50 A.M. Keeney and Mooney set out by taxi to overtake the army. Urging the driver to hurry, they moved along the
river road to Marmet, then turned up the familiar Lens Creek
road, bouncing in and out of the creek at speeds up to twenty
miles per hour, past the old encampment where the march had
started.

Hour after hour they jolted along the tortuous road up the
creek and over the ridge, down Short Creek, through Racine and
Peytona, then up Drawdy. All the way they passed armed miners, thousands of them, some camping, some marching, a large
body of them having lunch at Peytona, and to all they shouted
that the march was over and they should turn back. Keeney
commented later he had never seen so many men on the march
before. "From Racine to Madison there must have been ten thousand men." They reached Madison at noon, having traveled fifty
miles in little more than six hours.

At Madison, hundreds of miners milled about, sprawled along
the streets, camped in the nearby hills and hollows, eating from
tin plates and cans, loitering in restaurants, pool halls, theaters,
and hotel lobbies.

Minutes before, the advance guard of the miners' army, marching with near military precision and discipline, had set out for
the Logan County line, twelve miles away. They had lined up,
an observer reported, when their leaders commanded, "Fall in!"
and, "At the command 'Forward March,' they swung away on
the road to Logan with fire and determination in their eyes, their
guns firmly grasped in their hands."

Keeney made a quick decision. At 2:00 P.M., he said, they
would have a meeting in the Madison baseball park. All union

miners were to attend. He ordered those around him to spread
the word and make the arrangements. Then he and Mooney
sped out of town toward Logan to overtake the marchers.

The advance guard had gone only a short distance out of
Madison. The taxi passed the column on the road and swung
in front of its head. Keeney jumped out and spoke. The column
halted. There was a heated exchange; the miners could not stop.
Keeney insisted and prevailed. The miners agreed to a temporary halt, turned around and marched back into Madison.

Back in town, Keeney and Mooney grabbed a lunch at a restaurant counter and circulated on the sidewalk outside, urging
men to go to the ballpark, hearing stories of their experiences
so far. Automobiles shuttled miners from the courthouse lawn
to the ballpark as time for the meeting approached.

When Keeney and Mooney approached the ballpark, they
found the bleachers nearly filled with miners, their guns glisten-
ing in a bright sunlight. Other men lay full length on the grass
in the shade of the high board fence. Guards manned the gates,
and miners gave a new password, "I come creeping." They turned
away newspapermen, a policy Keeney endorsed. The men were
in an angry mood, he told one newsman.

Keeney spoke from the hood of the taxi. "A lot of you men
are going to disagree with me," he began, "but don't interrupt.
I am telling you facts, and you will find that this is no time to
argue."

It was suicide to continue the march, he said. He told them
that orders to stop the march had emanated from President Harding, himself; that President Harding had sent General Bandholz to Charleston; that General Bandholz had called the governor and Keeney and Mooney out of bed that very morning,
had told the two union officials they and the rest of the union
leadership would be held responsible if the march got out of
hand. There was no question Bandholz would see that the march
was ended; the entire might of the national government and the
United States Army would be used, if necessary, to stop it.

Fighting Governor Morgan or Sheriff Chafin or the Baldwin-
Felts thugs and Mingo County coal operators was fair enough.
But the miners, if they continued, would not be fighting these
traditional enemies; they would be up against the army of the

United States, the same army in which many of the miners had served in France. "Return to your homes," Keeney said.

Mooney followed Keeney. Union men, he said, didn't balk federal authority. Union men were loyal to their country. It was time to give up the march. Trains would be dispatched to Madison and Danville to take them home, back to their jobs.

Others spoke, generally agreeing that the march should be abandoned, at least for now. An aged black miner rose: "Boys, he's right," he said of Keeney's warning about federal power. "You ain't foolin' no more. This is your daddy talkin'. It's your real Uncle Sam."

The decision emerged. They would go home. Slowly, the men began edging out of the ballpark.

Many started immediately on the long march. Others waited in Madison for the promised trains. Word spread into the hills and hollows and back along the line of march.

Keeney and Mooney rode back into Madison and checked into a hotel. Keeney got a shave at a barbershop. Mooney called Charleston to arrange the special trains.

As darkness fell, miners built campfires in the hills around Madison and talked of their adventure, waiting for the trains. The march, they thought, was over. So much for Sid Hatfield's brutal murder.

15

"By God, we're goin' through"

I

As Keeney made his ballpark speech, an airplane droned overhead in a long, slow sweep across the sky. The pilot looked down on the miners as they dispersed from the Madison ballpark, and he turned the aircraft toward Logan.

There, Chafin already knew of the ballpark speech and plans to end the march on Mingo. A Madison informant had telephoned him with the news almost as soon as the men knew it themselves.

At three o'clock, Chafin recalled his troops. Cars and trucks carried the word to the front, where more than a thousand men waited in trenches and barricades, and that evening the first contingent of dusty, weary defenders came marching through Logan in a long column, all at ease, their rifles over their shoulders. Like returning heroes, they were cheered and applauded as they came through town, and they turned over their guns and ammunition at the commissary in the courthouse.

Chafin addressed them in the courtroom: "You have been in defense of our rights. Logan County will not forget it."

The word that the miners' march was over raced through the county. The *Logan Banner* quickly remade its front page with a headline screaming triumphantly, "ATTEMPTED INVASION FAILS."

The local coal operators association president issued a statement: "We took steps to defend the sovereignty of Logan County only when it appeared that the Kanawha County government, and the Boone County government, had not been able to cope with the situation." Many of the men went from the courthouse to the Aracoma Hotel, where Logan's ladies pushed on them quantities of food, and they ate a meal, smiling and laughing and enjoying each other.

II

Thousands of armed miners lounged in the streets and hollows and loitered along the hillsides around the adjoining towns of Danville and Madison. Many awaited the trains that Keeney had promised. But, by no means, were all ready to go home.

Ed Reynolds was far from ready to call off the march. He gathered with other self-proclaimed leaders. Keeney, they agreed, had faked his ballpark speech. Keeney, in fact, had told them after the speech that he had had to tell them to turn back in order to save the union. Actually, one miner told the others, Keeney had said "We could do what we please." They had gotten no orders to turn back, and they didn't intend to. Sid's death could not go unanswered. "By God," they said, "we're goin' through."

With little notice, more than three hundred miners walked out of Madison on the road to Logan, rifles in hand, red bandannas around their necks.

III

In Washington, reports of the end of the miners' march brought relief in the War Department and White House. Assistant Secretary of War J. Mayhew Wainwright and Army Deputy Chief of Staff Major General James G. Harbord conferred with President Harding and told him of developments. The president discussed the miners' march with his Cabinet.

Detailed accounts were given of Bandholz's actions and decisions. When it appeared definite that the march was over, Harbord wired Bandholz in Charleston: "Secretary War much pleased with your handling of situation through Keeney and Mooney."

IV

Although word of Keeney's ballpark meeting spread across the nation Friday afternoon, it was slow in traveling the dozen miles along the marchers' planned route to the little town of Blair. There, along Spruce Fork and the base of Blair Mountain – beneath the breastworks and guns of Chafin's army – armed, rebellious miners had no intention of calling off their march. Telephone and telegraph wires lay useless along the roads, and armed patrols of miners blocked the path of unfriendly visitors. It was an iron curtain through which truth had trouble passing, and miners behind it went on as before, continuing to prepare for their march.

Few union miners along Spruce Fork had known Sid Hatfield personally, but they well knew the problems he had confronted. On the edge of Logan County, they continually were harassed by Logan deputies, and refugees from Logan and Mingo frequently came to the Spruce Fork–Blair Mountain area for work in union mines.

On Thursday night, nearly five hundred armed miners gathered at the union hall in Blair. Using passwords, "I come creeping" and "Mingo," they marched along the railroad, stopped passers-by, and ordered residents to "contribute" money for ammunition needed in the march.

Late that night, they ran through the mining camps of the area, rousing families from their beds, calling men out to fight, announcing the mines would be closed on Friday. When morning came, the mines, indeed, had to close for lack of men.

All government, law, and industry in the area now rested in the hands of armed miners. Women and children fled as refugees. "Bad Lewis" White, one of the most belligerent of the miners, brutalized those who did not cooperate; at one time he instructed a group of miners to shoot at an incoming train because, he said, state police would be aboard.

Late Friday, word arrived of Keeney's ballpark speech. Union leaders could not believe it. They sent a delegation of miners who talked with men at Madison. Returning to Blair, they fired pistols into the air to attract a crowd and made their announcement: it was not true, they said, that the miners' march was over. They still planned to march on Mingo.

V

One of Chafin's aircraft taxied across the infield and lifted into the air from the Logan ballpark. It climbed hesitatingly, then dropped. The aircraft clipped a treetop, flipped over on its back on the cupola of a house. Unhurt, the pilot and his observer scrambled from their cockpits and down from the rooftop.

VI

Paul Curley, 17, son of a Madison grocer, had permission to use his dad's car. With two friends, he set out for Danville two miles away to see a motion picture show.

Armed miners lined both sides of the road to Danville; they filled the right-of-way, the vacant spots, and Paul often had to stop to let a miner walk out of the path of the automobile.

The teenagers sensed danger. This did not look like a good night for the movies. Paul turned the car around and started home.

They nosed slowly through masses of men. Suddenly, the men closed around the car. It could not move without hitting miners. Several men pointed their guns at Paul.

"I would like to get your car," a miner said, his gun pressed against Paul's side. Other miners pushed their guns through the windows and against Paul. "We want that car, and we want it quick," one said.

Paul tried to slide out of the driver's seat. He found a gun barrel pointing directly in his face. In fright, he threw back his head and tried to push the gun away; it went off, and the bullet ripped through his hand.

He was taken to the nearby Coal River Hospital and treated.

VII

In Charleston, crowds gathered at the makeshift landing field along the river east of the city. Three "monster olive-green planes" of the Army Air Service sat wingtip to wingtip, armed with machine guns and bombs.

One of them bore the pennant of the fleet flagship on its rudder, signifying it as the *Seagull,* the aircraft of Billy Mitchell, the nation's famous airman and assistant chief of the air service. Mitchell was there, himself; he had flown in during the afternoon, and he strolled around the landing field, talking to admirers.

Mitchell had come from bombing exercises against navy warships off the Virginia coast, where he demonstrated the power of aircraft in sinking the battleship *Ostfriesland.* He saw in West Virginia another opportunity to demonstrate the effectiveness of air power. Airplanes, he argued, could quell civil disturbances in remote locations. And he came winging in from Bolling Field outside Washington and strutted around, wearing a pistol, spurs, and rows of ribbons.

The miners' march interested him as a tactician. "All this could be left to the Air Service," Mitchell said to reporters. "If I get orders I can move in the necessary forces in three hours."

How would he handle masses of men under cover in gullies, he was asked.

"Gas," said the general. "You understand we wouldn't try to kill these people at first. We'd drop tear gas over the place. If they refused to disperse then we'd open up, with artillery preparation and everything."

Citizens flocked around to gaze at the famous general, the great flying machines, and the handsome pilots whose Sam Browne belts sagged with the weight of their sidearms. Mechanics in greasy jumpers bent over the machines while trucks brought in gasoline and supplies. Veterans of the war came out to take new looks at their old planes, and children sucking ice cream cones swarmed everywhere. A tall, bronzed lieutenant shooed them away when they came too close.

VIII

The evening passenger train puffed along the C&O tracks alongside Coal River, and the engineer, Charles A. Medley, looked out at the moving coal miners. Never had he seen so many, walking, loitering, shouldering their guns. He had read of Sid Hat-field's death, and he had followed news of the miners' rebellion, but somehow he felt it would not affect him.

When his train stopped at Madison at five o'clock, Medley saw hundreds of miners. He pulled out and headed up Little Coal River, then southward along Spruce Fork. The train passed through one coal camp after another: Jeffrey, Clothier, Sharples, Blair, Sovereign. The sun was low, and the cars cast long shadows. At Sovereign he turned around and headed back. On schedule, he pulled in at Clothier at 7:00 P.M. to lay over for the night.

Late that night, Medley played pool in a Clothier pool hall when a half dozen armed miners came in and approached him. They wanted his train, they said. They motioned for him to go with them. He didn't argue. With their guns playing casually on him, he walked with them to the depot. Other miners there already had taken prisoners of the brakeman and firemen. The crew was complete except for conductor, and he would not be needed.

They mounted the train and fired up the engine. The engine pulled out, headed north toward Madison. The miners ordered Medley not to shine his headlight, and the train moved through the darkness, Medley leaning out from the cab and peering ahead, an armed miner riding behind him.

The train passed through Madison and went on to Danville. There, under orders from the gunmen, they unhitched the engine, and Medley turned it around so that it would push the cars on the return trip.

"Bad Lewis" White, apparently one of the miners who had commandeered the train, appeared on the Danville depot platform, wearing two revolvers, and he called and yelled to all who would listen that the train was headed for Blair on the march to Mingo. All miners should get on the train, he yelled, to continue their march across Logan County. Logan deputies, he shouted, had come into Blair killing women and children; the help of other union miners was needed. It was all a lie.

Keeney had called off the march, someone yelled back. They were waiting for trains to take them home.

"To hell with Keeney," Bad Lewis replied. "They are killing women and children up at Blair."

Several miners boarded the outlaw train. Medley was told to move out, and the train rolled on to the Madison depot where it stopped again.

Again, Bad Lewis yelled to miners. Hundreds surrounded the Madison depot; many had built fires on the hillside next to the depot and sat around them talking, waiting for the trains to take them home. Again, Bad Lewis and others yelled that the miners were needed at Blair to fight the Logan deputies. "All you fellows that have high power rifles, come get on this train," someone yelled.

Miners ambled down and got on the train. Medley was given the word, and the train pulled out. As it returned up the river, Medley was told to stop at every station. At each one, more armed men boarded. Bad Lewis walked ahead through the coaches, checking, talking, supervising. In the early morning hours, when the train stopped just outside Blair, more than three hundred men filed off, ready to march on Mingo.

IX

Jack Brinkman, 32, of Terre Haute, Indiana, played piano for a traveling production called "The Old Kentucky Show." He was pleased at the large number of miners who attended Friday evening's performance at Danville, even if they did carry guns. Afterward, with nothing better to do, Brinkman followed some of them to the Danville depot. A train was in the station.

At the station, Bad Lewis shouted at Brinkman to get on the train to go help fight Logan deputies. Brinkman didn't move. Another miner turned on him with a .38 pistol and ordered him onto the train. Brinkman said he was not a miner; he was simply observing.

"Are you with us?" the miner asked.

"Certainly," Brinkman responded nervously, "if that will do you any good."

Several armed miners drew their guns and ordered Brinkman to get on the train. Brinkman boarded, and the train pulled out.

X

It was not easy to recall Don Chafin's army. His men were spread along a ten-mile front in mountain passes and wild, remote country not connected by road. Chafin had begun calling them back to the courthouse in mid-afternoon, but it was nearly midnight when the last soldiers reported back.

Chafin prepared to go home. It had been a long day. Suddenly the telephone in the outside hall rang. It was Walter Hallinan, state tax commissioner in Charleston, with news. Miners had commandeered another train, he said, and had loaded it with miners. They planned to resume the march on Mingo to avenge Sid Hatfield's death and free Mingo's miners from jail. Blair was filled with angry, armed miners ready to head up the mountain and across Logan County. Some did not think the threat was great; Hallinan did, however, and he thought Chafin should know. Chafin agreed with the assessment.

At 12:05 A.M., Logan's fire siren screamed out again. Men scrambled from their beds where many had just settled in. They hurried into Logan and drew their guns from the commissary in rapid time, thanks to the previous experience. Model T's materialized again on the darkened streets and, loaded with armed defenders, jolted out of town toward George's and Blair mountains. By morning, eight hundred men looked down from machine-gun nests and rifle emplacements into the valley below.

16

"We wouldn't revolt against the national guv'ment"

KEENEY AND BILL BLIZZARD struggled into the temporary state capitol Saturday morning in Charleston, exhausted; they had been up all night. They had a good report for General Bandholz: the miners' insurrection was all but over; the men were going home. Trains had arrived at Danville and Madison in the early morning hours to take miners back to their homes; other trains were picking them up along Coal River. Hundreds more were returning on foot. Keeney and Blizzard had returned with the men from Madison, nearly eight hundred of them, on a special train that took them to Saint Albans; there they changed to trolleys, which rolled eastward along the Kanawha River through Charleston to Marmet and Paint and Cabin Creeks where many of them had started the adventure.

Bandholz was pleased but not entirely convinced. Disquieting reports continued: a train had been commandeered; reports from Logan and Blair were not reassuring. To make sure, Bandholz decided, he would make a personal inspection of the front. He would go to the Coal River and look for himself.

Because of exhaustion, Keeney begged off taking the trip. He had brought Blizzard along to help, he said, and Blizzard volunteered to accompany the general, "to keep the boogers off," he joked. Bandholz laughed. He was in a good mood. Wearing puttees and flicking a little swagger stick, he led the other men outside to waiting cars, bantering and joking as they left.

Bandholz, Blizzard, Colonel Ford, and a reporter boarded one car; Major Thompson and John Charnock, West Virignia's new adjutant general, took another, and Jessie V. Sullivan, Governor Morgan's secretary, followed in a third with a group of news reporters.

The caravan headed east along the now familiar road, past the Kanawha City airfield, where crowds still swarmed about the military aircraft parked along the river. At Marmet they separated, Major Thompson continuing up the river to Cabin Creek to inspect the situation there, Bandholz, with Sullivan close behind, heading up the Lens Creek road along the line of the miners' march.

Bandholz was hardly prepared for West Virginia's rural roads. He muttered and grinned good-naturedly as the car pitched along the gulley that was known as the Lens Creek Road, bouncing over embankments, sinking again and again into the rock and water and mud of the creek, kicking up dust when they emerged from it. All along, they passed miners returning to their homes, on foot and in cars, and the miners waved, smiled and saluted as the general passed. The miners' cars were loaded with supplies no longer needed.

They reached the headwater of Lens Creek and plowed up through the mountainside wilderness, spinning wheels and churning dust, and then went over the ridgetop, pitching downward into Boone County, where they got into another creek to make their way. Finally, nearly two hours after their departure, they emerged on Coal River and moved into Racine. They had come twenty miles.

At Racine, the two cars stopped, and the men looked out. On the other side of the little river, near the railroad track, scores of husky, grizzled men stood, eyeing the new arrivals. Their guns were a "veritable forest," one of the newcomers observed. Bayonets and steel helmets glistened. Most of the men in the cars hesitated, but not Bandholz. He climbed stiffly from his car. Colonel Ford followed, and everyone else came, too.

Bandholz walked to a dilapidated swinging bridge, put himself on it, and advanced across the river. The others followed. The miners continued staring. No one spoke. Rapping his little swagger stick against his thigh, the general walked silently into the midst of the armed miners, looking intently into their faces, one by one. The men pushed forward, shuffling their feet. They surrounded him, standing close around him. Finally, one spoke:

"Are you General Pershing?"

"No, I'm General Bandholz, and I'm here for the United States Government."

His voice was kind. The men stared. Silence. Then, with perfect timing, Bandholz talked:

"There are service men among you. You know what the army means, know what it can do, know that it never bluffs but always calls them.

"I don't want martial law here. Neither do you. I've seen enough men killed. I don't want to see any more die. But if it must be, then we will go under martial law. I don't want it, but I must obey orders.

"They tell me you men are going home. I'm glad. It's the right thing to do. Go back. Let law and order take their course. Are you all going home?"

The ice broke. They all began talking. They pushed forward; everyone wanted to see this real general. "My Gawd, we wouldn't revolt against the national guv'ment," one said. Yeah, they sure were going home. Just as soon as the train came to get them. Several tried to tell Bandholz about their military service. They joked and laughed. They called him "Buddy." They invited him to stay for lunch. Bandholz, looking old and grandfatherly, smiled and joked and enjoyed them.

Suddenly, a train whistled on the nearby track. It was their transportation home. They yelled and called and milled around, crowding toward the train, in disorder, yet accomplishing the desired result: they got on the train. A half dozen Red Cross nurses were with them, one old and maternal, and the others young and fresh, and they were the last to board. The train pulled out, the men leaning out the windows, waving and laughing their farewells and calling "Hey Buddy" to the general, and the march was over. Sid Hatfield was all but forgotten.

Bandholz was convinced of it. This was no crazed army of maddened anarchists. These were warm-hearted American boys who had been led astray. The general was deeply moved. He and his party climbed back into their cars, which wheeled around and headed back over the mountains toward Charleston.

There, Major Thompson had a similar report; the men of

Cabin and Paint creeks also were returning home. "I think it's over," Bandholz said, and he sent off wires. The troops being held in readiness, he advised the War Department, would not be needed immediately, but they should be kept in readiness in case of emergency. He and Colonel Ford caught the night train for Washington.

17

"The thugs are coming"

STATE POLICE had a score to settle before the end of the miners' march on Mingo. They still remembered the incident in early August, twelve days after Sid Hatfield's death and before armed miners assembled on Lens Creek, when a mob of fifty union miners captured, disarmed, and humiliated several state policemen and deputy sheriffs near Clothier in Logan County. Since the incident, they had obtained the names of more than twenty miners who had participated, including "Bad Lewis" White, the leader. To maintain law and order, to show who was in control of southern West Virginia, it was important these men be arrested and made to pay the penalty for their crime. That would clean up the last remnant of the rebellion.

The order to arrest the men came incidentally. At two o'clock Saturday morning, Governor Morgan ordered Captain Brockus and his state police to move immediately from Mingo County to Logan County to reinforce Sheriff Chafin. It was a precautionary move; the miners' march was all but over; still, reinforcing Chafin at this juncture would help seal its fate.

In the pre-dawn hours, as the men prepared to leave, Major Davis and Chafin talked by telephone and added a new assignment for the expedition: not only would the state police move to Logan, they could go on to Sharples and Clothier to arrest the miners who had humiliated state police in early August.

Brockus and some seventy state troopers set out from Williamson at 6:00 A.M. All morning the line of trucks and cars threaded its way over high-pitched mountains, through gorges and some of the wildest country of West Virginia, where even the railroad had not reached, inching around horseshoe bends, splashing through creeks, moving through heavy timber, bouncing over rocks and into ruts on a so-called road that was hardly a trail. At two o'clock in the afternoon, they had gone forty miles in eight hours, and they reached a railroad. Abandoning their vehicles, they rode in the relative luxury of boxcars the remaining ten miles to Logan Town.

Chafin met them at the depot, and he and Brockus made plans while the troopers grinned from the boxcars at a gathering crowd. With Chafin aboard, the train rattled on for the short distance to Ethyl, field headquarters of Chafin's army. There, the troopers ate supper, and Chafin assigned some two hundred deputies from his army to Brockus' force. At six o'clock, Brockus and his detachment, now numbering nearly three hundred men, set out on foot toward Clothier, Sharples, and the hotbed of rebelling coalminers, to make the arrests that would atone for the humiliation state police had suffered two weeks before.

They followed a creek upward toward Blair Mountain and walked north along the ridgetop. The country opened up. As darkness fell, Brockus formed an advanced guard of state police with two local guides, and they moved out again, guns ready. In darkness, they followed a rough horse trail called the "county road," descending gradually into the Spruce Fork Valley, union territory. The road led them to the head of Beech Creek, and they followed it down toward Sharples.

The Boone County Coal Corporation operated a series of mines along Beech Creek, separated by half-mile intervals, connected by railroad, each mine numbered consecutively: Boone No. 5 at the top, No. 4 next one down, and so on to No. 1 near Sharples at the bottom. Brockus's men passed Boone No. 5 and walked rapidly down the hollow alongside the railroad and creek. Lights went on in miners' cabins, and uncertain voices called out. The column had stretched out, and several minutes were needed for all the men to pass. Miners and their families came to their front porches in alarm. Some took fright. Some ran down the road calling to the miners who lived below, "The thugs are coming!" Alarm changed to rumor which spread down the hollow like wildfire: the thugs had come to kill union miners and their wives and children, one man yelled. A Hungarian family hid in terror.

Someone telephoned from the No. 4 camp to a foreman's home at the No. 2 mine and asked for "a union man." One was found; he listened, and then went out on the front porch where a crowd had gathered. Hundreds of state police had passed No. 4, he announced; they were taking prisoners of all who stood in the way. Men in the crowd yelled angrily. Someone shot a gun into the air. Others got their guns and moved up the road to meet the police.

By this time Brockus, indeed, was taking prisoners. When he reached No. 4, a detachment of armed miners, standing guard, called out in the darkness for the invaders to halt and identify themselves. They were state police patroling the roads, Brockus said, and he ordered the miners to surrender. Five armed miners came forward and surrendered. Brockus arrested and disarmed them. The column moved forward again, the prisoners marching at gunpoint ahead of the advance guard.

Minutes later, they confronted a car moving up the road with armed men inside. At Brockus's command, the car stopped and men threw their guns from its windows. Brockus arrested them and placed them with the other prisoners at the head of the column.

Again, the column moved downward, and immediately they came upon a second automobile. Two men inside were disarmed, arrested, and placed with the other prisoners. When the column moved out again ten prisoners led the way at gunpoint.

The column moved on. Just outside the No. 2 camp, a dozen armed miners confronted them, lined up across the road. A bright light shone on them from a company store. Standing in the light, their guns silhouetted, two miners commanded the police to identify themselves. Brockus walked forward within ten feet of them; they were state police, he said, and asked why the miners were armed.

"By God, that's our business," one replied.

"We've come after you God damn miners," someone yelled from Brockus's force.

And at that instant, shooting started.

As usual, no one knew who shot first. Police and deputies

blazed forth at point-blank range while several miners fired from the front and sides. Brockus's men jumped over an embankment behind the road and continued shooting. Bullets had ripped through their clothing, but all escaped injury.

Three miners fell at the first volley. One, William Greer, formerly of Matewan, was killed instantly; he had come to Sharples from Matewan after Baldwin-Felts detectives evicted him from his home on May 19, 1920, setting off the Matewan battle that had made Sid Hatfield famous. Another miner, William M. Morrison, fell fatally injured. Cecil Clark was hit three times and fell with critical injuries, which he survived. A fourth miner suffered a slight injury.

Brockus's ten prisoners, meanwhile, found themselves in the middle of the crossfire. All threw themselves on the ground and rolled over the embankment. Miraculously, none were hit. Five escaped into the darkness.

Bullets ricocheted and whined along the little valley, tearing through miners' cabins. In one cabin, a bullet ripped through a wall and into a pillow on a bed; a baby was unhurt on the bed.

Miners turned on outside lights, brilliantly illuminating the area. Brockus, still behind the embankment, took stock: if they were to advance through Sharples as ordered, they would have to shoot their way through. There was no telling how many more would be killed. At last, he began to question the wisdom of his actions. He gave orders to turn back.

The deputies and troopers began sneaking away, moving back up the mountain in the darkness; they regrouped a little higher and marched together, faster, talking loudly, whistling, laughing excitedly. They still had five prisoners.

18

"There was a different feeling"

FRIGHTENED MINERS, their wives, and children spilled out
of their cabins along Beech Creek, shouting and crying: the thugs
had come, had shot people, had killed people. They hurried out
onto the road. The bodies lay there, blood still flowing from
them, bathed in bright, unearthly light of floodlamps from the
company store. Greer was dead, Morrison dying. Clark seemed
near death. Women screamed, babies cried, men cursed and
yelled. Some families ran, panic stricken, back to their cabins and
hid in their cellars. Some pointed to bullet holes in their homes
and tried excitedly to count them. Several moved the bodies
into a boarding house and tried to give them first aid. Someone
sent for a doctor. In a cacophony of voices and dialects, the
people blurted out to each other their own versions of what had
happened. This time it was not rumor. The police, the deputies,
the thugs had come down secretly in the night from Blair Mountain, hundreds of them, and opened fire with their guns on the
miners where they lived in their homes with their wives and
children, killing them, riddling their homes with their bullets.
It was the Sid Hatfield murder all over again. And it was real.

In terror, women and children streamed down the road,
wailing they had no protection; they could stay in their homes
no longer. The story of the battle spread down the creek to
Sharples, along Spruce Fork to Blair, Clothier, Sovereign; up
and down the company streets of every mining camp. Miners
and their families came out onto their front porches in the early
morning hours Sunday to hear the news. At Mifflin, they didn't

believe it and sent a runner back to Sharples; he returned with confirmation.

It spread on to Madison and Danville, through Boone and Raleigh Counties, on to Charleston and it swept up along the Kanawha River and through the mining camps of Cabin Creek and Paint Creek, where men still returned from the preceding week's march. It was thug justice, and as the story spread it grew to fantastic proportions: thugs at Sharples were shooting women and children; there were so many dead they had to stack bodies in piles; six dead children lay in a single pile; miners were needed instantly at Sharples to stop the slaughter.

Suddenly, the miners' rebellion, which Keeney had largely defused, leaped back to life with white hot intensity. What was outrage over Sid's death now was blazing fury. Men who had put away their guns on Saturday took them out again Sunday.

A motorist returning from vacation set out Sunday on the Lens Creek Road, his grips held on the running board by an accordion lattice, and he found miners moving toward Logan County again, guns in hand. Wasn't the mine war over? "No, by God," answered a miner who had just taken a shot at an airplane.

Along the base of Blair Mountain, armed patrols grew larger. Women and children refugees crowded depots and roads, trying to get out of the battle zone. Miners with guns went into the hills as pickets to intercept any new invasion by the thugs. Boys of thirteen and fourteen came forth to fight with their dads. Miners strode along the paths and roads with two pistols in their belts, rifles over their shoulders. They forced their way into private homes to search for weapons. They demanded food at gunpoint from local coal companies.

William M. Wiley of Sharples, vice-president of the Boone County Coal Corporation, heard the gunfire Saturday night from his home. When he learned what happened, he recognized immediately there would be open warfare. He set out at daylight to see the governor; he would have left Saturday night but for fear he would be shot in the darkness.

French Estep, 33, learned the news on his front porch near Blair, and he and other miners gathered at a schoolhouse. "There was a different feeling," he said. The men were "uneasy and scared, talking of watching every point on the mountain so they would not be surprised again." To the outrage over Sid's death now was added a deep-seated fear and a seriousness of purpose.

Roads filled with automobiles hurrying south toward Sharples and Blair, loaded with miners and guns. Men yelled with new vigor they'd "hang Don Chafin to a sour apple tree."

Along the Kanawha and its tributary creeks, in Raleigh, Boone, and Fayette counties, miners poured from their homes again. From Edwight, Ameagle, Boomer, Dry Branch, Longacre, Nellis, Glen Jean, and Kelly's Creek they came on the same roads they had used before. This time they did not assemble on Lens Creek; on foot and in cars they moved straight through, all the way through Racine, up Drawdy Creek and down to Madison, along Spruce Fork to Blair and Sharples, at the foot of Blair Mountain, ready to attack Chafin's entrenched army.

As they moved, observers noted the "different feeling" that Estep saw at Blair. They "went through quite fast," one observer said, "with very set, determined expressions on their faces."

Their fury tolerated no slackers. At Ameagle, miners announced that anyone who didn't march would be driven like animals.

They commandeered every kind of transportation: automobiles, trucks, teams of horses and mules, trains. Commandeering automobiles was a quick operation: they simply stopped cars at gunpoint, forced the drivers out, and drove the vehicles off, loaded to overflowing with guns and miners. If a vehicle broke down, they abandoned it, commandeered another and went on.

Near Charleston, they halted a truck with a piano in the back, set the piano out on the road, loaded it up with miners and forced the driver to take them to Blair.

Hundreds arrived at Blair Sunday on regular passenger trains, but there was not enough of them. They commandeered trains, both passenger and freight, so often that regular train runs were discontinued. Men rode the freights sitting on flatcars, guns in their laps, legs dangling over the sides. One train arrived with a huge banner on the front of the locomotive proclaiming "Bound for Mingo." Another locomotive carried across its front a banner reading "Blue Steel Special." Men rode the cowcatchers, on the roofs, in the engine cabs, in boxcars, everywhere there was space.

S. P. Embry, the Clothier railroad man whose car had been shot up August 12, was roused from his bed to take a train at gunpoint to Whitesville. With armed men riding on the front of the train and in the cabin with him, he made the seventy-mile round trip picking up men and provisions at every stop on the way back. He was relieved in the afternoon, after picking up more than seven hundred men. A new crew took over, still working for the miners.

Jack Brinkman, the pianist who had been shanghaied into the rebellion, joined in commandeering three trains.

W.H.B. Mullins, Boone County prosecuting attorney, reported seeing an early train pass through Madison with only twenty riflemen aboard, but it returned that afternoon packed with so many miners that they rode the fender and clung to the sides of the coaches. He telephoned the governor's office for help, saying armed miners were pouring out of every hollow. Boone County Sheriff D. M. Griffith watched helplessly as the commandeered trains passed. He had five deputies to stop them.

Red neckerchiefs became more numerous as the miners' mood turned uglier. Nonminers stayed in their homes, afraid to venture forth. A doctor was allowed to make calls only after he made white crosses of adhesive tape on the two black headlamps of his automobile; other cars were stopped and commandeered.

Black miners pushed into Jim Crow restaurants and demanded food, and it was served.

W. B. Wade, a Madison attorney, described the trains that passed his house at night: "They were all crowded as a rule with men who had high powered guns. I saw some machine guns going by on the train during the day . . . I saw one or two machine guns go by there in automobiles. They were streaming by in automobiles all day long . . . they were commandeering machines all over the country."

Thirty armed miners moved up the mountain from Sharples toward Logan, following Brockus's men, and captured four Logan County deputies who had lost their way. Triumphantly they handcuffed their prisoners and brought them back to Jeffrey. That night, miners slapped and punched the deputies in a cabin and tried to force them to give information about Chafin's army.

Monday afternoon, the prisoners were turned over to Bad Lewis White, who treated them well. By then, miners had taken a fifth prisoner, Elbert Gore, a school teacher who lived on Beech Creek, son of a Logan deputy. Gore, too, was turned over to Bad Lewis.

With his prisoners safely put away, Bad Lewis sent word to Chafin the miners held five prisoners of war.

19

"I, Warren G. Harding . . . do hereby command"

IN WASHINGTON, the War Department had trouble keeping up with events in West Virginia. General Bandholz returned Sunday morning, unaware of the Sharples battle that had renewed the march on Mingo in even greater fury. As union miners rose again in insurrection all over West Virginia on Sunday, he reported his findings of Saturday morning: that the rebellion was all but over.

To make the misjudgment greater, his report apparently did not reach President Harding and Secretary of War Weeks until Monday, when thousands of armed miners were on the march again. While newspapers reported the new outbreak of fighting, Secretary Weeks issued a statement, with the president's approval, citing Bandholz's recommendation that no troops be sent and stating that West Virginia had made "only a feeble attempt to check the growth of the insurgent movement or keep in reasonable touch with its progress."

Back in West Virginia, Governor Morgan was beside himself. On Sunday night he sent his new Adjutant General John Charnock and a union officer, A. C. Porter, to the Sharples area to investigate conditions in the battle's aftermath. The men returned to Charleston Monday filled with alarm. Porter compared the Sharples-Blair area with Belgium in the early days of the World War, "a monster powder keg awaiting only the smallest of sparks to launch one of the bloodiest industrial wars in the history of the world."

"Males were in arms and women and children were fleeing

in panic," Charnock told the governor. When the two tried to persuade miners at Clothier to go home, the miners not only refused but threatened to blow up the train that had brought them. When they tried to go beyond Clothier, the train engineer refused unless someone went ahead and cleared the track. At Sharples, Charnock threatened martial law if miners refused to surrender, and no one moved. Porter read a letter from Keeney asking the men to be moderate, and the miners branded the letter as a fake.

Morgan's reaction was predictable. In a telegram to President Harding and Secretary Weeks, he pleaded for federal troops again. Delay would be "most disastrous." "Large forces," he said, were "leaving the Cabin Creek district tonight for the Logan border." There were "imminent dangers of loss of life," and Sheriff Chafin's defensive army at Logan "will be utterly unable to repel the attack."

Morgan's telegram arrived Tuesday morning. To follow it up, West Virginia's Senator Sutherland, former Governor W. A. McCorkle and a delegation of other prominent West Virginians met with Weeks and Bandholz to describe the turn of events. Without disbanding, the entire group went straight to the White House and conferred with Harding.

Morgan telephoned while they were meeting; conditions were still worse, far beyond state control, he said. He called again in the afternoon to say matters had deteriorated since morning. He promised to organize a National Guard immediately within several days—under legislation enacted by the West Virginia legislature in the previous spring. The War Department suggested he convene the legislature to declare martial law, a suggestion he answered by telegram: "Danger of attack on Logan County by armed insurrectionists is so imminent that Legislature cannot be assembled in time."

Secretary Weeks prepared a proclamation, and Tuesday afternoon President Harding signed it, setting federal power finally into motion. Citing the insurrection in West Virginia and the president's powers to suppress insurrection, the proclamation gave the miners less than forty-eight hours to disband:

Now, therefore, I, Warren G. Harding, President of the United States, do hereby make Proclamation and I do hereby command all

persons engaged in said insurrection to disperse and retire peaceably to their respective abodes on or before 12 o'clock, noon, of the
first day of September, 1921, and hereafter abandon said combina-
tions and submit themselves to the laws and constituted authorities
of said State.

That was not all. The president ordered Bandholz back to
Charleston to observe the effect of the proclamation on the miners and to determine whether they obeyed it. Orders were dispatched to the Twenty-Sixth Infantry at Camp Dix, New Jersey,
and to the Nineteenth Infantry at Camp Sherman, Ohio, for the
two regiments to be prepared to move to West Virginia on September 1 if the miners should refuse to disperse. The Camp Sherman troops could reach their destination in West Virginia in
slightly more than three hours and those from New Jersey in
little more than that, the War Department advised.

20

"Bring your raincoats and machine guns"

AS THE MINERS' REBELLION reescalated, an emotion of war swept across West Virginia. Sheriff Chafin's dramatic pronouncement—"No armed mob will cross Logan County!"—stirred leading citizens to the marrow of their bones, awakening patriotism that had been dormant since American boys had gone "Over There." Sid Hatfield's death now was fast receding into history; what seemed at stake was full-fledged civil war, and West Virginia's established citizenry responded accordingly. In an outpouring of feeling, hundreds of West Virginia's most prominent young men came forward as volunteers to help Logan County fight off the invading "rednecks."

McDowell County, where Sid was shot, was first to respond. In a fleet of private automobiles driven by the ladies of Welch, McDowell volunteers bounced and pitched over forty miles of rugged mountains to the nearest railhead and there caught special trains into Logan Town. The first of them arrived Sunday and took positions along the defensive line. Four hundred more from McDowell arrived by train Tuesday, and a great cheer went up from townspeople as they stepped down from the coaches at the Logan depot, assembled in formation, and marched through the streets. By Wednesday, nearly six hundred McDowell men were on the line. In one contingent, the group reported proudly, were "six lawyers, one bank cashier, one bank vice president, six bank clerks, fifty prominent businessmen and every doctor who could be spared from practice." McDowell County was so caught up in the spirit that citizens back in the county organized a "home defense unit" to defend McDowell if Chafin's line should fail. Chafin was so grateful that he made a speech to one group of McDowell volunteers: "If ever they faced peril," he said, "I hope and believe that the men of Logan would rally to the support of McDowell loyally and bravely, as the McDowell men have done on this occasion."

By then, volunteers arrived from all over southern West Virginia. A company of Mingo County's newly organized militia hiked across the mountains to fight under Chafin's banner and took positions along the line of defense. At Huntington, some sixty-five socially prominent young men, most of them officers in the World War, left for the Logan front carrying rifles and a machine gun.

In Bluefield, the American Legion organized a special company of two hundred men to fight the miners. A telegram from state police ordered them to Logan: "Bring your raincoats and any ammunition and automatic rifles or machine guns that may be found in Bluefield." A blast of the city's fire whistle brought them to the main street where they formed, answered roll call and marched to the depot like heroes going off to war. At the depot, a crowd of fifteen hundred cheered and waved as the column marched through, boarded the train, and the train moved off.

Governor Morgan sent Charnock, his new adjutant general, to Logan Tuesday in a special train with more than one hundred cases of state-owned army rifles and ammunition. Logan men rushed the arms to the courthouse, cleaned them, and issued them to arriving volunteers.

As reinforcements rolled into Logan on special trains, enthusiasm for the war mounted throughout the state. The marching of detachments of newly arrived volunteers through Logan streets became a common sight, and townspeople never failed to cheer them from the sidewalks. Frequently, the units halted along the streets; field kitchens were set up, and they were fed. Some marched into the Aracoma Hotel where Logan's ladies generously heaped food on their mess kits and plates.

Chafin moved his headquarters from the courthouse to the Aracoma to be nearer the contingents of men who were joining his army. There, in the lobby, ladies established a supply station with steaming hot foods sitting on tables at all hours for volunteers as they came from the depot or the front. Several times a day they dispatched truckloads of food and clothing to the men on the mountain passes, and bananas, oranges, cigarettes, and cigars were available to all who came through. Logan's most prominent matrons donned aprons for the work and lent themselves to it with a happy feeling of contribution. A *New York Times* reporter watched incredulously as they served rations to some five hundred men in the lobby.

On the streets of Logan, cars sat bumper to bumper on both sides, their drivers sitting at the wheels ready to move to the front with a load, while space was allowed in the center for only one lane of traffic. On the sidewalks, every other man had a rifle, and an air of optimism, and an esprit de corps pervaded among all, from those who leaned on their rifles in the streets to the women ladling soup and proffering cakes in the Aracoma.

Chafin's army included many nonunion coalminers who volunteered with little enthusiasm, some still under "fight or be fired" ultimatums. Some Logan men joined the defensive army for the excitement, intensified by moonshine whiskey, and the army accepted fourteen- and fifteen-year-old boys seeking adventure.

In Charleston, leading citizens called meetings of veterans at the YMCA to recruit for Chafin's army. To their distress, union miners appeared and heckled, jeered and sang, "We'll hang Don Chafin to a sour apple tree," until police forced them to leave. Nevertheless, many Charlestonians signed up for Chafin's army and left immediately for the war. Governor Morgan, involving himself increasingly in Logan's defense, called for volunteers for temporary duty in his new National Guard, and veterans and college students who responded were sent posthaste to Logan.

Joe W. Savage, 22, who had been a pilot in France during the war and was now a student at West Virginia University, was allowed to shake the governor's hand when he signed up for Logan duty. He changed into hunting clothes, borrowed a .38 Smith and Wesson and left. He and his friends traveled to Logan in the dark of night on a special three-coach train, in which the lights were extinguished as they neared the battle zone. Deputies met them after midnight at the Logan depot and marched them to a lodge hall where they slept a few minutes on mattresses that covered the floor. At 2:00 a.m. they were aroused and marched to the courthouse where they were issued rifles, ammunition, and cartridge belts. The courthouse looked like an arsenal, the wide hallways stacked with rifles and boxes of ammunition.

Back on the streets, the men loaded into Model T's in the bluish light of a streetlamp, and they rattled off to the front, bumping over dirt roads for a dozen miles, headlights dimmed and air choked with dust. At last, a flashlight halted them, and a voice commanded them to fall out.

Chafin's army, like the miners' army, now had a password, and a deputy grouped them close around him and whispered they must remember it: "Holden."

"Holden," someone repeated.

"Don't say it," the deputy growled. "Just remember it."

They marched along a ravine through woods up Crooked Creek Mountain as the Model T's headed back for more men. At the top they used the password successfully, and defenders greeted them warmly. The Charleston men slept a few more minutes on the ground and then were marched off in small groups to reinforce positions along the line.

In Charleston, meanwhile, Governor Morgan hastily established his National Guard. He designated two National Guard companies in Charleston, two at Huntington, two at Welch, and one each at Logan and Bluefield. He named William E. Eubanks, native of Welch and veteran of the Mexican border and the World War, as colonel of the National Guard in charge of all troops at Logan.

Eubanks arrived in Logan Tuesday and immediately went into conference with Chafin and Charnock. They planned their defense; forces would be concentrated at Blair Mountain, Crooked Creek, Mill Creek, and Beech Creek. Chafin turned over command of the entire defensive army—twenty-eight hundred men— to Eubanks and expressed pleasure at the support from the state. Despite the change in command, the army remained Chafin's in popular perception.

The organization of National Guard units, militias, American Legion companies, and volunteer groups to help police and deputies fight the miners created confusion. Some men were sworn in for duty in their hometowns, some were sworn in on arrival at Logan, some were sworn in more than once and in more than one organization, and many did not know what they were sworn into. Defenders variously called themselves deputy sheriffs, militiamen, state police, volunteers, national guardsmen, and constabulary. John Charnock, son of the state adjutant general, got to Logan without being sworn into anything; when he told Colonel Eubanks this, the colonel told the young man to hold up his right hand, administered an oath, and said, "Now you are a God damned militiaman," and the young Charnock headed for the front.

Discipline was lax or nonexistent. Volunteers drank, both in Logan and on the line. Eubanks drank heavily while on duty. Accidents were numerous. A Charleston volunteer inadvertently fired his rifle while riding in a car toward the front, blowing a hole through the roof. Another volunteer accidentally fired his rifle into a sidewalk in downtown Logan while trying to extract a shell from it; the bullet shattered the sidewalk, and flying concrete injured him and several passersby.

At Ethyl, a laborer accidentally discharged a rifle, and the bullet struck and killed a state policeman, George Duling. It was the first fatality in the defensive army.

21

"Bullets were hissing back and forth"

I

BLAIR MOUNTAIN was wild, hilly, wooden country, with underbrush so thick in places one could hardly see twenty feet. The mountain actually is a twin mountain, with a pass separating the two sides. A dusty road ran down the pass. Don Chafin's deputies and volunteers, looking down from their defensive line into the valley, could see the road as it turned sharply left below them, ran along the face of the left side of the mountain for about a quarter mile, then dropped down toward Blair. They considered the road as the battle line. On the crest of the mountain to their right, eight hundred feet above Blair, several of them operated a machine-gun nest. Between the road and the machine gun, lining the edge of the hill, others waited in rows of breastworks. On the left side of the road, atop the other twin mountain, was an outpost, and below it other men waited, rifles ready, in trenches or behind breastworks at scattered positions along the mountains.

Northward from these positions ran Spruce Fork Ridge, of which Blair Mountain was a part, and Chafin's army manned similar emplacements along the entire ridge line, ten miles long. Heaviest fire power and fortifications were concentrated at the passes, named for the creeks that formed them: Crooked Creek and Mill Creek on the Logan side, Beech and Hewitt creeks on the Blair side.

On Wednesday morning, August 31, 1921, the West Virginia mine war – the civil war that had smoldered and popped

under Sid Hatfield's leadership in Mingo County for more than
a year and had accelerated into two fighting armies because of
Sid Hatfield's death—finally erupted in hot warfare. Fully ten
thousand men—and some estimates go to twice that number—
were involved as the two armies began exchanging shots along
a ten-mile front. George Washington had fewer soldiers at the
Battle of Trenton, the engagement which changed the course of
the American Revolution.

II

The Logan air force—Chafin's three little biplanes—swooped low
over the miners' line along Blair Mountain Wednesday morning, and from the planes pilots hurled thousands of leaflets which
fluttered to the ground in the morning sunlight. They carried
the printed words of President Harding's proclamation, ordering the miners to lay down their arms and return home by Thursday noon.

The pilots might as well have dropped confetti. Few miners
apparently picked up the leaflets or even saw them, and many
who did found them hard to read. There was no sign of posi-
tive effect.

But in Blair, Major Charles F. Thompson was under orders
to assure that the miners paid attention to the president's proclamation; he was to read the proclamation personally to the rebelling miners. Major Thompson, who had more firsthand information about West Virginia's mine war than anyone in the
army, probably understood fully how futile his orders were, but
he carried them out like the good soldier that he was. Late Tuesday night, he and A. C. Porter of the United Mine Workers took
a special train, consisting of only a locomotive and single coach,
into the war zone. All through the night, the little train made
its way slowly up Coal River on the C&O track and pulled into
the depot at Blair Wednesday morning.

The town consisted of the railroad depot, several large wooden
houses and stores, a swinging bridge, company store, school
house, and a scattering of miners' whitewashed cabins, their front
porches facing Spruce Fork, Blair Mountain towering overhead.
Several hundred armed miners milled about the station as the

little train steamed in, and they took interest as the smartly uniformed officer stepped from the coach.

The men moved toward him. Thompson opened his briefcase, took out the proclamation, and announced it was issued by the president of the United States. He began reading: "Whereas the Governor of West Virginia has represented that domestic violence exists in said State which the authorities of said State are unable to suppress; and, Whereas, it is provided in the Constitution of the United States that the United States shall protect each State . . ."

The words tumbled out, long, legal terms, "whereases," "whereofs," "aforesaids," phrases like "in pursuance of the above," and references to the executive and legislature and laws that must be duly executed. Miners pushed in close around Thompson to listen, understood nothing, and gave up. Several tried to interrupt. One claimed it was not the president's proclamation because the president had not signed it personally. Others argued the point. Several tried to argue with Thompson. Others tried to tell him about the unhappy situation in Logan County, about the Sharples battle, about their problems and the wrongs inflicted upon them by Baldwin thugs. An old miner broke down and cried as he tried to tell Thompson of their troubles.

As they talked, the little train pulled forward from the depot and disappeared down the track. It was to turn around, to be headed back toward Charleston when the major was ready to leave.

The scene degenerated in front of the depot. Thompson told the men it was not *his* proclamation; it was from the president of the United States; *he* was there simply to read it.

This angered the miners. Several moved toward Thompson menacingly. A few drew guns.

As the miners watched, Thompson tacked the proclamation to a telephone pole. He announced he thought the place needed two proclamations, and he moved to tack up another one on the side of a building.

At that moment, the little train came back down the track into the depot. Armed miners rode on the engine and on the roof of the coach. The train stopped so that the platform on the rear of the coach was positioned immediately behind Thompson. On the rear platform stood a middle-aged miner, brandishing a gun threateningly at the major. The miner yelled angrily, "Here's this train. Come on and get out of there."

Thompson was not to be dismissed so easily. "Now, just a minute. This is a government train. I am here representing the president, and I am not ready to go."

"You have not got a damn bit of business here," the miner shouted back. "Get on here and get out of here."

Thompson told the men the best thing they could do was to lay down their arms and go home. A miner yelled the best thing he could do was to get on that train if he wanted to get out of Blair alive.

In the crowd was a physician, Dr. L. F. Milliken of Blair, who grew increasingly alarmed as the confrontation became more heated. The miner on the coach platform, Milliken believed, was ready to shoot Major Thompson. Like every other man in Blair, Milliken carried a gun, and he quickly drew it from his pocket. If the miner on the train started to shoot Thompson, Dr. Milliken decided he would shoot the miner first.

Dr. Milliken stepped up on a little bridge abutment and looked down into the crowd. He saw one of Blair's most respected, elderly miners, a cooperative man who had strong influence.

"Uncle Charlie," he called quietly to the old man. "Call that man off!" He nodded at the miner on the coach platform.

In his dignified, country voice, Uncle Charlie yelled at the man on the train: "Get down from there!"

The words were like magic. Instantly, the armed miner jumped down from the platform. Just as quickly, Major Thompson jumped onto the train. Immediately, the engine lurched forward, picked up speed, and the train disappeared down the track, speeding toward Charleston.

III

John E. Wilburn had been conspicuous among the miners milling around Blair's depot. A coal miner who lived with his wife and eight children in one of the large miner's homes across the creek from the depot, Wilburn was a self-proclaimed Baptist minister. He organized revival meetings and frequently preached in area Baptist churches. A tall, swarthy man, Wilburn was deeply disturbed by the events of recent weeks; the police attack on Sharples had outraged him. "The time has come," he moodily told his friends, "for me to lay down my Bible and pick up my rifle and fight for my rights."

Caught up with the excitement of the march on Mingo, Wilburn assembled a group of followers at the Blair School Tuesday evening. It was time for the laboring man to fight for his rights, he told the group. As a minister of the gospel, he would lead them in march to meet the enemy; they would attack into the face of Chafin's army dug in at the top of the mountain above them; they would take no prisoners.

As evening came on, more than seventy armed miners, black and white, including two of his own sons, joined Wilburn's force, ready to march, and he assumed command of them enthusiastically. He lined them up in two columns, took position at their head, waved his hand in a forward motion, and shouted orders to move out: "We'll eat dinner in Logan tomorrow!" The group moved up the mountain.

That night, high on the mountainside, they camped, put out guards, and slept. Next morning, they were awakened by shooting along the ridgetop. Without breakfast, the men marched around the hillside, through light woods, toward the sound of shooting. They reached the top and followed a little road along a sag in the ridge. They had gone nearly a mile when the column stopped. Ahead, three men stood on the hill, cradling rifles across their arms. The three looked down at Wilburn's column. They were deputies in Chafin's army.

John Gore, leader of the trio, made a sign for Wilburn's men to come forward. Gore was a well known Logan figure, a deputy for nearly ten years, father of nine children (one of whom, Elbert Gore, had been taken prisoner by the miners after the Sharples battle). He carried two pistols and a rifle. The others were John Cofago and Jim Munsie, nonunion miners. They had spent the night on Chafin's defense line and had set out in the morning to reconnoiter.

At Gore's motion, Wilburn and his men moved forward cautiously. The two groups looked at each other intently, questioning, neither recognizing the other. Both had passwords—"I come creeping" for the union miners, "Amen" for the Logan defenders—and decided simultaneously to use them. When they were six feet apart, both Wilburn and Gore asked each other for the password. Suddenly the realization struck both of them. They were facing the enemy. There was a reaching for guns. Someone in Gore's group managed to call out the word "Amen," and then everything exploded in gunfire.

All three of the Logan men fell, mowed down by the fusillade from Wilburn's men. Gore managed to get a shot off before he fell, and the other two may also have shot. Eli Kemp, a black in Wilburn's column, turned to run when a bullet hit him in the small of the back and ripped through his chest. He pitched forward into the grass.

The shooting stopped as suddenly as it began. Wilburn and several of his men walked forward stealthily. Gore and Cofago already were dead. Munsie twisted in agony. They had shot the wrong man, he moaned, and he begged them not to shoot again. Henry Kitchin, a union miner, stood over Munsie, placed the muzzle of his rifle to the man's forehead and said he would now get his revenge on the "God damned son of a bitchin' thug." He pulled the trigger.

Munsie's head jumped off the ground. A witness described it: "The blood welled out like water would out of a hose where you turn it on and the pressure is light."

The union miners took Gore's gun. Suddenly, the wail of a train from the valley made them pause. Reinforcements might be on the way. Wilburn and all his men turned and ran back down the mountain toward Blair.

Jack Brinkman, the Indiana pianist, was with Wilburn's group, and he and one of Wilburn's sons picked up the wounded Kemp and carried him along. Kemp was dying; blood flowed from his wound. Frequently Brinkman and young Wilburn stopped to drain the wound. The boy fainted momentarily on one such stop, but they went on. Exhausted, they placed Kemp under a tree, hurried down to Blair, returned with a stretcher, and carried Kemp on it to Dr. Milliken's office in Blair. There, as the physician pulled Kemp's shoes off, Kemp died.

That night, several miners from Wilburn's force had dinner in a store at Blair. They didn't eat much. "Just a few bites," one said.

IV

With fighting all along their line, Chafin and Eubanks sent reinforcements wherever fighting seemed heaviest and worried
about what they considered a substantial handicap to their forces:
the governor had told them they could not counterattack.

At the Blair Mountain breastworks, a machine gun chattered,
and several hundred deputies and volunteers maintained a steady
rifle fire. The fighting became increasingly heavy. Eubanks sent
a state police captain with sixteen picked veterans to help, and
for two hours they exchanged shots with miners. A veteran of
France and the Rumanian outbreaks, the captain returned reporting, "I never experienced anything like that battle . . . bullets were hissing back and forth all around our heads."

Toward noon, action shifted to Crooked Creek and Hewitt
Creek, the center of the defensive line. Chafin and Eubanks considered their forces insufficient there and shifted a contingent
of McDowell volunteers from Mill Creek to meet the new assault.
An Associated Press reporter, looking down on the sweep of the
valley from a machine-gun nest, saw a group of buildings a mile
distant, behind which as many as fifty armed miners hid. "Time
and again," he reported, the miners moved forward, "but at each
attempt machine guns and rifle fire drove them back."

The shooting became so heavy that Logan defenders began
to doubt their ability to stop the miners. As a precaution, Chafin
and Eubanks organized a second line of defense encircling Logan
Town, while panic began to seize the townspeople. In midafter-
noon, Walter R. Thurmond, president of the Logan Coal Operators Association, telegraphed a congressman in Washington: "Unless troops sent by midnight tonight, the Town of Logan will
be attacked by an army of from four to eight thousand reds and
great loss of life and property sustained."

The defensive line held, despite almost continuous firing at
Blair, Crooked Creek, Beech Creek, and Mill Creek. Recruits continued to arrive from Bluefield, Huntington, and Charleston,
and Chafin's automobiles hurried them to the front. All the remaining state police in West Virginia arrived to further reinforce
the line, and Chafin and Eubanks began to gain confidence.

Chafin had still another tactic. In the preceding weeks, he

had gotten chemists from Charleston to fashion a number of explosive and gas bombs, and late Wednesday afternoon one of his aircraft swooped down over a ravine where miners were thought to be concentrated, and a bomb was dropped. It was a twenty-four-inch pipe, four inches across, filled with TNT, and it exploded as it crashed to the ground, shaking the mountains to either side with its deafening sound, and the explosion echoed and re-echoed. Like most of the shooting, it caused more noise than damage; no miners were in the area, and none were hurt.

By evening, Chafin had regained full confidence. He issued a statement (immediately termed "an official communique" by the press) citing the miners' many attacks and triumphantly reporting success in defending his line: "At all points our forces succeeded in driving back the invaders and in each instance regaining lost territory." He acknowledged the loss of Gore, Cofago, and Munsie and expressed fear for the lives of his men who had been taken prisoner.

By then, he had lost another prisoner. Samuel Hulme, an Englishman and veteran of campaigns in Egypt, Mesopotamia, India, Africa, and France, had joined Chafin's army from a non-union Logan mine. He and two others had been sent out on a scouting expedition, and several union miners cut them off from their lines. Hulme was captured as his two comrades fled. His captors, several of them black, took him to a barn where one struck him with a rifle and another threatened to shoot him. They finally turned him over to Bad Lewis White, now recognized as custodian of the miners' prisoners, who handcuffed him for the duration.

V

The Logan army was not alone in being reinforced. Commandeered trains arrived regularly at Blair bringing armed miners to the front. Union men commandeered a freight train Tuesday night and used it to carry supplies to Jeffrey and to the men on Hewitt Creek. On Wednesday, they commandeered a passenger train and sent it back toward Madison, picking up three hundred miners who had crossed the mountain from the Big Coal River. It deposited them at Jeffrey, where they could move up Hewitt Creek to join the fighting.

Commandeered trains became the rule, rather than the exception. The C&O abandoned its schedule, and trains ran when the miners moved them. Miners even put together their own trains, hitching together engines, freight cars and coaches to suit their needs, and they called them "Miners' Specials." Because railway systems were not working, motor section cars ran along the tracks ahead of the locomotives as a precaution. At night, locomotives and motor section cars moved through darkness burning only red lanterns and flares as warning. The passenger train that normally lay over at Clothier every night was commandeered so regularly that miners joked about its new schedule. Most commandeered trains, however, were freights that carried food, ammunition, weapons, and other supplies, as well as men. One carried six dairy cows to the front to provide milk and butter for the men.

As the trains reached the villages along Spruce Fork, miners swarmed off, and eventually they headed up the mountain in groups of five or ten, fifty or sixty, sometimes several hundred. Wilburn's force was one of them. "Red" Thompson, a black from Opperman mine, led another force of seventy-five men up from Blair. Wearing khaki riding pants, leggings and shirt, and a broad-brimmed white hat, Thompson led his men directly toward the shooting. As the men moved, many shot their guns into the woods ahead of them, toward the top of the ridge, while others simply hid in the woods or stopped short of the more dangerous areas. Both sides fired without aiming and without targets. Casualties were rare. A black miner told of it later: "Well, one crowd climbs up one side of a hill and the other crowd climbs up on the other side of the hill, and they both shoot at the top of the hill."

With so much lead, some casualties could not be avoided. Dr. W. F. Harliss of Clothier made a daily climb up Hewitt Creek and usually found a wounded man or two needing treatment. Dr. Milliken treated those hurt on Blair Mountain. Throughout the battle zone, miners converted school buildings to headquarters and hospitals where nurses administered first aid to the sick or wounded. Miners gave area doctors passes to allow them access to the battle areas.

Both sides thought the miners' army was suffering more casualties than were actually inflicted. Chafin's men assumed they were killing scores of miners; Chafin once estimated at least fifty miners had been killed, and former Governor Henry D. Hatfield, who worked with Chafin in Logan, reported as many as two hundred miners might be dead. The miners, too, thought they were suffering heavy losses. One miner ran down the mountain to Blair shouting, "The deputies are mowing the men down with machine guns," and he reported fifteen to twenty already had been killed. Reinforcements headed up the mountain to replace the miners thought to have been lost.

Men on both sides of the Battle of Blair Mountain made up for the inaccuracy of their shooting by the quantity of shot they fired. The sound of gunfire became a continual roar. Dr. Milliken, a veteran of the Spanish-American War, said he heard as much shooting at Blair as he did at Manila. A front line soldier in Chafin's army said requirements for the front were "cotton to plug the ears and aspirin to kill the headaches caused by the concussions of the rifles firing." At Blair, a miner described the shooting in a miner's language: "You could hear it, seemed like, for miles down the river–seemed like you could hear it–you couldn't tell so much–sometimes you could think they were right down in Blair. Machine guns cracked up there, you would think the whole place was coming down on you."

Nightfall brought no relief; in fact, at times there was more shooting by night than by day. Men on both sides enjoyed shooting into the darkness and seeing the flames spit out from their gun barrels. Miners built large fires at night, hoping to lure the deputies to attack, when they would rush in from the sides, but the deputies didn't fall for it. A Bluefield volunteer with a writing talent described night fighting by Logan's defenders on Blair Mountain:

Someone spies the dark shadow of an armed man stealing along the road and lets go at it. Immediately the whole face of the two mountainsides spit forth angry protesting tongues of flame from which bullets whistle and ricochet down the road. The miners returned the fire–the report of the first rifle shot hardly begins to echo before the pinkish mushroom of flame and the following crack of a revolver or rifle tell the tale.

Both sides included soldiers who didn't want to fight. A reluctant union miner rode to the front in a commandeered train, he said, because other miners forced him to. Another hid under his cabin for most of a week to keep from going to war. On the other side, a miner who was drafted into Chafin's army spent the battle sitting on a log in a secluded spot in the woods. Both said there was more danger at the front from their own men than from the enemy. "We'd just shoot at anything that moved," a union miner said. "You were more likely to be shot in the back by your own troops than you were by the opposition." A non-union miner in Chafin's army agreed: "You was in more danger from another greenhorn than any miner getting to you from the other side."

22

"Things slacked off after we ate"

I

President Harding's deadline passed at noon Thursday. The miners to whom it was directed simply ignored it. At the time of the deadline, they controlled five hundred square miles of southern West Virginia, and within that area they took automobiles and trucks from citizens at will; they operated the C&O trains and controlled the railway tracks, stations, and railyards; they patrolled the highways and regulated automobile and pedestrian traffic and issued passes to authorize citizen movements within the battle area; they refused to allow mines to operate; they commandeered school buildings and used them as mess halls, first aid stations, meeting halls, and sleeping quarters. Sheriffs, judges, and other public officials in the area looked on helplessly. When Boone County Prosecutor W.H.B. Mullins appealed to the governor's office for help, miners reprimanded him and ordered him to make no further such appeals.

It was the duty of General Bandholz to determine officially whether the miners obeyed the president's ultimatum, and at 11:30 A.M. Thursday, a half hour before the deadline, he arrived in Charleston and set to work. He first met with the governor, to whom he presented his orders signed by the secretary of war. When he tried to see Keeney and Mooney, he learned they had fled the state after being indicted in Mingo County for complicity in one of the killings in the Three Days Battle of May. Bandholz talked, instead, to Bill Petry, vice-president of District 17 of the miners' union.

All reports led Bandholz to one conclusion: the miners had paid no attention at all to the president's proclamation, but to confirm it he sent his staff to the battle zone for first-hand impressions. Major Thompson, freshly returned from Blair, Colonel Ford and Petry hurried back by special train to the battle area, and at every stop they found the miners in full rebellion. At Sharples, they ran into Philip Murray, international vice-president of the UMWA, who had come to persuade the rebelling miners to lay down their arms. The miners not only refused to listen to Murray but threatened his life for interfering. Trying to stop the miners, a coal executive told Murray, was like trying "to sweep up the Atlantic with a broom." Murray, Petry, Thompson, and Ford returned to Charleston together.

They found Bandholz in his hotel room, in his pajamas, considering other reports Thursday night. Eubanks had reported heavy fighting all day and, in a glamorous statement like a general under siege, promised, "We intend to hold our line with all the power at our command." Governor Morgan had wired President Harding that armed men were mobilizing again along the Kanawha and were "commandeering automobiles and conveying dynamite and other explosives up Lens Creek to the trouble zone." Former Governor W. A. McCorkle wired: "The whole mining country is practically on the march," and former Governor Hatfield wired: "Many lives of innocent people will unquestionably be sacrificed within the next twelve hours unless Federal troops are dispatched." A congressman wired the president: "Your proclamation is being contemptuously ignored."

It was after midnight when Ford and Thompson gave their reports. After listening to them, Bandholz summoned the governor and told him his decision: there was no alternative other than to call in federal troops. Morgan agreed completely. Bandholz sent off a telegram at 2:00 A.M. to the adjutant general, marked "Immediate Attention": "The invaders have not obeyed the President's proclamation and there is no apparent intention to do so. It is therefore recommended that the troops now held in readiness be sent to West Virginia without delay."

Padding down hotel corridors in his pajamas, Bandholz gave the news to reporters. They turned to the governor.

"I have nothing to say," Morgan replied. "I am through."

II

Armed miners arrived in wave after wave along Spruce Fork and the Little Coal River Thursday, as commandeered trains shuttled back and forth, moving men and supplies to the front. Five hundred miners from Fayette County and two hundred from Raleigh, many of them wearing red bandannas, came on commandeered trains, and a Boone County official estimated eight to ten thousand rebelling miners in the area.

Streams of men filed through the villages and coal camps back of the fighting line. They moved without smiles or songs, intent, silent, sitting around depots or school houses with shoulders humped. They thought only of "eating breakfast in Logan Town," one observer said. In every town they asked for high-powered rifles.

G. C. Williams, 33, of Sharples, a bookkeeper for a mining company, walked six miles up Hewitt Creek to a commandeered school house, listening to machine-gun and rifle fire. "I observed along the road and in rest, 1,500 to 2,000 men," he said, "some men eating, washing their clothes, some cleaning up. . . . About one mile from the school house I encountered a patrol of about forty men armed with high powers holding up everyone going in, telling them in order to get in and out they required a pass."

At Blair, a railroad foreman watched at the town's little school house as men brought in food that had been cooked elsewhere and set it out for the men. Miners lined up and moved through a mess line, each receiving a ration of canned fruit, bread, or meat. In another room of the school house, nurses in white uniforms tended several patients who lay on pallets on the floor. Miners clustered around outside, talking, preparing for battle, or resting from battle.

At Sharples, Williams watched as a company of eighty men, most wearing blue overalls and red neckerchiefs, marched into town and halted opposite the depot on command of a man acting as captain. The captain faced the men forward and called roll, using numbers instead of names:

He called the roll call and started with man No. 1. He said "Here."
He got down to thirty nine. Thirty nine was absent. He called a man

from the rear of the company, probably a lieutenant, to know where the man was. Later he ordered the men to throw down their tin cups; he said they were going into action that night and he didn't want anything to rattle.

Ed Reynolds led his force of three hundred men in red necker-chiefs and blue bib overalls up Hewitt Creek, the men armed with rifles, pistols, and a Gatling gun and five thousand rounds of ammunition. They ate dinner at a school house and camped there Thursday night, then moved into battle Friday under heavy fire. They went only a short distance when three were hit. Romeo Craigo, 23, of Smithers was struck by a bullet in the left leg; Emory Sutphin, 22, was hit by a bullet that ripped through his forearm from elbow to wrist, and Jim White fell with an un-disclosed wound. All were helped down the mountain to a school house where nurses treated them with iodine and bandages. Later, a physician in Jeffrey treated them and sent them to their homes or to hospitals.

Five miners were reported killed Thursday and Friday, al-though details of the killings are scarce. James Roberts, 23, was hit on Blair Mountain, and his body was taken down the moun-tain by tight-lipped miners who refused to answer reporters' ques-tions. Frank Hastings of Dry Branch also was reported killed in the Logan fighting, and his body was taken to his home. Two other miners, not identified, were killed on Blair Mountain, and their bodies were taken to Logan. The *New York Times* reported that a third, unidentified miner, brought wounded to Logan Hos-pital, died Friday night after saying he had been hit by machine-gun fire. The fatality reports were casual, incomplete, and un-substantiated for the most part. No apparent effort was made later to verify the deaths in detail. The number of miners killed probably was smaller than the number reported.

Fred Hall, 19, of Alcott, in Kanawha County, rode a flatcar on a commandeered train into Blair Thursday night and, after five hours of sleep, climbed Blair Mountain Friday with some seventy other miners. "We was to fight our way through," he said, but a bullet stopped him. He lay on the mountainside, shot through the left shoulder, for eight hours before Logan deputies found him and carried him to the Logan hospital. He remained there twelve days and was then removed to Logan's jail.

Manuel Dooley, 27, of Dorothy, was shot through the left knee as he lay prone firing in front of Blair. Clarence Jarrell, 20, of Whitesdale was shot through the back reportedly while leading an attack against Chafin's line. At Madison, a physician treated two wounded miners, one shot in the arm and the other who said he had fallen off a cliff.

Total casualties were low. Most miners who moved up Spruce Fork Ridge never brought themselves to the ultimate in ground warfare: charging directly into enemy fire. They lagged behind; they feinted; they went through the acts of warfare, but they stopped short of that final massive charge over the top. Perhaps they needed more discipline, or trained officers to command them, with the death penalty awaiting any who refused. Perhaps had more time elapsed, they would have brought themselves to that point on their own. They very likely would have. But they didn't.

Instead, they arranged, without conscious effort, for as many of the trappings of war as possible. Increasingly they fought in the unofficial uniform of blue bib overalls, leggings and red neckerchiefs, with scores of variations. Some tied red bandannas to their arms; some tied them to their automobiles. Large numbers continued to appear in World War I uniforms, many with the "tin derby" trench helmets. They carried ammunition in cloth bags over their shoulders; some wore homemade cartridge belts, and some wore great bandoliers heavily laden with bullets. One miner wore the uniform of a captain in the Italian army.

Union locals issued passes to nonfighting citizens authorizing them to move in the fighting zone. All physicians received such passes so they could treat the injured, and special passes were given individuals. When a local union president learned that seventeen-year-old William Arbaugh, visiting an uncle at Opperman, had to start home to Ohio for school, he quickly issued a pass enabling the youth to get through roadblocks in safety.

Secrecy surrounded the miners' army. It was against the miners' tacit rules to ask for names. Everyone was "Buddy." Miners watched for spies or suspects. After C. W. Waldron came under suspicion of signaling to Logan deputies, four miners knocked on the door of his house on Hewitt Creek and took him prisoner until the end of the mine war.

With all telephone and telegraph wires cut, news reporters had to do extra duty to get usable information from the miners and worked still harder to get it out to the world.

Reporters tried continuously to learn something of the leadership of the miners' army, endlessly conjecturing about some unknown miner "general" who sat somewhere – everyone thought in Jeffrey – issuing orders controlling the movements of the miners' army. No military organization could operate as smoothly as this one without central direction, they reasoned. A typical analysis was given by the *Charleston Gazette*:

They have a smoothly operating food commissary. They are divided into companies whose strength is unknown, and officered, just as army companies are commanded, from captains down to corporals. Who the general of this army, which is equal almost to an entire army division, is nobody knows. That's one secret that never comes out. It's believed few of the miners really know who issues the orders from Jeffrey Headquarters, but that these orders are issued is a certainty. For everything is done with system. Every man is accounted for. Every little detail is seemingly worked out in advance.

The analysis was excessively kind to the miners. Actually, little was done with system; every man was not accounted for; the details were not worked out in advance.

Leaders, indeed, emerged, and they served as corporals, sergeants, lieutenants, and captains. Ed Reynolds, Bill Blizzard, Walter Allen, Dee Munsie, John Wilburn, Savoy Holt, Romeo Craigo, "Bad Lewis" White, "Red" Thompson, Charlie "Popcorn" Gordon – the latter two blacks – all were leaders of the rebellion, and there were more. But they were not generals. No one of them commanded the miners' army. They assumed leadership by their own personalities and abilities, not by official recognition; their leadership waxed and waned according to individuals and circumstances. In some groups, discipline was enforced and roll calls taken; in others, discipline and roll calls did not exist.

In the more than half century since the rebellion, many have discussed the fabled "general" of the miners' army, but no such person has emerged. It is inconceivable that the commander of such an enterprise could have remained hidden. The answer, of course, is that there was no general.

Wiley, the perceptive general manager of the Boone County Coal Corporation, made a conscious effort at the height of the rebellion to find the commander. "I never got anywhere near anybody in authority," he said. The leader of his union committee "seemed to object to discussing it and seemed to object to putting me in touch with any other person."

Many have said Billy Blizzard was the general of the miners' army. Indeed, Blizzard was active throughout the fighting as a leader, making speeches to groups of miners, urging them to do this or that, and often groups obeyed him. But he did not command the army; he did not make its decisions or issue its orders. His acquittal in his later trial for treason demonstrated that. One of the miners in later years told of Blizzard's leadership: "A lot of people will tell you that Bill Blizzard was the leader of it all. Now Bill's one of the finest people that's ever lived, don't get me wrong. . . . But he wasn't the leader any more than any of the rest of us was, from the way I see it. We was just all leaders, in a manner of speaking."

"We was just all leaders." It could hardly be expressed better. The miners' army was a singular example of working anarchy, held together for a time by a common drive, a common understanding, a set of common emotions, added to a touch of muscle, a bit of mob rule, and occasional terror tactics. The men knew where they wanted to go and how to get there, and they were united in this knowledge. They moved in groups, comparable to platoons or companies, because they ran in groups from their own mining camps and union locals. In most groups, leaders already existed; where there were none, leaders emerged, as they always do.

The rest came naturally. They brought guns and food because they needed guns and food; they organized their supplies because supplies moved more quickly that way. No "general" was needed to tell them all this, or that they needed cars, trucks, trains, and guns, or how to get them. By the law of averages and by the varying interests and judgments of miners, hundreds of uncoordinated separate decisions somehow resulted in a collective harmony, a leaderless army that was incredibly efficient.

III

Bugles sounded "Assembly" at Camp Dix Friday morning, and soldiers of the Twenty-Sixth Infantry Regiment fell out, packs and guns and equipment ready for war. Husbands kissed wives good-bye, and the first of the regiment's three battalions marched down New Jersey Avenue to the railroad station, each man carrying a rifle, one hundred rounds of ammunition, the "tin derby" steel trench helmet, blanket roll, and shelter half. Major General David Shanks, division commander, reviewed them as they marched, and the first long troop train pulled out, carrying French 75's, camp kitchens, mules, caissons, mortars, baggage wagons and coaches filled with men. In Ohio, Kentucky, and Indiana, soldiers of the Nineteenth Infantry Regiment boarded troop trains at Fort Benjamin Harrison, Camp Sherman, Camp Knox, and Columbus Barracks. They were off to West Virginia.

IV

As fighting increased in intensity Friday, the people of Logan Town and the volunteers of their defensive army received joyously the word that federal troops were on the way. Some feared the town would be overrun by murderous union miners if troops did not arrive soon. Thursday night, State Police Captain I. C. Hollingsworth rushed into the town from the front in a panic; a machine gun had jammed at the Crooked Creek pass, he said; miners had broken through the line and swarmed over the ridge, driving deputies down the hill before them. The town was thrown into a frenzy. Eubanks, beginning to show the effects of heavy drinking, hastily sent Captain Lawson with reserves and a new machine gun to close the gap, and the men hurried off into the night, while townspeople waited fearfully. Before daylight, heavy gunfire broke out within a mile of the town, and Eubanks reported driving back a patrol of attacking miners. Townspeople, awakened by the shooting, were calmed in the morning when Eubanks announced the entire line was intact and no territory had been lost. The situation probably never had been as serious as represented.

Crooked Creek pass remained the center of action. Isaac

Brewer, Sid's old friend who had turned state's evidence in the Matewan trial, showed up there as a machine gunner in Chafin's army. He told reporters proudly how he repelled an attack through a cornfield by shooting where shaking cornstalks betrayed advancing miners. Richard Gough, a machine salesman from Huntington serving as a volunteer, was shot in the hip in one attack on Crooked Creek. Toward evening, the battle shifted back toward Blair Mountain.

Volunteers from Huntington, Bluefield, and Charleston had been on the line more than twenty-four hours, and many began to feel like veterans. They lounged around breastworks and in trenches, shooting haphazardly, talking like men on a hunting trip. When new men showed up, the veterans greeted them with just a touch of superiority. Joe Savage of Charleston found himself with a dozen such twenty-four-hour veterans in a long, narrow fissure in a massive rock formation at the Crooked Creek pass. The men lolled about inside this natural fortification, smoking cigarettes and telling stories. From the rim of the crevice, they could look far down the valley. A desolate farm house could be seen in a small clearing; pole beans and corn were growing in the garden. The farmer's cow had been killed by gunfire, and the carcass could be seen through field glasses, sprawled across a path. Machine guns sprayed the area periodically.

All through Friday morning, rifles and machine guns sounded. Savage and his compatriots responded in kind, and if the interval between volleys was overly long, someone would fire a few rounds toward the invaders and set off another round of heavy fire. When midday came, Savage recalled:

I was pumping some lead downward through the trees when a fellow named Jerry Sizemore grasped my arm and told me to lay off. He pointed down the sheltered side of the mountain, and I saw two men bringing a pack-mule toward us; one leading and the other threatening the animal from the rear. Firing eased up all along the ridge. The two men stopped some fifteen or twenty feet below us, extracted a large packet of sandwiches and a dozen or so bottles of pop, and the smaller of the two slithered up to our crevice and delivered our noon-day repast. . . . The sandwiches were all made with bologna, but the slabs and the bread slices were thick and we made out very well.

After lunch, firing was intermittent, and Sizemore said it had been the same the day before. "Things slacked off after we ate."

Sizemore was a farm boy from Lincoln County, and during the lull he told the others a story about how his father had sold their cow for thirty-five dollars, changed the dollars into nickels, and put all the nickels into a slot machine at a local pool parlor.

"Every last nickel?" someone asked.

"Took him two days," Sizemore said. "We didn't even know where he was."

"You get on slot machines you can't stop," someone said. Savage asked Sizemore about his mother's reaction. "She never said a word," Sizemore said proudly.

The story was a good morale-builder. Everyone seemed to relax, and several defenders were able to get in a nap before the heavy shooting resumed.

As the fighting shifted back toward Blair Mountain that evening, Eubanks decided to bomb the miners again. Chafin's aircraft swooped over the lines and again let loose their bombs. One tore a huge hole in the ground in a hollow near Blair; there were reports of other bombs exploding, and a newspaper reported a bomb caused miners to scatter. No one was injured or killed.

Several bombs failed to explode. Miners found one, a large device of four-inch pipe containing five pounds of explosives and a collection of nuts and bolts intended as projectiles. They passed it around and on Saturday placed it on display in the United Mine Workers office in Charleston.

Eubanks also brought in gas bombs, which exploded in a cloud of gas that caused vomiting among those touched by it. One fell behind a railroad car near Blair but caused little problem. Later, miners picked up the remnants, and a crowd gathered. The only injury from gas bombs occurred when Bob Greever, a Logan defender, toyed with one behind Chafin's line; it broke open, spilling a liquid that burned through his clothing and shoes and severely blistered his leg. He was hospitalized.

Eubanks and his staff apparently thought the bombing was inflicting heavy casualties. The *New York Times* reported after the bombing that the attacking miners had retired and "carried their dead and wounded away with them." Actually, there is no evidence of any miner being hurt by the bombs.

V

The Industrial Workers of the World, that federation of labor organizations dedicated to the overthrow of capitalism before World War I, never made much headway among West Virginia's coal miners, but the IWW's – "Wobblies," they were called – did show up in the state from time to time. In the midst of the mine war, at the height of the miners' attack, a Wobbly somehow managed to arrive in Logan Town.

We have only his last name: Comiskey, a bricklayer who got off the train from Huntington with an IWW card in his pocket. Those who know Logan could have told him he would not last long there.

He was arrested within minutes. Sheriff Chafin said he was drunk and disorderly and had "criticized" unnamed Logan citizens. A local press report said only that the man "gave utterances of his position and was immediately placed in jail."

Next night, about seven o'clock, Oscar White, the jailer's eighteen-year-old son, entered the jail cell area. He carried a revolver for which he had no permit. His father had told the boy to exercise the prisoners.

The boy unlocked a large jail cell and let Comiskey and a dozen other prisoners out into the corridor. There, the boy said, Comiskey swung at him, knocking him to the floor. From the floor, his head against the wall, young White fired his revolver, and Comiskey fell, shot through the groin. He died several hours later. That was the way Chafin told it.

Another prisoner in the jail filed an affidavit swearing that Comiskey was "shot down in cold blood murder" and two deputies dragged the body by the feet from the jail.

We do not know which story is true. We know the Wobbly lasted less than thirty-six hours in Logan.

VI

Chafin's deputies brought in eighteen prisoners of war from the miners' army Friday afternoon, several of them wearing red arm bands, and they were crowded into the Logan jail, where more than thirty other men—most of them prisoners of war—were being held.

Chafin called in newspapermen to interview three selected prisoners. Two said they had been forced to fight in the miners' army, and the third said he was on the way to surrender when captured. Few believed him.

One prisoner bolted from his captors on a Logan street, but he ran only a few feet before volunteers on the street captured him again.

On the other side, Bad Lewis White took increasing pride in his job as guard of the miners' five prisoners, perhaps because he was the brother of Chafin's jailer. Bad Lewis moved his prisoners from place to place, always keeping them handcuffed together. At one point he kept them in his own cabin and at another time in the mouth of a mine. He fed them well and even stopped other miners from harming them.

The wife of Howard Young, one of the imprisoned deputies, gave birth to their first son in Logan while he was a prisoner. Elbert Gore, a sixth prisoner who was separated in Jeffrey, learned from the newspapers that his father had been killed on Blair Mountain while he was a prisoner, but he was not allowed to attend the funeral.

23

"These strange new craft"

AT 11 O'CLOCK THURSDAY MORNING, Lieutenant Rex K. Stoner's twin-cockpit Dh-4B biplane taxied down the runway at Langley Field and lifted into the air. Behind him, sixteen other army planes, equipped to carry bombs and machine guns, prepared to follow on a trip into the West Virginia mountains.

Billy Mitchell selected the 88th Air Squadron at Langley in Virginia to perform West Virginia duty. When President Harding issued his proclamation, Mitchell alerted the squadron, and he issued the field order at 10:30 that morning, a half hour before the first take-off.

The movement had been planned carefully. In addition to the Dh-4B's, several Martin bombers from the Washington area were ordered to carry extra ammunition, medical supplies, a flight surgeon and replacements; a photographic detachment and communications section also would move to West Virginia by air. The Langley aircraft planned to refuel at Roanoke, Virginia, about half way to Charleston, before flying across the Allegheny ridges to Charleston. Mitchell alerted Roanoke officials to their coming.

At 1:15 that afternoon, Roanoke's Mayor Boxley and other city officials hurried out to a twenty-acre alfalfa and corn field north of the city to witness the arrival of war planes in the Appalachians. They had hardly arrived when Stoner's plane appeared as a dot on the horizon, grew larger, and, as excitement increased, flew over the city, banked around and came in for a perfect landing in front of the mayor. Two trucks had brought in fuel, and a crowd of excited citizens began to gather. As Stoner climbed from his cockpit, the mayor greeted him, "We are at your service, Lieutenant."

The crowd grew steadily during a long interlude before the next plane arrived. About four o'clock, as a reporter described it, "eight black specks, which looked like a covey of birds, were seen coming over the top of the mountains east of the city." The crowd became so excited Stoner had to quiet them. As all watched with bursting admiration, Stoner's mechanic spread a twenty-foot square sheet on the ground to designate the landing area, and Stoner, with another white cloth, signaled to them their approach.

One by one, their engines roaring with deafening noise, the aircraft came in, the pilots guided by "signals known only by the men in the air service of the United States Government," the *Roanoke Times* reported knowingly.

The new pilots reported a rainstorm approaching. Indeed, at 4:20 P.M., the tenth and eleventh planes came in, and the pilots were barely from their cockpits when the rain poured down. In the midst of the downpour, the twelfth aircraft arrived, could not find the landing field because of the rain, and set down in a field several miles away; there, the pilot sat out the downpour and then "soared into the air, located the landing place and glided down to his position."

About five o'clock, the thirteenth and fourteenth craft arrived, flying through the rainstorm, and landed safely on the alfalfa field. A half hour later, the last three came in, led by Major Davenport Johnson, Squadron Commander.

The Roanoke hosts took the airmen like war heroes to the city's fashionable Shenandoah Club for dinner and installed them in the fine accommodations of the Hotel Roanoke. Volunteers from the American Legion proudly stood guard over the planes that night.

"Seventeen planes left Langley field, and seventeen planes arrived here," Johnson told a reporter with obvious pleasure. That record, unfortunately, would be badly tarnished during the ensuing days.

Next morning, because the rain had so softened the cornfield, the first plane, again piloted by Stone, took off two hours late. Others took off at half hour intervals. All day the planes roared into the air as Roanoke citizens turned out in huge crowds. By noon, a serious traffic jam blocked roads in the area as festive throngs came to watch.

As the third aircraft was leaving the ground, its left wing struck a corn shock, and the plane glanced off into a telephone pole, nosed down in an adjacent field and came to rest upside down. The pilot, Lieutenant Valentine S. Miner, and a cadet emerged unhurt from their cockpits, but the plane could fly no more.

Two other aircraft were found to have suffered engine problems and were held back for minor repairs.

Of the fourteen aircraft that got into the air at Roanoke, one developed engine trouble over West Virginia and was forced down on a rough field near Beckley. In landing, it hit a mound of dirt, blew a tire and broke an axle. The pilot and his assistant emerged unhurt.

Of the remaining thirteen, two lost their way in a fog and spent Friday night at Mooresburg, Tennessee. Heading again toward Charleston Saturday, they ran into a storm; one of the pilots tried to land, hit a ditch, wiped off the landing gear and demolished the plane. The other pilot, seeing what had happened, flew on seeking a better landing field. Running low on gas, he finally landed on the side of a hill near Beckley, hit a fence and crashed. The two crewmen scrambled from their cockpits as the plane was engulfed in flames.

The remaining eleven aircraft landed successfully at Charleston, creating a sensation below wherever they flew. A rebelling miner from the miners' army was buying rifles at a hardware store at Beckley when one of the planes flew over; he, the hardware merchant and all other customers dropped everything to run out and look skyward. The weekly *Fayette Tribune* reported when the planes flew eighty miles per hour directly over Fayette County, "thousands were afforded their first view of these strange new craft." When one plane circled low over Fayetteville, the newspaper reported: "chickens took to shelter, cows bawled and ran at top speed for home and dogs with tucked tails sought protection of their masters."

Meanwhile, four big, awkward, boxlike Martin bombers were

winging their way toward Charleston from Aberdeen, Maryland. One was blown off course. As darkness approached, the pilot tried to set the big biplane down on a small field near Fairmont in northern West Virginia. The plane struck a fence and wrecked. Again, neither the pilot nor any of his three crewmen was injured. Of the twenty-one aircraft ordered to Charleston, only fourteen arrived. The problems still were far from over.

On Friday, General Mitchell, at Langley, wired Davenport Johnson ordering three Martin bombers to return from Charleston to Langley, and next day the three big biplanes took off from Kanawha City and headed over the mountains toward the coast, flying in formation at seventy miles an hour at four thousand feet. In the lead plane, Lieutenant Harry L. Speck, the pilot, sat in the big open cockpit in front of the wings. It was the same plane that six weeks earlier had led the final attack on the German ship *Ostfriesland* off the Virginia coast in a demonstration of the remarkable power of aircraft to sink ships at sea.

A short distance out of Charleston the three aircraft ran into a storm. Apparently intending to return, Speck banked his big plane to the left. Suddenly, to the horror of the other pilots, the plane went into a nose dive and then a tailspin, falling slowly to the ground. There, the four tons of canvas, spruce and iron springs burst into flames on a wooded mountainside, its tail pointing upward.

The other aircraft circled. One returned to Charleston while the other landed on a farm a mile from Oak Hill. Police, the army, county sheriffs, and hundreds of citizens fanned out across Nicholas County in southeastern West Virginia in search of the fallen aircraft. On Monday, September 5, two days after the crash, a searcher ten miles northeast of Summersville heard faint cries of help. Pushing through the brush, he came upon the plane. Four of the five crewmen – Speck, Lieutenant William S. Fitzpatrick, Sergeant Arthur R. Brown, and Private Walter B. Howard – were dead, but the fifth, Corporal Alexander Hazelton of Wilmington, Delaware, was still alive. Despite two broken legs, a dislocated hip, internal injuries, and a broken back, Hazelton had managed to crawl from the burning wreckage to safety. As he did, he saw the bodies of three of the crewmen hanging upside down from the wreckage, their heads nearly touching the ground. The fourth was buried underneath. Hazelton waited in agony.

Searchers carried Hazelton more than a mile through the woods on a makeshift stretcher, then took him by automobile to Summersville and finally to a hospital at Montgomery east of Charleston. He lived, but his legs remained paralyzed for life.

The aircraft of the 88th Squadron made a half dozen or so reconnaissance flights for General Bandholz over the mine war area during the next several days but fired no shots and dropped no bombs; the planes, in fact, carried no ammunition or bombs on these flights. Miners fired at the planes and slightly damaged several of them. For the most part, the planes sat on the Kanawha City field where Charlestonians flocked to look at them and to laden the pilots with cigars, cigarettes, and pails of ice cream.

Gradually, the planes of the 88th Squadron returned to Langley during September with only two more mishaps. The wheel of one collapsed in landing at Kanawha City following a routine flight, damaging wheel, propeller and radiator. Another, forced down in the mountains at Narrows, Virginia, suffered a broken axle landing on a small, mountain field. The crewmen of both planes scrambled away unhurt.

The Martin bomber that had landed near Oak Hill, meanwhile, found itself stranded because of the small size of the field on which it sat. It was only a short distance from the Fayette County Fair, and thousands of fairgoers visited it for the next ten days as air service men tried to figure out how to get it airborne. Finally, stripped of its bombs and excess equipment and with only the pilot aboard, it sailed out of a clover field into the air in mid-September.

The 88th Squadron claimed in later years, when it became the 436th Bombardment Squadron, to be the only Air Corps unit ever to have participated in a civil disturbance. Billy Mitchell, pleased with his West Virginia operation, boasted that it had provided "an excellent example of the potentialities of air power, that can go wherever there is air."

24

"The miners have withdrawn their lines"

I

WEST VIRGINIA'S MINERS periodically had risen in varying degrees of violence since the turn of the twentieth century, although never to the extent of the rebellion following Sid Hatfield's death and the subsequent killing of miners at Sharples. Despite their trigger-happy ways, despite their cruel treatment by many coal operators, despite the dangers and outrages of their vocation, they had never entertained real thoughts of trying to overthrow their national government. The idea, in fact, was totally unthinkable to them. Their enemy was nearer home: the coal operator; the deputy sheriff hired by the operator to enforce the law the way the operator liked the law enforced; and, above all, the private Baldwin-Felts detectives and others collectively known as "thugs," who, protected by the operator-paid deputies, broke both the laws of man and the principles of morality that others adhered to, by spying, by bullying, by violence, by gun.

But when the moment came that they must fight federal troops, who were serving in the same army in which they, the miners, had served, there was no question in their minds. The refusal by operators to let them join a union; the eviction at gunpoint of their wives and children from their homes; their imprisonment without charge or hearing; the savage, brutal, planned murder by operator-employed detectives of Sid Hatfield and Ed Chambers with their wives on their arms; the killing of miners and shooting into miners' homes late in the night;

even the dropping of bombs on them – all paled into insignificance when compared with shooting at soldiers of the United States Army.

The miners knew this so well they did not need to talk about it. There was no decision, no judgment to make. They would not, could not, make war against their own country.

II

A train of ten cars carrying two hundred soldiers rolled out of Saint Albans Friday night and moved up the C&O tracks along Coal River. The engine pushed three flatcars, placed end to end, ahead of it, a safeguard against explosive mines, and two soldiers stood at the front of the lead flatcar looking ahead into the darkness for objects that might derail the train. The coaches were dark, except for cigarettes glowing here and there; the only other light came from the engine searchlight beaming ahead over the flatcars and track, and from the fire box which cast a red glare against clouds of black smoke pouring from the smokestack. As it circled around horseshoe bends in the mountains, the soldiers looked out and caught sight of the engine and the two soldiers riding lookout on the flatcars.

The train clicked along at a steady twenty miles per hour, often alongside a mountainside so steep that rock cliffs literally hung over the train. It would have been easy, soldiers observed, for a miner to drop a bomb by hand on the train. They noticed frequently above them cabins perched on the mountainsides, and families looked down at the train from their front porches. When it passed through villages, small clusters of men and women watched and occasionally cheered.

Aboard were two companies of combat veterans of the Nineteenth Infantry from Fort Thomas, Kentucky, under the command of Captain John J. Wilson of Williamsbridge, New York. They carried rifles and machine guns, enough to hold off any attack until heavier equipment could be brought up. Word already had spread that one of the soldiers was Sergeant Samuel Woodsill who had killed more enemy in the World War than anyone except Sergeant York.

As the train wound its way up Coal River, other military units moved in many places toward the West Virginia war zone. Three large trains had set out from Camp Dix, and other trains still were in transit from Indiana and Ohio. At Philadelphia, a boy at the station stared at the long string of cars carrying soldiers, howitzers, horses and caissons of the Twenty-Sixth Infantry from Camp Dix and asked, "Where's the war?" A leather-skinned face at the window responded, "This ain't no war," and there was general amusement. The train pulled out, moving slowly toward Washington; three battalions, a machine gun company and a howitzer company formed the Twenty-Sixth.

At Huntington, Colonel Thompson met the trains as they came in from Indiana and Ohio and directed them to Saint Albans or Logan, and at Saint Albans Colonel Ford directed them up Coal River. When the Nineteenth Infantry passed through Huntington, soldiers hung out windows and traded questions with a crowd of citizens.

In Charleston, Bandholz directed the military investiture from new offices in the Chesapeake and Potomac Telephone Company building, a huge topographic map covering one wall. He divided the war zone into three districts: one from Saint Albans to Blair along the Coal River, one along the Kanawha River, and the third the Logan area. On Friday, he ordered an air reconnaissance: "You will under no circumstances drop any bombs or fire any machine guns or do anything to unnecessarily excite the invaders." Bandholz planned a pincer movement involving 2,100 troops: the Nineteenth would move up Coal River from Saint Albans to Madison, Danville, Sharples, Jeffrey, and Blair, behind the miners' lines; the Fortieth Infantry from Camp Knox would move to Logan to relieve the Chafin-Eubanks army, and the Twenty-Sixth from New Jersey would reinforce the Nineteenth around Madison, with additional companies stationed along the Kanawha at Marmet, Lens Creek, Cabin Creek, and Montgomery.

Captain Wilson's train rolled into Madison shortly after ten o'clock, and a sharp-eyed little man in a wrinkled suit swung aboard, the assistant prosecutor of Boone County. "We're glad you're here," he said, and he told the soldiers the last commandeered train of union miners had left, loaded with miners and headed for the front, only forty-five minutes earlier. "It has been just terrible."

The train stopped. A bugle sounded, a sergeant yelled "Packs and guns – fall in!" and soldiers piled out of the coaches and formed on the cinder right-of-way. Half were sent out as sentries; machine guns were posted up and down the tracks, and the remaining soldiers climbed back into the train to sleep.

Billy Blizzard, who had hurried from Charleston on a gasoline motor track car, suddenly appeared, wearing a suit that appeared to have been slept in for a week, his necktie knotted wrong side out against a soiled white collar.

"Are you the general of the miners' army?" someone asked. "What army?" Blizzard answered with a smile. Then he added: "I guess the boys'll listen to me all right." He told Captain Wilson that if he would send a squad up the line with him, "I can get all our fellows out of the hills by daylight."

Blizzard talked to several news reporters who had come along: the Logan deputies, flying a "Baldwin-Felts plane," had dropped a half dozen bombs on the miners that day, but only one exploded, and it hurt no one. He told of a bomb that dropped between two women but failed to explode. Three miners had been killed in the day's fighting, he said, and he didn't know how many wounded. He consistently referred to the "enemy" as "Baldwin-Felts thugs," "Don Chafin's thugs," or simply "dogs."

Captain Wilson searched Blizzard and took a pistol from him. Blizzard produced a permit signed by the Kanawha County sheriff, and Wilson returned the gun.

"Does this mean you are going to allow only men with permits to keep their guns?" Blizzard asked. Wilson nodded affirmatively.

"The men on the other side of the ridge will keep theirs?" "If they have permits, yes."

Blizzard's eyes flashed. "Know what that means? Our boys'll be unarmed and those Baldwin-Felts thugs will just shoot 'em down whenever they please." It was typical West Virginia justice in his eyes; the miners, he said, would refuse to turn over the guns if the deputies did not have to.

Then he disappeared into the night.

Meanwhile, another troop train had started up the Coal River from Saint Albans, bringing horses, howitzers, pompoms, field kitchens, and Colonel C. A. Martin, commander of the Nineteenth Infantry. The train pulled in at Madison at 4:45 A.M. as Wilson's two companies lined up for breakfast. The captain reported immediately to the colonel.

Blizzard appeared again; he had been gone four hours. He had been to Jeffrey and the fighting front. "The miners have withdrawn their lines," he said, and were awaiting the troops' arrival.

Colonel Martin ordered both trains to advance toward Jeffrey. The first moved out at 5:30 A.M., and the second twenty minutes later; Major Charles T. Smart was in command of the second train, with Captain Wilson and his men aboard. Their armament was strengthened with a howitzer and two pompoms. Blizzard and several news reporters continued to ride along.

Wilson's soldiers were in a jovial mood, hanging out the windows like schoolboys, calling to "the natives." They passed overalled men in Ford flivvers, five and six to a car, none armed, bouncing down the road toward Madison. The miners waved and grinned at the soldiers. A gray mist wreathed the mountains, and tangled telegraph and telephone wires lay along the road and tracks. Miners' cabins were scattered along the track, and miners and their families stood on their front porches and watched the train pass.

Blizzard rode on the rear platform. During the night, he told officers and reporters, he had talked to miners at the front and told them of the army's plans to take guns only from those without permits, meaning the miners but not the "thugs." As a result, he said, the miners were hiding their guns. "That's why you don't see guns. When we need 'em again, we'll know where to look for 'em."

At Jeffrey, the lead train pulled off onto a siding, and miners lined up on both sides of it, looking with curiosity at the soldiers, occasionally acknowledging by the wave of a hand the friendly greeting of a soldier from the train. They stood dirty, tired, stubble-bearded, dressed in overalls and khakis: blacks, white natives, and Europeans. The troops got off the train.

The second train passed through Jeffrey and pushed up the

valley between steep, green mountains. It disappeared briefly into a cloud bank that covered across the tracks and emerged on the other side. At 6:35 A.M., the train crossed the Logan County line. At Clothier, miners called to the soldiers pleasantly. "Howdy, boy," one said to a soldier at the window.

At Sharples, so-called "capital" of the rebellion, the train stopped, and Captain Wilson's men climbed out. Rebellious miners were everywhere. Black and white, they thronged around the station, blanket rolls over their shoulders, several still carrying guns. The troops and miners mingled and talked about the war. A reporter told of one conversation between black miners and the soldiers, a story that reflected the prejudices of the time. The blacks, the reporter wrote,

told the regulars about their fighting experience with rolling eyes showing a lot of the white.

"Yes, suh, they b'en a hauling of d'ed men out these yer mountains every hour of the day and night. Three hundred and ninety-seven men killed. Yes, suh, three hundred and ninety-seven." The regulars were far from believing. "Do ye hear him," said the sergeant listening from a boxcar, "he says three hundred and ninety-seven. He must be their adding machine." The other regulars whooped and laughed.

Major Smart, meanwhile, was having difficulty. He ordered several armed miners to surrender their guns, and the miners ignored him. In frustration, he turned to Blizzard. Blizzard talked to the miners, and they immediately turned in their arms. Some of the unarmed miners, after listening to Blizzard, crossed Spruce Fork on a bridge, disappeared up the mountainside for ten or fifteen minutes, and returned with their guns which they had hidden in the mountains. As Major Smart watched, very much impressed with Blizzard's power, the miners surrendered these guns, too.

Under Major Smart's direction, some four hundred union miners boarded the train on which the soldiers had come, and the train headed back to Madison. There, soldiers surrounded it and searched it from engine to caboose, finding several pistols and rifles the miners had hidden under coach seats. From

Madison, the train went on to Saint Albans, taking the miners back toward their homes.

A third troop train arrived at Madison carrying the Nineteenth's regimental headquarters company, and soldiers detrained to establish Colonel Martin's headquarters. Madison took on a martial aspect, with field ranges, sidecars, army automobiles, caissons, artillery and horses.

Just outside Madison, the soldiers recaptured a "Miner's Special," a train the miners had made up for themselves and had run almost constantly for a week. The miners gave their train up cheerfully.

III

At Logan, fighting continued. Miners, ignoring the federal troops moving up on their rear, kept up their fire on Blair Mountain and succeeded in wounding two Logan defenders at Crooked Creek. The machine guns of Chafin's army rattled on as if by habit, although most defenders were not busy. A heavy rain drenched all on the mountain Saturday afternoon. A Welch physician on the front line was struck by lightning and injured slightly.

At 1 P.M., in the middle of the rainstorm, the first troop train pulled into Logan with three companies of the Fortieth Infantry from Camp Knox, bringing machine guns, trench mortars, 37 millimeter guns, a radio outfit, and fifty mules. Logan townspeople and volunteers hailed the troops as they stepped from the train, and when the first of them entered the Aracoma lobby the women and ministers serving food broke out in applause. Soldiers set up wireless equipment atop the Aracoma Hotel as Logan citizens watched in awe.

Colonel Thompson had accompanied the men from Huntington, and he and the unit commander, Colonel G. A. Shuttleworth, immediately set out to inspect the Logan situation. They found Eubanks drunk. Eubanks and his staff, Thompson said later, were "so unmistakably under the influence of liquor as to render them unfit in our opinion for an orderly transaction of business." Thompson had suspected from previous telephone conversations with Eubanks that the Logan commander was drinking. On his inspection he found so much confusion in the defensive army, he said, he was satisfied "that there had been dissension among the leaders, lack of a carefully organized plan of defense, and that the state of intoxication found upon our arrival had endured for at least most of the preceding twenty-four hours."

Despite his intoxication, Eubanks sent out word to his men announcing the troops' arrival. During the night, under a desultory rain, the soldiers moved out to Blair Mountain and Crooked Creek in cars, on mules, and on foot. Shuttleworth set up headquarters two miles outside Logan toward the front. The defenders were awakened at their barricades and in their trenches and sent back toward Logan all through the night. The relief went off with few mishaps, although a McDowell volunteer accidentally shot himself in the foot in the Aracoma Hotel lobby where he chose to unload his rifle.

IV

Among those getting off Major Smart's train at Sharples were four news correspondents trying to reach the battle front. Chief among them was the famed war correspondent of the *New York Tribune,* Boyden Sparkes, and with him were H. D. "Al" Jacobs of United Press, Donald Craig of the *New York Herald,* and Mildred Morris of International News Service, the only woman correspondent covering the action. With Blizzard's help, they secured an automobile driven by an electrician, Nicholas Ball, and set out up the Blair Mountain Road with Ball, his wife and small baby.

Like all visitors to West Virginia, they were impressed first with the primitive roads; the road they followed from Sharples to Blair dipped into and out of the water of Spruce Fork. The driver, Sparkes noted, "followed the bed of this river for a while, took a so-called road for a change, found it worse, and got back in the stream."

They turned up a hollow, and Ball secured a second car driven by a friend. In the two cars, they moved on through country Sparkes compared to the Argonne. Ball's wife and baby got out and went home, and they pushed on. About a mile up the hollow, the lead car sank hub deep into muck, blocking the road to the second car. An old miner in overalls, his face covered with scrubby white whiskers and a green celluloid patch over his right eye, happened along, leaned one arm on the higher side of the stranded car, and struck up a conversation: "The machine guns a'crackin' up yere at the head of the crick." About three hundred miners had been holding the hollow, he said.

They set out walking, and soon they heard sporadic rifle and machine-gun fire ahead. Ball whistled loudly as he walked and suggested the reporters "keep a'talking. Some of these boys are careless about shooting." The reporters began talking loudly.

As they neared the top of the mountain, Ball admitted he might be lost. Two miners came along in bib overalls and offered to lead the group, now numbering seven, to the top. "This is Blair Mountain," they said. "The top of it was nearly shot off the other day."

They began scrambling up the steep, slippery mountainside, along a path, until they were within fifty feet of the summit. There they stopped to rest. As they started up again, a barrage of gunfire suddenly erupted. All seven threw themselves to the ground as bullets splashed up leaves and earth at their feet. The shooting went on. The reporters shouted, "Friends!" Someone shouted "Unarmed," the others joined in. Finally the firing stopped.

"Stick up your hands if you are unarmed," a man yelled from the top of the hill. All seven held up their hands and began struggling to their feet.

As he tried to get up, Sparkes discovered he had been shot in the calf of his right leg, the bullet coming out cleanly on the other side. Another bullet had creased his head, and blood ran down his face. Nonetheless, he stood up and walked without trouble. One of the miners had been shot in the ankle.

They climbed to the top of the mountain and faced their assailants. They were state police. Before they could talk, someone down below began shooting, and the police poured bullets down the mountainside again, shooting at unknown persons. The new outbreak subsided, and the police turned back to the reporters. One officer went to a telephone hung on a tree and called headquarters at Ethyl. He asked for cars for "six rednecks we just got."

V

President Harding signed a second proclamation establishing martial law in the disturbed areas of West Virginia, but he did not promulgate it. Instead, General Bandholz was to use the martial law declaration only if necessary. As events unfolded, it became increasingly apparent the martial law edict would not be necessary, and Bandholz's reports to Washington reflected that. When Secretary Weeks left his office Saturday, he expressed optimism to reporters and cancelled orders to hold another infantry regiment in readiness for movement to West Virginia.

Samuel Gompers of the American Federation of Labor called on President Harding and urged him to adopt the suggestions of John L. Lewis that a conference of miners and coal operators be called to settle the West Virginia controversy. Harding replied his first interest was in establishing the authority of the United States and in maintaining law and order. Lewis, meanwhile, conferred with Secretary of Labor James J. Davis, himself a West Virginian, in Chicago about the West Virginia situation and then told reporters he hoped government officials would disarm the coal operators and extend the miners the right to bargain collectively.

In Charleston, Bandholz kept his thinking to himself. Asked if he would disarm the deputies as well as the miners, he begged the issue nicely: "They are now under the control of Federal authorities, and they will do just as they are told."

Both sides of the controversy were pleased with Bandholz's leadership. Coal operators praised him, and the *UMW Journal* reported the general "is ever smiling and good natured, with time to see everybody, but there is doubt in the minds of none that he is boss. In the claims and counterclaims of either side he has no interest."

VI

Freedom of the press was a concept little understood by either side in the miners' rebellion. Reporters covering the event found that many of their most basic rights, rights they took for granted elsewhere, were not tolerated in southern West Virginia. Both operators and miners tried to control the press by the most direct methods, including force. In Logan, the local newspaper effectively did what the coal operators and Sheriff Chafin asked, and across the mountain at Madison coal miners informed a newspaperman he could not send out dispatches unless they were censored by miners. James J. Brady, photographer for the *Philadelphia Inquirer,* arrived at the miners' front with a written recommendation from the Attorney General of the United States, but it got him nowhere with the rebelling miners. They took his camera, destroyed his film and held him prisoner for most of a day.

At Logan, Sparkes and his colleagues could hardly believe the treatment accorded them by Sheriff Chafin and his deputies. Al Jacobs and Mildred Morris, the UP and INS correspondents, respectively, irritated Logan officials and found themselves under guard as they tried to write their stories. Miss Morris was outraged: "My guard, an insolent youth, insisted on going with me into the bedroom assigned to me," she wrote. "When I objected, he said he was acting under orders." To avoid such indignity, she said, "I was compelled to sit in the hotel lobby while more insolent youthful members of the state police made insolent queries and threatened me if I refused to answer." West Virginia's mine war, she concluded, was "not war as civilized nations carry on against each other, but war without mercy, carried on by men lusting for blood." Both she and Jacobs left Logan in a huff.

Sparkes, a more agreeable person, remained to cover the mine war despite his minor wound. Borrowing a typewriter, he went to his room in the Aracoma and wrote a story about the trip up Coal River. In his own office, Sheriff Chafin worried about what the New York reporter was telling the world, and he asked George Coyle, prominent young man among the Charlestonian volunteers, to find out what Sparkes was writing. Coyle, sensitive to the issue of freedom of the press but not wishing to anger Chafin, went to Sparkes's room, entered, and self-consciously lay down on the bed for a few moments, then left without bothering the reporter.

Chafin decided to take more direct action to control the report. When Sparkes finished his story, Major Tony Gaujot, well-known Logan citizen, informed the reporter his dispatch would have to be approved before it could be sent to his newspaper. Gaujot was to be the censor.

Reluctantly, Sparkes turned his article over to Gaujot for review. Gaujot began reading but soon stopped, pointed to a portion of the story, and said, "Cut that out." He pointed to a sentence which read: "Gaunt-faced women, barefooted and expressionless watched the troops pass. Some of them waved half-heartedly."

"No sob stuff for those rednecks," Gaujot said, and struck the passage.

A moment later Gaujot objected to a line saying: "Daybreak at Madison was greeted by long blasts from the whistle of arriving troop trains."

"Cut that," he said. "We don't want any patriotic stuff from those people."

Sparkes explained that the whistle blasts were blown by the train engineer, not by the miners.

"Don't want it in there," Gaujot said, and the sentence came out.

Gaujot went over with special care several lengthy quotations of Blizzard and told Sparkes he could not quote Blizzard as referring to the "Baldwin-Felts men." "The defenders here are not Baldwin-Felts men," Gaujot said, "and we are not going to let them call us that."

Sparkes explained that, although the defenders were not Baldwin-Felts men, the miners referred to them as such, or by even less flattering terms, and Sparkes felt compelled to report the references truthfully. It made no difference. "Take that out," Gaujot concluded the discussion.

Gaujot then struck the following passage entirely as "sob stuff for the red necks":

As Blizzard talked on the rear of the troop train he watched a tall, thin, stubbly-faced miner who sat on the porch of his small house near the tracks. On his overalled lap was a baby. His wife held one of his hands and with her free calico-clad arm waved smilingly to the soldiers. Two other children stood beside them, looking happily into the face of their "Pappy." They seemed to feel that the trouble was over and their parents out of it unscathed.

Sparkes tried to explain that the paragraph was intended to show that the miners were not merely footloose men of the migratory worker type but men who had left their homes and families to participate in a rebellion against their state and county authorities.

Major Gaujot listened attentively, pursed his lips thoughtfully and finally shook his head. The paragraph came out.

After reviewing the remainder of the article and striking another Blizzard quotation, Gaujot affixed his name and OK to the last page and gave it back to Sparkes. It was suitable for publication.

25

"It was Uncle Sam did it"

I

ALL WEEKEND, West Virginia's rebelling miners surrendered in large numbers to the United States Army along Coal River and Spruce Fork. Some came forward voluntarily, surrendered their arms, gave their names to federal officers, and were carried away from the battle zone on special trains to Saint Albans. A larger number hid their guns in the mountains or in the cabins of their friends and simply made their way home – on foot, riding in flivvers, on horseback, or in wagons.

Colonel Martin set up headquarters at Madison and established strong detachments at Sharples, Jeffrey, and Clothier. By Saturday evening, six hundred miners had formally surrendered, and thousands more simply had gone home. Those who surrendered turned in only eighty guns.

The little mining towns took on a military appearance as uniformed soldiers patroled the streets, and army pup tents and field tents appeared in the hollows. The last shot was fired Saturday evening, and on Sunday miners and their families strolled along the streets of their communities, talking with each other but not with the soldiers. Military authorities forbade fraternization between soldiers and natives and declared no gatherings of citizens would be permitted. The soldiers broke up little knots of people as soon as they formed. Miners gathered in union halls, where meals were served, and stopped often to exchange tidbits of information, moving on as sentries approached them.

Passenger trains continued moving down the river carrying

miners, and each train was searched as it passed through Madison. Soldiers searched pedestrians on the roads, and patrols walked the streets of Madison both night and day.

Refugees who had fled from the battle area to Huntington, Charleston, and Saint Albans moved back into their homes along Spruce Fork. Boone County Sheriff D. M. Griffith made himself known to the federal troops, and a lieutenant reported, "Persons in the country state that this is his first appearance since the trouble started."

Nearly two hundred men of the Twenty-Sixth Infantry moved into Blair Sunday morning, and Colonel Martin personally accompanied them to supervise the surrender. As the train pulled in, miners lounged around the depot. Others came down from Blair Mountain. About four hundred, half of them armed, surrendered, and they turned in some two hundred firearms.

Rumors continued that scores of miners had been killed, their bodies scattered along Blair Mountain ridge. Martin sent a company of soldiers, with miners as guides and stretcher bearers, up onto the mountain to search. They found no bodies. He sent out patrols through the countryside, covering all roads and trails. Miners who insisted they had seen bodies were sent, themselves, to help find the bodies they reported, but they, too, found none. Gradually, all began to realize the death toll was smaller than some had feared. Since the start of the rebellion on Lens Creek, about sixteen persons had been killed, all but four from the miners' army. The precise number would never be known.

The surrendering miners at Blair climbed onto a train that headed back down the valley. As usual, soldiers searched the train at Madison. They found some twenty pistols and a thousand rounds of ammunition.

II

In Logan, Don Chafin's army rapidly demobilized. Soldiers of the Fortieth Infantry replaced the last of the Logan defenders on the Blair Mountain line early Sunday, and the deputies and volunteers moved down toward Logan Town. As they came down from the line, their pathways merged; young men from Charleston, Huntington, Bluefield, and Welch walked along together;

the air was filled with greetings, reunions, and loud talk. They assembled at the bottom in crowds of a hundred or more, and wheezing cars whisked them off along the rutty, bumpy roads into Logan Town.

Joe Savage and several friends rode in with a horse doctor who told them Bill Blizzard was getting ready to attack the federal troops with hand grenades. They asked who Bill Blizzard was, and the horse doctor withered them with scorn and said Blizzard commanded the miners' army. At the Aracoma, Savage and a friend were asked for the password, and for a moment neither could remember it. "You're the only two men in Logan who don't know it," the guard said, and let them pass.

The lobby of the Aracoma was like a military headquarters. Army officers moved about, talking with deputies and state police officers. Ladies solicitously served sandwiches and coffee.

Logan was overrun with defenders and with country folk who had come to see the activities. The defenders exchanged stories of their adventures as they awaited their special trains. One big defender with an ancient squirrel gun proudly showed two bullet holes in his shirt sleeve, the result of fighting on Mill Creek Knoll.

Many defenders marched through Logan's streets as they returned from the front, carrying rifles and revolvers, their cartridge belts bulging. One by one, special trains pulled into the Logan depot, loaded quickly, and headed off to carry the volunteers back to their homes.

They rolled out of the station amid cheers and screeching of automobile horns, and men stuck their heads far out of the coach windows to cheer and shout, "If you need us again, just holler."

Mingo County's volunteers, with Brockus at their head, hurried away in a special train Saturday, before the rest, after receiving a report that fighting had broken out again along the Tug.

By Sunday evening, women and children appeared in numbers in Logan's streets for the first time since the war began. Newcomers and citizens motored out over the mountain roads, now cut with deep ruts and bumps, to look at the soldiers.

Newspaper correspondents filed their last stories and left, signaling better than anything else that the war was over.

The two divisions of Bandholz's pincer movement linked up along Blair Mountain, and the investment was complete.

Many of the defenders came home as heroes. At Bluefield, despite a drizzling rain, a crowd of citizens was at the depot to cheer and welcome their boys back home. In Logan, the townspeople held a giant celebration in the circuit courtroom Monday evening, passed resolutions of thanks to the people who helped from other counties, and cheered Chafin for his firm stand. They gave a rousing cheer to a speaker who said they would now change Chafin's famous slogan, "They shall not pass," to "They did not pass."

III

In Charleston, Bandholz was pleased. His soldiers made no arrests, fired no shots, dropped no bombs. He decided it would not be necessary to implement the proclamation of martial law. On Sunday afternoon he wired the War Department that, as of noon, "Federal troops had replaced both state and county forces and the invading miners throughout the disturbed area. Up to the present time there has been no hostile act on the part of anybody toward the United States troops. . . . If conditions are as good as they appear to be, I shall recommend the prompt return of the Twenty-Sixth Infantry to its station."

At Madison, army intelligence officers investigated possible Communist influence in the miners' rebellion but found little. "I cannot find that any organization except the United Mine Workers of America are operating in this field openly," an intelligence officer reported, but he added, "A small amount of I.W.W. and Bolshevist literature has been taken from departing miners."

Coal operators later displayed circulars issued by the Central Executive Committee of the Communist Party of America calling on workers elsewhere in the nation to "help your struggling brothers in the mines of West Virginia! To your task! All as one in the name of working class solidarity! . . . The miners' fight for a union must be made the fight of all organized labor and of all workers of America! On with the struggle! On to victory!"

At Saint Albans, the rebellious miners swarmed off their special trains and climbed aboard streetcars, which were hitched together into little trains. They were going home, this time for good. The little streetcar-trains crossed the river and moved into Charleston's central business district, traveling on tracks with automobiles and horse-drawn wagons on either side. Charleston citizens, alerted to the movement, thronged downtown, and the streetcars passed down Capitol Street, the city's busiest, before thousands. The miners leaned out of their windows, laughing and acting foolish, yelling and waving. Some waved flags from their streetcars. "It was Uncle Sam did it," one yelled, and he expressed the pride of all that neither Sheriff Chafin nor Governor Morgan had stopped their march.

That was the miners' victory, their only victory: they had compelled the nation to pay attention to them and forced the army to come to West Virginia. Sid Hatfield's murder had not been avenged. The men who killed him were still free and working as Baldwin-Felts detectives. Mingo's miners were still in jail, and the union still was not recognized along the Tug. The police who killed the miners at Sharples still kept their power, their authority, their guns. Don Chafin, instead of hanging from a sour apple tree, was a hero in the eyes of the coal operators. Even Governor Morgan could claim the army was on his side.

They had accomplished nothing they set out to do, except for that one thing which gave them life and hope: for a few days, at least, they had gotten the nation's attention, had made the people of America a little more aware of the conditions of life of the Appalachian miner.

They could only hope that nation would not forget.

Epilogue

THE SUPPRESSION of the West Virginia miners' rebellion did not end with the surrender of the miners.

During September and October of 1921, special and regular grand juries in Logan County returned 1,217 indictments for complicity in the insurrection, including 325 murder charges and 24 indictments for treason against the state of West Virginia.

Hundreds of union miners were jailed, and many of the cases were transferred to other sections of West Virginia for trial.

In the most celebrated of these, Billy Blizzard was tried for treason in Charles Town in West Virginia's eastern panhandle, in the same courthouse where John Brown was convicted of treason in 1859 and only a few steps from where John Brown was hanged. After a thirty-day trial in April and May of 1922, a jury found Blizzard not guilty, and cheering miners carried him from the courthouse on their shoulders.

Walter Allen, tried for treason in August and September of 1922, was the only defendant convicted of the charge. He was sentenced to ten years in prison but jumped bail and was never heard from again.

The Rev. J. E. Wilburn and his son, John, in separate trials, were convicted of murder in the death of Deputy John Gore and sentenced to eleven years each in the state penitentiary. Governor Morgan reduced their sentences to five years each, and Governor Howard M. Gore pardoned them after they had served three years.

Keeney and Mooney (who had been hiding in Ohio) returned

home in mid-September, surrendered to Governor Morgan, and were placed in the Mingo County jail, where they stayed in preference to being arrested by Sheriff Chafin for leadership in the insurrection. Facing numerous charges, they later were transferred to the Kanawha County jail in Charleston and, in early 1922, spent several weeks in the Logan County jail, where a procession of deputies and miners looked at them like caged animals. Keeney was tried for treason at Charles Town, but in the midst of the trial the judge granted a change of venue on grounds of prejudice. The trial was moved to Greenbrier County and then to Fayette County where the charges were dismissed.

The remaining cases also were transferred to Fayette County, where the population sympathized with the miners. Hopelessly discouraged by this development and the failure to convict Keeney, the operators directed their attorneys to dismiss all remaining indictments.

The badly weakened strike in Mingo continued, and hundreds remained in tents along the Tug through the winter of 1921–22 and into the following summer and fall. In October 1922, the executive committee of the United Mine Workers finally called off the strike. It had cost two million dollars, enough to bankrupt District 17 of the UMWA and to lead to the resignation of its leaders, and more than twenty persons had been killed, not counting those killed in the march. Those then still living in tents were moved to union coalfields where they found jobs.

Partly because of the failed strike in Mingo County, membership in the United Mine Workers in West Virginia slumped from its peak of about fifty thousand in 1920 to about six hundred in 1929. It was not until the Roosevelt administration that the mines of southern West Virginia were unionized. Once started, however, organization swiftly spread through the mines of the state in the 1930s.

The Matewan battle trials also sputtered out. Fred Burgraff and Reece Chambers were tried in Pocahontas County for the murder of J. W. Ferguson, one of the detectives killed in the battle, and were freed by a hung jury. The cases against the remaining defendants were continued from time to time and gradually dropped.

Lively was tried for the murders of Sid Hatfield and Ed Chambers in December 1922 in the McDowell County Courthouse in Welch, the same courthouse where he had shot them. His attorneys argued self-defense, and he was acquitted. Lively worked in the coal mines around Mt. Hope, West Virginia, for several years afterward and later as a railroad detective and hotel operator in Roanoke, Virginia. He died in Huntington in 1962 at the age of 75.

Sheriff Chafin was not so fortunate in the courts. One of his deputies, arrested for dispensing liquor in a tavern just outside Logan in violation of Prohibition laws, disclosed Chafin was his partner in the liquor business and received half its profits. Chafin was tried, convicted, and sentenced to two years in the state penitentiary. After serving the sentence, Chafin continued as one of West Virginia's most colorful figures, lobbying for coal interests in the West Virginia legislature and living in Huntington until he died a wealthy man in 1954.

Sallie Chambers married Harold Houston, the UMW attorney who had defended Sid and Ed in the Matewan battle trial.

Jessie Hatfield, Sid's widow, married a state policeman and moved to Huntington. She later divorced her third husband and married a fourth. She lived with her son in the last months of her life and died in 1976 at age 82.

Sid lived on in the memories of West Virginia's miners. For more than fifty years, his grave across the river from Matewan was marked only by a small plaque put there by the United Mine Workers. More recently, after the circumstances of his life and death gained publicity, a large headstone was erected with his picture engraved on it, over the words: "Defender of the rights of working people, gunned down by Felts detectives on the steps of the McDowell County Courthouse. . . . His murder triggered the miners' rebellion at the Battle of Blair Mountain."

Notes

With the exception of the introduction, the backnotes are keyed to the main text by a page number and an identifying phrase and by a short title of the book, article, or document cited. The full title is given in the bibliography.

INTRODUCTION

1. U.S. Coal Commission, *Report* (5 vols. [Washington, D.C.: Government Printing Office, 1925]) and Edward E. Hunt, *What the Coal Commission Found: An Authoritative Summary by the Staff* (Baltimore: Williams Wilkins, 1925) provide detailed contemporary descriptions of the coal industry during this era. Richard M. Simon deals with the industry's decentralization in "The Development of Underdevelopment: The Coal Industry and its Effect on the West Virginia Economy, 1880–1930" (Ph.D. dissertation, University of Pittsburgh, 1978), 104–47, esp. tables 31–33.

2. John Alexander Williams, *West Virginia and the Captains of Industry* (Morgantown, W. Va.: West Virginia University Press, 1976), 17–67.

3. Joseph T. Lambie, *From Mine to Market: A History of Coal Transportation on the Norfolk & Western Railway* (New York: New York University Press, 1954), 223–26, 240, 252–53.

4. Two federal investigations documented railroad consolidation and the use of coal car distribution to reward favored producers. See U.S. Senate, Committee on Interstate Commerce, *Railroad Combination in the Eastern Region, Part 1 (Before 1920)*, Senate Report 1182, 76th Congress, 3rd Session (Washington, D.C.: Government Printing Office, 1940) and "In the matter of the relation of common carriers subject

to the act to regulate commerce to coal and oil and the transportation thereof," Records of the Interstate Commerce Commission, National Archives, Record Group 134 (docket 869 [1906], volume 22).

5. Curtis Selzer, *Fire in the Hole; Miners and Managers in the American Coal Industry* (Lexington, Ky.: The University Press of Kentucky, 1985), 34–41.

6. Selzer, *Fire in the Hole*, 24–33, offers a concise view of the growth of unionism in the coal industry before 1920. See also David Corbin, *Life, Work and Rebellion in the Coal Fields: The Southern West Virginia Miners, 1880–1922* (Urbana: University of Illinois Press, 1981).

7. James H. Thompson, *Significant Trends in the West Virginia Coal Industry, 1900–1957* (Morgantown: West Virginia University Bureau of Business Research, 1958), 6.

8. Irving Bernstein, *The Lean Years: A History of the American Worker, 1920–1933* (Baltimore: Penguin Books, 1966).

9. John Alexander Williams, *West Virginia: A History* (New York: W. W. Norton and Company, 1976), 95–129; Altina L. Waller, *Feud: Hatfields, McCoys, and Social Change in Appalachia, 1860–1900* (Chapel Hill: University of North Carolina Press, 1988), 1–16, 235–249.

10. The most recent such analysis (and a considerably more thoughtful one than is usually the case) is by David Hackett Fischer, who posits endemic violence in Appalachia throughout its history and attributes this to cultural traits shaped by endemic violence on the English-Scots border in medieval and early modern times and brought to America by the colonial settlers of the highlands. (*Albion's Seed: Four British Folkways in America* [New York: Oxford University Press, 1989], 618–668).

11. Ronald D. Eller, *Miners, Millhands, and Mountaineers: Industrialization of the Appalachian South, 1880–1920* (Knoxville, Tenn.: University of Tennessee Press, 1982), 132–134.

12. Williams, *West Virginia*, 141–43. For a view of West Virginia progressivism and its achievements, see Williams, *West Virginia and the Captains of Industry*, 196–254.

13. Corbin, *Life, Work and Rebellion*, 61–86, and Ronald L. Lewis, *Black Coal Miners in America: Race, Class, and Community Conflict, 1780–1980* (Lexington, Ky.: University Press of Kentucky, 1987), 119–164.

14. Corbin, *Life, Work and Rebellion*, 1–60; Williams, *West Virginia*, 139–142; Selzer, *Fire in the Hole*, 18–22.

15. Maurer Maurer and Calvin S. Senning, "Billy Mitchell, the Air Service and the Mingo War," *West Virginia History* 30:1 (October 1968), 339–350.

Chapter 1: *"On To Mingo"*

3. "Nearly a thousand miners": Testimony of Fred Holley, State vs J. E. Wilburn (hereafter called Wilburn trial).

4. "Gather across the river": words of Savoy Holt, testimony by Charles Tucker in State vs Walter Allen treason trial (hereafter called Allen trial).

4. "Now it is up to us": testimony of J. S. McKeaver, Allen trial.

4. "Every drop of blood": Bituminous Operators' Special Commission Report to U.S. Coal Commission, August 1923, p. 68.

4–5. Departure of miners from camps described in Allen and Wilburn trials.

5. "Coal River Hellcats": *West Virginia Coal Fields,* Hearings Before the Committee on Education and Labor, U.S. Senate (hereafter referred to as *W. Va. Coal Fields*), p. 848.

5. "Miners have been murdered": Communist circular quoted in *W. Va. Coal Fields,* pp. 938–39.

6. "Throw the harness on": testimony of Burrell Miller, Allen trial.

7. "Baby needs shoes": *Charleston Gazette* (hereafter referred to as *Gazette*), Aug. 21, 1921, p. 1.

8. "If the white people got guns": testimony of Charles Tucker, Allen trial.

8. "They mean business": *Bluefield Daily Telegraph* (hereafter referred to as *Daily Telegraph*), Aug. 24, 1921, p 1.

9. "I've interfered time and again": *Huntington Herald Dispatch* (hereafter referred to as *Herald-Dispatch*), Aug. 15, 1921, p. 1.

9. Blankenhorn's report: *The Nation,* Sept. 14, 1921, p. 288.

Chapter 2: *"Everyone called him 'Sid'"*

10–11. Construction of Norfolk and Western Railway through Tug Valley described in *From Mine to Market* by Joseph T. Lambie, pp. 125–30.

11. Widow and children evicted without compensation: interview with Jesse Boyd of Matewan.

12. "Affiliate with or assist": from contract signed by Stone Mountain Coal Co. miners in Matewan, *United Mine Workers Journal* (hereafter referred to as *UMW Journal*), July 15, 1920.

12. Sid's height and weight: *Gazette,* May 21, 1921, p. 1.

13. Description of Testerman's store by his son, Jack Testerman, in interview.

13. Matewan was "the worst governed town in the state": *Gazette,* Jan. 3, 1911, reprinted in *West Virginia Hillbilly,* Oct. 6, 1973, p. 5.

13. "A little shooting match": *W. Va. Coal Fields,* p. 219.

14. John L. Lewis's statement: *Fayette* (W. Va.) *Tribune,* Feb. 5, 1920, p. 1.

14. "As long as there is any respect": *W. Va. Coal Fields,* p. 11.

15. "We want this 27 percent raise": ibid., p. 80.

15. Sid's candidacy announcement: *Williamson News,* April 6, 1920.

16. "If it puts 100 men in jail": *Philadelphia Public Ledger,* March 2, 1921, p. 6.

16. "If I wouldn't be a union man": *W. Va. Coal Fields,* p. 215.

17–18. Mother Jones speech: U.S. Senate Committee on Education and Labor hearings, *Conditions in the Paint Creek District, West Virginia,* 63d Congress, 1913, p. 2263.

18. Efforts to "buy" Sid Hatfield's cooperation: *W. Va. Coal Fields,* p. 212.

CHAPTER 3: *The Battle of Matewan*

19–24. Matewan battle description drawn from many accounts, chiefly: testimony in *W. Va. Coal Fields* by Charles Lively, pp. 383–86; W. E. Hutchinson, pp. 81–91; Sid Hatfield, pp. 205–12; Sheriff C. T. Blankenship, pp. 487–90; and Thomas L. Felts, pp. 881–905; interviews with several witnesses; and daily coverage by the *Gazette, Herald-Dispatch, Philadelphia Public Ledger,* and *New York Times* of Sid Hatfield's murder trial, January 19 to March 21, 1921. It should be noted that other accounts of the battle vary from this one, notably the assertion by Felts that Sid Hatfield not only fired first but shot Mayor Testerman.

CHAPTER 4: *"We have organized all the camps"*

25. Union official shook hands with himself: *W. Va. Coal Fields,* p. 363.

25. "Them sons of bitches had it comin'": interview with Jesse Boyd.

26. "Our boys would have dropped": *Gazette,* May 21, 1921, p. 1.

26. John L. Lewis' statement: *Herald-Dispatch,* May 22, 1921, p. 1.

26. Papers on Felts's body: *W. Va. Coal Fields,* p. 212.

27. Report that Sid was seen strolling with Jessie along banks of Tug before the Matewan battle is from notes of Charley Lively, in possession of Lively's son, Paul Lively.

27–28. Sid's and Jessie's arrest and marriage: *Herald-Dispatch,* June 2 and 3, 1921, p. 1.

28. "We have organized": *UMW Journal,* July 15, 1921.

29. Mother Jones's speech: *Williamson Daily News,* June 23, 24, and 25, 1920, p. 1. Her photograph with Sid and others in *UMW Journal,* July 15, 1920, p. 11.

29. "We have nothing to discuss": Responses by coal operators, *W. Va. Coal Fields,* pp. 111–13.

30. Attack on Freeburn: *W. Va. Coal Fields,* pp. 277–301.

31. "I never heard of those letters": *Williamson Daily News,* Aug. 28, 1920, p. 1.

CHAPTER 5: *"The most complete deadlock of any industrial struggle"*

32–33. Mohawk attack: *Daily Telegraph,* Sept. 5, 1920, p. 1; *W. Va. Coal Fields,* pp. 370–73.

33. Lively's double life: *W. Va. Coal Fields,* pp. 355–92.

34. "A protest to our legislators": *Gazette,* Sept. 16, 1920, p. 1.

35. "For immediate shipment": *W. Va. Coal Fields,* p. 158.

36. Martin Justice's letter: *UMW Journal,* Nov. 1, 1920, p. 17.

36. "Yaller dog" contract: Winthrop D. Lane, *Civil War in West Virginia,* p. 65.

37. Injunction: *W. Va. Coal Fields,* pp. 755–56.

37–38. Waddill's injunction: Lane, *Civil War in West Virginia,* pp. 71–72.

38. "And if I have to recall them": *Herald-Dispatch,* Sept. 29, 1920, p. 1.

39. Governor's proclamation: *W. Va. Coal Fields,* pp. 272–73.

39. "The most complete deadlock": *Coal Age,* Nov. 18, 1920, p. 1037.

39. "Political bankruptcy": quoted in *Literary Digest,* Dec. 18, 1920, pp. 16–17.

40. "Inside, on a 'cot'": International News Service, reprinted in *UMW Journal,* Jan. 15, 1921, pp. 14–15.

40. NY Times reporter's visit: *Times,* Dec. 7, 1920, p. 1.

CHAPTER 6: *"It's good to have friends"*

42–49. Material in this chapter primarily from coverage of trial by *Gazette, Herald-Dispatch, Philadelphia Public Ledger, New York Times, Charleston Daily Mail* (hereafter called *Daily Mail*), *New York Evening Post,* Jan. 19–March 21, 1921.

42. The twenty-three defendants: N. H. Atwood, William Bowman, Jesse Boyd, Isaac Brewer, Albert Burgraff, Fred Burgraff, Ed Chambers, Hally Chambers, Reece Chambers, Van Clay, William Coleman, Sid Hatfield, Charley Kiser, Calvin McCoy, Ben Mounts, Doug Mounts, Clare Overstreet, James Overstreet, Ben R. Page, William Starr, Lee Toler, Fred Webb, Art Williams.

43. Singing of black prisoners: Interview with Jesse Boyd.

48–49. Story of juror described in interview of Willard Smith.

CHAPTER 7: *"Our citizens are being shot down like rats"*

50. *UMW Journal* editorial: issue of April 1, 1921, p. 13.

50. Description of apartment over jewelry store furnished by Mayor Testerman's son, Jack Testerman, in interview. Lively's hurried departure from Matewan after trial was described by his son, Paul J. Lively, in interview.

51. "Marked man": *New York Herald,* Aug. 2, 1921, p. 1.

53. "Slapped him down": *W. Va. Coal Fields,* p. 217.

53. "Nothing short of 100 percent": Morgan to Weeks, May 14, 1921.

53. "Our citizens are being shot down": C. R. Wilson to Weeks, May 14, 1921.

54. "Do not see justification": Thompson to Commanding General, Fort Benjamin Harrison, May 13, 1921.

54. "The President is not convinced": *Gazette,* May 18, 1921, p. 1.

CHAPTER 8: *". . . to clean up Mingo County"*

55–56. Meeting of "better people": *New York Times,* May 19 and 20, 1921, p. 1; *Gazette* of May 19; *Herald-Dispatch,* May 19; *W. Va. Coal Fields,* pp. 338–40.

57. Exclusion of foreign-born and blacks from militia: *W. Va. Coal Fields,* p. 345.

57. Lavinder's arrest: *NY Times,* May 24, 1921, p. 1.

58. "Military dictatorship:" Undated memorandum from Mooney to District 17 locals of UMW, in papers of Allen trial.

59. The miners lay down: interview with Willard Smith.

59–60. Lick Creek raid: much testimony on this in *W. Va. Coal Fields,* notably pp. 307, 336, 476, 332, 574, 303–21, 335, 581–82.

61. Murray's and Davis's agreement: *UMW Journal,* Aug. 1, 1921, p. 3.

61. Sid's Williamson visit: *NY Times*, May 25, 1921, p. 1.
62. Jail key incident: *NY Times*, May 29, 1921, p. 15.
63. Affidavit: *W. Va. Coal Fields*, p. 166.
63. "A soft-nosed bullet": ibid., p. 166.

CHAPTER 9: *"You saw nothing wrong in that?"*

64–67. Entire transcript of hearing found, of course, in *W. Va. Coal Fields*.
66. Montgomery's advice to Sid, Sid's arrest, Montgomery's statement: *Wheeling Intelligencer*, July 29 and 30, 1921, p. 1.

CHAPTER 10: *"Don't shoot him anymore!"*

68–71. Detailed narrative of Sid's death: mostly from testimony by Jessie Hatfield and Sally Chambers, *W. Va. Coal Fields*, pp. 730–41, and in *UMW Journal*, Sept. 1, 1921, p. 10, as well as newspaper accounts. Tom Felts and Charles Lively deny many of these details.
70. Contrary to this narrative, several law officers testified Sid and Ed were armed and fired back at detectives in front of courthouse.

CHAPTER 11: *"There can be no peace . . ."*

72–73. Funeral descriptions: *Gazette, Herald-Dispatch, Wheeling Intelligencer,* Aug. 3 and 4, 1921, p. 1 in all newspapers, and Fred Mooney, *Struggle in the Coal Fields*, p. 89.
74. Mother Jones's reaction: Fred Mooney, *Struggle in the Coal Fields,* p. 89.
74. Sheriff Hatfield's statement: *Herald-Dispatch*, Aug. 10, 1921, p. 1.
74. Sally's and Jessie's interview: *Herald-Dispatch,* Aug. 4, 1921, p. 1.
74. *UMW Journal*'s comment: Aug. 15 and Sept. 1, 1921, p. 3, 10, respectively.
75. Mass meeting: Governor Morgan describes in Allen trial, roll 2-A of microfilm, pp. 185–211.
75. Incident at Clothier: *W. Va. Coal Fields*, pp. 512–13; also described in testimony of A. R. Browning, A. C. Porter, and G. C. Parker in Allen and Wilburn Trials.

CHAPTER 12: *"We'll hang Don Chafin to a sour apple tree!"*

77. "Gonna go clean through": Most quotes from *The Nation,* Sept. 14, 1921, p. 288. Song about hanging Don Chafin from numerous sources.

77. "Men are pouring into Marmet": *Daily Telegraph,* Aug. 24, 1921, p. 1.

78. "Take this damn scab": *Bituminous Operators Report,* op. cit., p. 71.

78. Mother Jones's speech: Numerous newspaper accounts; Governor Morgan's testimony in Wilburn trial, testimony of Mrs. Jessie Nichols and H. L. Hundley in Allen trial.

79. Gillespie told of telephone incident in Allen trial, roll 2-A, p. 264.

80. Reynolds also testified in Allen trial, roll 2-A, p. 140.

80. "Lie down, watch where the bullets": *The Nation,* Sept. 4, 1921, p. 289.

80. Bantered into the night: *Daily Telegraph,* Aug. 26, 1921, p. 1.

CHAPTER 13: *"No armed mob will cross Logan County"*

81. "No armed mob": G. T. Swain, *History of Logan County, West Virginia,* p. 163.

82. Chafin's wealth: *W. Va Coal Fields,* pp. 1055–66.

83. Fifty UMWA organizers' visit: Arthur Gleason, "Private Ownership of Public Officials," *The Nation,* May 29, 1920, pp. 724–25.

83. "The *Banner* regrets": *Logan Banner,* Aug. 26, 1921, p. 1.

83. "Anyone who doesn't come fight is fired": These quotes from *On Dark and Bloody Ground,* oral history project, pp. 62 and 68, courtesy of Anne Lawrence, project director.

84. "Inflamed and infuriated": *New York Times,* Aug. 26, 1921, p. 1.

84. "Ready to move": War Department telegram to Commanding General, Fifth Corps Area, Aug. 25, 1921.

CHAPTER 14: *"It's your real Uncle Sam"*

86–87. Bandholz's trip: described by Bandholz, Allen trial, and Wilburn trial; by Colonel Ford, *W. Va. Coal Fields,* pp. 1032–35; and by Mooney in Wilburn trial.

87. "There must have been ten thousand men": *NY Times,* Aug. 28, 1921, p. 6.

87. "At the command 'Forward March'": *Fayette Tribune,* Sept. 1, 1921, p. 6, quoting *Huntington Advertiser.*

88–89. Ballpark scene and Keeney's speech: Ed Reynolds's testimony in Allen trial; Cabell Phillips, "The West Virginia Mine War," in *American Heritage,* August, 1974, pp. 58–62, 90–94, and *Fayette Tribune,* op. cit.

CHAPTER 15: *"By God, we're goin' through"*

90. Chafin knew of ballpark speech: Chafin related this in Allen trial testimony.

90. "You have been in defense": *Herald-Dispatch,* Aug. 27, 1921, p. 1.

91. "We could do what we pleased": Ed Reynolds testimony, Allen trial.

91. "Secretary War much pleased": General Harbord to Bandholz, Aug. 26, 1921.

93. Paul Curley incident: he told of it in Allen trial; also *W. Va. Coal Fields,* p. 531.

94. Mitchell's visit: *Gazette,* Aug. 27, 1971, p. 1; Blankenhorn, "Marching through West Virginia," op. cit., p. 289.

94–96. Medley's story: he tells it in Wilburn trial.

96. Brinkman's story: he tells it in Allen and Wilburn trials.

97. Hallinan's phone call: Chafin tells of it in Wilburn trial.

CHAPTER 16: *"We wouldn't revolt against the national guv'ment"*

98–99. Bandholz's trip: Bandholz describes it in testimony in Allen and Wilburn trials. Colonel Ford describes it in *W. Va. Coal Fields,* pp. 1032–33.

100–01. Delightful exchange between Bandholz and returning miners: *Gazette,* Aug. 28, 1921, p. 1, article by James E. Cutlip, Jr.

CHAPTER 17: *"The thugs are coming!"*

102–05. Material in this chapter largely from testimony by Major Davis in Allen trial, Governor Morgan in Allen trial, and by Captain

Brockus in both Allen and Wilburn trials, as well as in separate Brockus report, National Archives, Central Decimal Files RF 407, Project Files AGO, 1917–25, West Virginia, Box 1580.

104. A Hungarian family hid in terror: testimony by John Bakos, a Hungarian miner, in Wilburn trial.

105. Talking loudly, whistling, laughing: *On Dark and Bloody Ground,* op. cit., p. 58.

CHAPTER 18: *"There was a different feeling"*

107. "No, by God": William Le Page testimony, Wilburn trial.

107. Wiley: his testimony, *W. Va. Coal Fields,* p. 518.

107. "There was a different feeling": testimony by French Estep, Wilburn trial.

108. They "went through quite fast": *Gazette,* Aug. 30, 1921, p. 1.

108. Commandeering trains: testimony of Sheriff D. M. Griffith, Allen trial.

109. Embry's experience: his testimony in Allen trial.

109. Blacks in Jim Crow restaurants: *W. Va. Coal Fields,* p. 531.

109. Wade's statement: *W. Va. Coal Fields,* p. 531.

109. Captured four Logan County deputies: one of them, Fulton Mitchell, told of his capture in Allen trial.

CHAPTER 19: *"I, Warren G. Harding . . . do hereby command"*

111. "Only a feeble attempt": *NY Times,* Aug. 30, 1921, p. 17.

111. "A monster powder keg": *Daily Telegraph,* Aug. 30, 1921, p. 1.

111–12. "Males were in arms": *Gazette,* Aug. 30, 1921, p. 1.

112. "Danger of attack": Morgan to Weeks, Aug. 30, 1921, National Archives, project Files AGO, 1917–25, West Virginia, RF 407, Box No. 1580.

112–13. Harding's proclamation: Archives, ibid.

CHAPTER 20: *"Bring your raincoats and machine guns"*

114. "Six lawyers, one bank cashier": *NY Times,* Sept. 5, 1921, p. 1.

115. "I hope and believe": Chafin's speech in *Herald Dispatch,* Aug. 29, 1921, p. 1.

115. Bluefield report: *Daily Telegraph,* Sept. 1, 21, p. 1.

116. Feeding operation: *NY Times,* Sept. 2, 1921, p. 1.

116. Use of fourteen-year-old boys in army: report of Maj. C. F. Thompson to Commanding General, Provisional Brigade, Sept. 6, 1921.

116. Savage's story: "The Armed March in West Virginia," by Joe W. Savage, the author's father, published in *Goldenseal* (Fall 1987), vol. 13, no. 3, p. 65.

117. Eubanks's story: his testimony in Allen trial.

118. "Now you are a God damned militiaman": interview with Charnock.

118. Volunteer accidentally fired his rifle: Grant Hall, of Charleston, recalled this incident in interview.

118. Duling's death: Capt. Brockus report, Aug. 28, 1921, National Archives.

CHAPTER 21: *"Bullets were hissing back and forth"*

119. Blair Mountain description: *Daily Telegraph,* Sept. 3, 1921, p. 1.

120. Fully ten thousand men: Concerning the size of the miners' army, David Corbin, after much research, wrote in *Life, Work and Rebellion in the Coal Fields* that "an estimate of between 15,000 and 20,000 is probably safe" (p. 219). Most contemporary estimates by responsible observers, however, were in the 6,000–12,000 range, and some were smaller.

120. "and from the planes pilots hurled thousands of leaflets": *NY Times,* Sept. 1, 1921, p. 1.

120–22. Thompson's experience: Dr. L. F. Milliken's testimony, Allen trial.

123. "The time has come": testimony of Alva Rowe Allen trial. Killing of Deputy Gore described in much detail in Wilburn trial.

125. "Bullets were hissing": *Gazette,* Sept. 1, 1921, p. 1.

125. "Unless troops sent by midnight": W. R. Thurmond to Rep. Goodykoontz, Archives, Proj. Files AGO 1917–25, West Virginia, RF 407, Box No. 1580.

126. "At all points": *Gazette,* Sept. 1, 1921, p. 1.

127. Moving dairy cows: *NY Times,* Sept. 5, 1921, p. 1.

127. "Well, one crowd climbs": *W. Va. Coal Fields,* p. 973.

128. "The deputies are mowing the men down": *Gazette,* Sept. 1, 1921, p. 1.

128. "You could hear it seemed": testimony of Ira Wilson, Allen trial.

128. "Someone spies the dark shadow": *Daily Telegraph,* Sept. 3, 1921, p. 1.

129. "You were more likely to be shot": *On Dark and Bloody Ground,* pp. 79–80; "You was in more danger": ibid., p. 68.

CHAPTER 22: *"Things slacked off after we ate"*

131. "Sweep up the Atlantic with a broom": *W. Va. Coal Fields,* p. 972.

131. Morgan and McCorkle telegrams: *Herald-Dispatch,* Sept. 2, 1921, p. 1.

131. "The invaders have not obeyed": *Daily Mail,* Sept. 2, 1921, p. 1.

131. "I have nothing to say": *Gazette,* Sept. 2, 1921, p. 1.

132. "Eating breakfast in Logan Town": *Gazette,* Sept. 3, 1921, p. 1.

132. Williams's statement: Allen trial testimony.

132–33. "He called the roll": G. C. Williams's testimony, ibid.

133. Fred Hall's story: testimony in Allen trial.

134. Uniform of Italian army captain: *W. Va. Coal Fields,* p. 550.

134. William Arbaugh's experience: testimony of Harold M. Richard, Allen trial.

135. "They have a smoothly operating food commissary": *Gazette,* Sept. 3, 1921, p. 1.

136. "I never got anywhere near anybody in authority": *W. Va. Coal Fields,* p. 971.

136. "A lot of people will tell you": *On Dark and Bloody Ground,* pp. 21–22.

137. Descriptions of fighting generally are from several newspaper accounts: *Gazette, Herald-Dispatch, NY Times,* and others.

137–38. Brewer's story: *Gazette and NY Times,* Sept. 3, 1921, p. 1.

138. "I was pumping": "The Armed March in West Virginia," *Goldenseal,* Fall, 1987, 13:3, p. 65.

139. Bombing stories: Eubanks described his use of bombs in testimony in Allen trial. Greever's injury by a bomb: *Logan Banner,* Sept. 2, 1921, p. 1. "Carried their dead away": *NY Times,* Sept. 3, 1921.

140. Comiskey's death: *Logan Banner,* Sept. 2, 1921, p. 1. *W. Va. Coal Fields,* pp. 1056–57, 1062, 1070–71, 1078; and Arthur Warner, "West Virginia–Industrialism Gone Mad," in *The Nation,* Oct. 5, 1921, p. 373.

CHAPTER 23: *"These strange new craft"*

142–46. Information in this chapter: *Roanoke* (Va.) *Times,* Sept. 2 and 3, 1921, p. 1; *Gazette,* Sept. 3 and 6, 1921, p. 1; *Fayette* (W. Va.) *Tribune,* Sept. 8 and 15, 1921, p. 1; and Maurer Maurer, and Calvin F. Senning, "Billy Mitchell, the Air Service and the Mingo War," from *West Virginia History,* October, 1968, p. 344, reprinted from *The Airpower Historian,* quarterly of the Air Force Historical Foundation, Maxwell AFB, Montgomery, Ala., April, 1965.

145. Billy Mitchell later was called on the carpet for ordering the bombers to return to Langley, as they were under General Bandholz's command. Mitchell defended himself saying Bandholz gave permission for the flight. Correspondence in National Archives.

146. Stories still circulate in West Virginia that Mitchell's aircraft bombed miners. The evidence of this is sketchy and seems highly questionable; evidence to the contrary is abundant and seems reliable.

146. Hazelton's injuries: *Gazette,* Feb. 4, 1923, p. 1.

146. "An excellent example": Maurer, Senning, op. cit.

CHAPTER 24: *"The miners have withdrawn their lines"*

149. "Where's the war?" *Gazette,* Sept. 3, 1921, p. 1.

149. "You will under no circumstances drop any bombs": Bandholz to Commanding Officer, Air Service Troops, Sept. 2, 1921, National Archives, MO-1 (loose bundle).

149. "We're glad you're here": *W. Va. Coal Fields,* pp. 878–79, quoting *NY Tribune* article by Boyden Sparkes. Much detail and dialogue here from that article.

151. "That's why you don't see guns": Boyden Sparkes's article from *NY Tribune,* Sept. 4, 1921, p. 1.

152. "Yes, suh, they b'en a hauling": ibid.

152. Major Smart told of experience with Blizzard in Blizzard's treason trial, roll 3 of Treason Trial Microfilms, West Virginia University Library.

152–53. Train movements: National Archives, Headquarters, Nineteenth Infantry, Madison, W. Va., Sept. 3, 1921, Record of Events.

153. Major Thompson's report of Eubanks's drunkenness: National Archives, Maj. Thompson to Commanding General, Provisional Brigade, Sept. 6, 1921.

155. Sparkes's story of his wounding: *Gazette,* Sept. 9, 1921, p. 2.

156. Bandholz "is ever smiling": *UMW Journal,* Sept. 15, 1921, p. 8.

157. Brady's letter of recommendation from U.S. Attorney General in National Archives, loose bundle.

157. Mildred Morris's report on incident: *UMW Journal,* Sept. 15, 1921, p. 8.

158–59. Sparkes wrote an article about the Logan censorship, and it was published in, among other periodicals, the *Roanoke Times* of Sept. 9, 1921, p. 4. The involvement of George Coyle was told by Coyle himself.

CHAPTER 25: *"It was Uncle Sam did it"*

160. Disposition of Col. Martin's troops: Lt. E. L. Brine to Director of Military Intelligence, Sept. 4, 1921, Archives, loose bundle.

161. "Persons in the country state": ibid.

162. "If you need us again, just holler": *NY Tribune,* Sept. 5, 1921, p. 1.

163. Bandholz's wire: *NY Times,* Sept. 5, 1921, p. 1.

163. Intelligence report on Communist influence: Brine to Director, Military Intelligence, op. cit.; Communist circulars in *W. Va. Coal Fields,* pp. 938–39.

EPILOGUE

165–67. Much information in epilogue from Kyle McCormick's *The New Kanawha River and the Mine Wars of West Virginia,* p. 161, and Howard B. Lee's *Bloodletting in Appalachia,* p. 14.

166. Disposition of remaining Matewan battle trials: J. Brooks Lawson, Jr., Williamson attorney, to Howard B. Lee, Nov. 2, 1961, in Lee's papers, West Virginia University Library.

167. Information about later lives of Charlie Lively and Jessie Hatfield from their respective sons, Paul C. Lively of Tucker, Georgia, and Jack Testerman of Naugatuck, West Virginia.

Bibliography

Books

Ambler, Charles Henry. *West Virginia: The Mountain State*. New York: Prentice-Hall, Inc., 1940.

Blankenhorn, Heber. *The Strike for Union*. New York: H. W. Wilson Company, 1924.

Coleman, McAlister. *Men and Coal*. Toronto: Farrar & Rhinehart, Inc., 1943; republished by Arno & *The New York Times*, New York, 1969.

Conley, Phil M. *Life in a West Virginia Coal Field*. Charleston: American Constitutional Association.

————. *History of the West Virginia Coal Industry*. Charleston: Education Foundation, Inc., 1960.

Connelly, Shirley. *The Hatfield-McCoy Feud Reader*. Parsons, W. Va.: McClain Printing Company, 1971.

Corbin, David Alan. *Life, Work, and Rebellion in the Coal Fields: The Southern West Virginia Miners, 1880-1922*. University of Illinois Press, 1981.

Cornwell, John J. *A Mountain Trail*. Philadelphia: Dorrance and Company, 1939.

Fetherling, Dale. *Mother Jones, the Miners' Angel*. Carbondale: Southern Illinois University Press, 1974.

Fink, Gary M. and Merl E. Reed, editors. *Essays in Southern Labor History*. Selected papers, Southern Labor History Conference, 1976. Westport, Conn.: Greenwood Press, 1976. Essays by David P. Jordan, "The Mingo War: Labor Violence in the Southern West Virginia Coal Fields, 1919–1921," and by David A. Corbin, "Frank Keeney Is Our Leader, and We Shall Not Be Moved: Rank and File Leadership in the West Virginia Coal Fields."

Finley, Joseph E. *The Corrupt Kingdom: The Rise and Fall of the United Mine Workers*. New York: Simon and Schuster, 1972.

Goodrich, Carter. *The Miner's Freedom*. New York: Workers Education Bureau of America, 1926.

Harris, Evelyn L. K., and Frank J. Krebs. *From Humble Beginnings: West Virginia State Federation of Labor, 1903–1957*. Charleston: West Virginia Labor History Publishing Fund, 1960.

Hatfield, G. Elliott. *The Hatfields*. Revised and edited by Leonard Roberts and Henry P. Scalf. Stanville, Ky.: Big Sandy Historical Society, 1974.

Hinrichs, A. F. *The United Mine Workers of America and the Non-Union Coal Fields*. New York: AMS Press, 1968. Columbia University Studies in the Social Sciences. Originally published 1923.

Jones, Mary Harris. *Autobiography of Mother Jones*. New York: Arno Press, Inc., and the *New York Times*, 1969. Originally published by Charles H. Kerr & Co., Chicago, 1925.

Jones, Virgil Carrington. *The Hatfields and the McCoys*. Chapel Hill, N.C.: The University of North Carolina Press, 1948.

Lambie, Joseph T. *From Mine to Market: The History of Coal Transportation on the Norfolk and Western Railway*. New York: New York University Press, 1954.

Lane, Winthrop D. *Civil War in West Virginia*. New York: Arno Press, Inc., reprint edition, 1969. Originally published in 1921.

———. *The Denial of Civil Liberties in the Coal Fields*. New York: American Civil Liberties Union, 1924.

Lee, Howard B. *Bloodletting in Appalachia: The Story of West Virginia's Four Major Mine Wars and Other Thrilling Incidents in its Coal Fields*. Parsons, W. Va.: McClain Printing Co., 1969.

Lunt, Richard D. *Law and Order vs the Miners—West Virginia, 1907–1933*. Hamden, Conn.: Archon Books, 1979.

McCormick, Kyle. *The New-Kanawha River and the Mine War of West Virginia*. Charleston: Mathews Printing and Lithographing Company, 1959.

McGovern, George S., and Leonard F. Guttridge, *The Great Coalfield War*. Boston: Houghton-Mifflin Co., 1972.

Mooney, Fred. *Struggle in the Coal Fields*. Morgantown: West Virginia University Library, McClain Printing Co., 1967.

Rochester, Anna. *Labor and Coal*. New York: International Publishers, Labor and Industry Series, 1931.

Ross, Malcolm. *Machine Age in the Hills*. New York: The MacMillan Company, 1933.

Spivak, John L. *A Man in His Time*. New York: Horizon Press, 1967.

Suffern, Arthur E. *Conciliation and Arbitration in the Coal Industry of America.* Boston and New York: Houghton-Mifflin Company and Cambridge: The Riverside Press, 1915.

Swain, George T. *Facts About the Armed Marches on Logan.* Charleston, W. Va.: Ace Enterprises, printed by Jones Printing Co., 1962.

———. *History of Logan County, West Virginia.* Published by Swain, 1927, printed by Kingsport Press, Kingsport, Tenn.

Tams, W. P., Jr. *The Smokeless Coal Fields of West Virginia.* Morgantown: West Virginia University Library, 1964. Printed by McClain Printing Co., Parsons, W. Va.

Williams, John Alexander. *West Virginia, a Bicentennial History.* New York: W. W. Norton & Co., 1967.

ARTICLES IN PERIODICALS

Blankenhorn, Heber. "Marching Through West Virginia." *The Nation,* Sept. 14, 1921, pp. 288–89.

Burkinshaw, Neil. "Labor's Valley Forge." *The Nation,* Dec. 8, 1920, p. 369.

Cain, James M. "West Virginia: A Mine-Field Melodrama." *The Nation,* June 27, 1923, pp. 742–45.

———. "Treason–to Coal Operators." *The Nation,* Oct. 4, 1922, pp. 333–34.

———. "The Battle Ground of Coal." *The Atlantic Monthly,* October, 1922, pp. 433–40.

Chenery, William L. "The Coal Strike Settlement." *Survey,* April 17, 1920, p. 112.

Dial, Wylene P. "The Dialect of the Appalachian People." *West Virginia History,* January, 1969, pp. 463–71.

Dickey, Carl C. "Must Murder Be the Price of Coal?" *Worlds Work,* March, 1924, pp. 510–24.

Gleason, Arthur. "Company-Owned Americans." *The Nation,* June 12, 1920, pp. 794–95.

———. "Private Ownership of Public Officials." *The Nation,* May 29, 1920, pp. 724–25.

"Gunmen in West Virginia." *The New Republic,* Sept. 21, 1921, pp. 90–92.

Hinds, Roy W. "The Last Stand of the Open Shop." *Coal Age,* Nov. 18, 1920, pp. 1037–40.

"Industrial Democracy and Gunmen." *The New Republic,* Feb. 9, 1921, pp. 318–19.

Lane, Winthrop D. "The Labor Spy in West Virginia." *The Survey,* Oct. 22, 1921, pp. 110–12.

———. "West Virginia – The Civil War in Its Coal Fields." *The Survey,* Graphic Edition, Oct. 29, 1921, pp. 177–82.

McCormick, Kyle. "The Historic Battle for Our State Police." *The Charleston Gazette Magazine Section,* July 28, 1957.

Maurer, Maurer, and Calvin F. Senning. "Billy Mitchell, The Air Service and the Mingo War." *West Virginia History,* October, 1969, reprinted from *The Airpower Historian,* April, 1965.

"The Mine Operators Explain." *The New Republic,* Sept. 28, 1921, pp. 118–19.

Phillips, Cabell. "The West Virginia Mine War." *American Heritage,* August, 1974, pp. 58–61, 90–94.

Quenzel, C. H. "A Fight to Establish the State Police." *Journal of Criminal Law and Criminology,* May–June 1943.

Savage, Joe W., "The Armed March in West Virginia." *Goldenseal,* Fall, 1987, 13:3, p. 65.

Searles, Ellis. "A Reply from the Union Miners to 'Must Murder Be the Price of Coal?'" *World's Work,* June, 1924, pp. 193–96.

"The Senators Tour West Virginia." *The Survey,* Oct. 1, 1921, pp. 23–24.

"The War in the Mingo Mine Fields." *American Industries,* October, 1921, p. 7.

Warner, Arthur. "Fighting Unionism with Martial Law." *The Nation,* Oct. 12, 1921, pp. 395–96.

Wheeler, Hoyt N. "Mountaineer Mine Wars: An Analysis of the West Virginia Mine Wars of 1912–1913 and 1920–21." *Business History Review,* Spring, 1976, pp. 69–91.

"What a Newspaper Reporter Saw in West Virginia." *The American Federationist,* October, 1921, pp. 865–66.

Government Documents, Private Papers, and Pamphlets

Axelrod, Jim, editor. *Thoughts of Mother Jones.* Huntington, W. Va.: Appalachian Movement Press, Inc., 1971. Pamphlet.

Houston, Harold W. "Brief on Behalf of the United Mine Workers Of America before the Committee on Education and Labor, U.S. Senate." 1921.

Lee, Howard B. The Papers of . . . West Virginia University Library.

Mooney, Fred. The Papers of . . . West Virginia University Library.

National Archives. Project Files of the Adjutant General's Office, 1917–1925, Washington, D. C. Declassification Review Project of the

War Department General Staff Military Intelligence Division, 1917–1941. Federal Mediation and Conciliation Service Case Files at the Washington National Records Center, Suitland, Md.

National Endowment for the Humanities. *On Dark and Bloody Ground.* Oral history published by Miner's Voice, Charleston, W. Va., 1973. Anne Lawrence, Project Director.

U.S. Coal Commission. *The United Mine Workers in West Virginia.* Report by Bituminous Operators' Special Committee to U.S. Coal Commission, 1923.

U.S. Senate. Senate Committee on Education and Labor. *Investigation of Paint Creek Coal Fields of West Virginia.* Senate Report 321, 63rd Congress, second session, 1913–14.

U.S. Senate. *West Virginia Coal Fields.* Hearings before the Committee on Education and Labor, United States Senate, 67th Congress, first session, 2 vols. Washington, D.C.: Government Printing Office, 1921–22.

West Virginia Department of Mines. *Annual Reports,* 1920 and 1921. Charleston, Department of Archives.

NEWSPAPERS

Bluefield Daily Telegraph. Bluefield, W. Va. May, 1920–September, 1921.

Charleston Daily Mail. Charleston, W. Va. 1920–1921.

Daily Telegram, The. Clarksburg, W. Va. August, 1921.

Fayette Tribune and Free Press. Fayetteville, W. Va. 1920–21.

Gazette, The. Charleston, W. Va. 1920–21.

Herald-Dispatch, The. Huntington, W. Va. 1920–21.

Huntington Advertiser, The. Huntington, W. Va. June, 1921.

Logan Banner, The. Logan, W. Va. January–September, 1921.

Mingo Republican, The. Williamson, W. Va. June 3 and July 8, 1921.

New York Evening Post. Dec. 1, 1920–March 31, 1921.

New York Herald. July–September, 1921.

New York Times. 1920–21.

New York Tribune. August–September, 1921.

Public Ledger, The. Philadelphia. January–March, 1921.

Raleigh Register. Beckley, W. Va. May–October, 1921.

Roanoke Times. Roanoke, Va. July–September, 1921.

The United Mine Workers Journal. 1920–21.

Wheeling Intelligencer, The. Wheeling, W. Va. July–August, 1921.

Williamson News. Williamson, W. Va. January–December, 1920.

Theses, Dissertations

Anson, Charles Phillips. *A History of the Labor Movement in West Virginia.* Ph.D. dissertation, University of North Carolina, 1940.

Barb, John Milliken. *Strikes in the Southern West Virginia Coal Fields, 1912–22.* Master's thesis, West Virginia University, 1949.

Eller, Ronald D. *Miners, Millhands and Mountaineers: The Modernization of the Appalachian South, 1880–1930.* Ph.D. dissertation, University of North Carolina, 1979.

Livingston, William John Bryant. *Coal Miners and Religion, a Study of Logan County.* Doctor of Theology dissertation, Union Theological Seminary, Richmond, Va., 1951.

White, Elizabeth. *Development of the Bituminous Coal Mining Industry in Logan County, West Virginia.* Master's thesis, Marshall College, Huntington, W. Va.

Other Sources

Personal interviews by the author of about twenty-five persons in Mingo County and Charleston area who remembered the events described in this work.

Records of Mingo County Circuit Court at Williamson, W. Va., and Pike County at Pikeville, Ky., including warrants, petitions, school records and other documents.

Transcripts, on microfilm, of the treason trial of Walter Allen and the murder trials of J. E. Wilburn and his son, John Wilburn, plus numerous documents, indictments and other court records, all resulting from the miners' march on Mingo County and all at the West Virginia University Library.

Written records of interviews, all unpublished, by Leo Peters, Charleston newspaperman, of several of the principals and participants in the armed march.

Index

Aircraft, 8, 83, 90, 93, 120. *See also* Air service; Mitchell, Billy
Air service, 84–85, 93–94, 142–46. *See also* Eighty-eighth Air Squadron
Allen, Walter, 4, 5, 75, 77, 135, 165
Ameagle, W. Va., 4, 108
American Legion, 115, 117
Anderson, Tim, 22
Anderson, Walter, 22
Aracoma Hotel, 83, 91, 115–16, 153
Arbaugh, William, 134
Army air service. *See* Air service
Atwood, Nathan H., 44

Bailey, R. D., 43, 44, 48
Baldwin-Felts detectives, 25; as cause of march, 4, 5, 9; cited at trial, 44, 48; in 1912 strike, 12. *See also* Evictions; Matewan, battle of
Bandholz, Harry H., 85, 86, 111–13; call by for troops, 130–31; and investiture, 149; praise for, 156; results of, 163; visits to miners by, 98–101
Battle of Blair Mountain. *See* Blair Mountain, battle of
Beckley, W. Va., 144
Beech Creek, W. Va., 103–05, 106, 117, 119, 125
Bennett, Oscar, 23

Big Coal River, 79, 83, 86. *See also* Little Coal River; Spruce Fork
Blacks: in battle, 109, 126, 127; as casualties, 78, 124; exclusion of from jury, 44; exclusion of from militia, 57; as immigrants, xvii, 11; leaders among, 135; at march origin, 4, 6, 7–8, 77, 78; prejudice against, 152
Blair, W. Va., 86, 92–93, 120–21, 161
Blair Mountain, W. Va., 86, 103, 107, 119, 155; battle of, 119–41, 125–26, 153–54; defenses on, 81, 82, 97, 117
Blizzard, Bill, 3, 5, 75, 77; and Bandholz, 98–99; as leader, 53, 135–36; at Matewan, 16; with Mother Jones, 78–79; with soldiers, 150–52; trial of, 165
Bluefield, W. Va., 115, 163
Booher, A. J., 23, 47
Boomer, W. Va., 77, 108
Boone County, W. Va., 83, 108
Borderland, W. Va., 30, 39
Bowles, James A., 59–60, 62–63
Bowman, William, 22, 45
Boxley (mayor of Roanoke), 142
Brady, James J., 157
Breedlove, Alexander, 59–60, 62–63
Brewer, Isaac, 24, 43, 45–47, 138
Brinkman, Jack, 96–97, 109, 124

Brockus, J. R., 30, 38, 65, 162; and martial law enforcement, 58–61; organization of militia by, 55–56; in Sharples battle, 102–05; in Three Days battle, 51–53
Brown, Arthur R., 145
Burgraff, Fred, 31, 36, 45, 166
Burkinshaw, Neil, 65
Burnwell, W. Va., 16

Cabin Creek, W. Va., 8, 99, 101
Cabin Creek Junction, W. Va., 6
Cantley, U. S., 5, 77
Carpenter, J. W., 55
Casualties, in mine war, 127–28, 129, 133–34, 161. See also Chafin's army; Miners' army
Central Competitive Field, xiv
Chafin, Don, 75, 81–82, 140, 157; in battle, 90, 97, 125; as hero, 163, 164; later life of, 167; middle-class backing of, xvi; slogans of, 77, 81, 108, 114, 164. See also Chafin's army
Chafin, Harry, 67
Chafin's army: casualties in, 124, 138, 139, 153; defensive positions of, 117, 119; demobilization of, 161–62; discipline of, 118; organization of, 81–83, 114–18; reinforcement of, 102–03; return of to front, 97
Chambers, Ed, 21, 30; funeral of, 72–74; murder of, 68–71; and Sid Hatfield, 31, 35, 50; trial of, 45
Chambers, Reece, 23, 30, 43, 166
Chambers, Sallie, 47, 68–71, 72–74, 167
Chambers, "Uncle Eb," 68
Charleston, W. Va., 3, 10; aircraft at, 84, 94, 144–46; Bandholz's operations at, 86, 98, 149, 163; Chafin's army at, 116; mass meetings at, 53, 75; panic in, 9
Charleston Gazette, 83–84

Charnock, John (adjutant general), 98–99, 111–12, 115
Charnock, John (son), 118
Chesapeake & Ohio Railroad. See Railroads
Christian, George, 54
Clark, Cecil, 105, 106
Clothier, W. Va., 75, 95, 102–05, 109, 152
Coal Age, 39
Coal camps, xi, xvii
Coal industry: in nation, xi–xv; in West Virginia, xv–xviii; in Tug Valley, 11, 29, 35; violence in, xv–xvi, 4–5, 8, 29–30, 38–39, 58–63, 170
Coal operators, 14, 29, 90–91, 166
Coal River. See Big Coal River; Little Coal River; Spruce Fork
Coal River Hellcats, 5
Cofago, John, 123–24
Comiskey (IWW member), 140
Communists, 163, 171
Congress. See Senate investigation
Conniff, John J., 42–49
Cornwell, John J., 26, 31, 33, 38–39
Cox, James M., 34
Coyle, George, 157
Craig, Donald, 154
Craigo, Romeo, 133, 135
Crooked Creek, 82
Crooked Creek Mountain, 117, 125
Crooked Creek Pass, 137
Crum, George A., 58
Cunningham, C. B., 23
Curley, Paul, 93

Damron, James, 42
Danville, W. Va., 86, 91, 93, 95, 96
Davis, James J., 156
Davis, Thomas B., 57–62, 102
Dooley, Manuel, 134
Drawdy Creek, W. Va., 86, 87, 108
Dry Branch, W. Va., 4, 108
Duling, George, 118

East Bank, W. Va., 68

Edwight, W. Va., 4–5, 108

Eighty-eighth Air Squadron, 142–46

Embry, S. P., 109

Estep, French, 107, 108

Ethyl, W. Va., 86, 103, 118

Eubanks, William E., 117, 118, 137, 153–54

Evictions, 16, 20–21, 46

Fayette Tribune, 144

Federal troops, 32, 38–41, 84, 131. *See also* Fortieth Infantry; Twenty-sixth Infantry

Felts, Albert, 16, 19; death of, 22–24; funeral of, 26; mention of in trial, 45, 46

Felts, Lee, 19, 22–24, 26, 45

Felts, Tom, 18, 26, 51

Ferguson, J. W., 24, 45, 47

Fitzpatrick, William S., 145

Ford, Stanley H., 98, 101, 131, 149

Fortieth Infantry, 153

Freeburn, Ky., 30

Gaujot, Tony, 157–59

George's Mountain, W. Va., 97

Gillespie, P. D., 79

Glen Jean, W. Va., 4, 108

Gompers, Samuel, 156

Gooslin, Ambrose, 52

Gordon, Charlie "Popcorn," 135

Gore, Elbert, 110, 123, 140

Gore, John, 123–24, 165

Gough, Richard, 138

Greer, William, 105, 106

Greever, Bob, 139

Griffith, D. M., 109, 161

Guinn, William, 78

Gunnoe, George, 31

Guyan Valley, W. Va., 82

Hall, Fred, 133

Hall, Herman, 39, 43

Hallinan, Walter, 97

Harbord, James G., 91

Harding, Warren G., 34, 46; cabinet of, 91; martial law considered by, 53, 111–13; proclamation of, 130–31; and requests for troops, 53, 84, 112, 131

Harliss, W. F., 127

Hastings, Frank, 133

Hatfield, Anse, 19, 21, 31, 44

Hatfield, Henry D., 128, 131

Hatfield, Jessie. *See* Testerman, Jessie

Hatfield, Sid: bribe attempts on, 16, 26; early life of, 10–13; fame of, 25, 50, 61–62; fear of for life, 51, 66–67; funeral of, 72–74, 167; indictment of, 30, 31; as law officer, 15, 31, 50, 62; marriage of, 26–28, 50; murder of, 4, 5, 7–9, 68–71, 74–75, 77, 107, 167; political life of, 15, 26, 34; and Senate hearing, 64, 66–67; as subject of injunctions, 36–37; and Three Days battle, 52–53; trial of, 42–49

Hatfield, William, 67, 70, 74

Hatfields and McCoys, xv, 10, 26, 44

Hazelton, Alexander, 145–46

Hewitt Creek, W. Va., 119, 125

Higgins, Troy, 22, 47

Hildebrand, C. B., 24

Holbrook, J. C., 73

Hollingsworth, I. C., 137

Holt, Savoy, 3, 4, 5, 77, 135

Houston, Harold, 38, 42, 47, 64, 84, 167

Howard, Walter B., 145

Howard Colliery, W. Va., 32

Hulme, Samuel, 126

Iaeger, W. Va., 68

Indian Creek, W. Va., 79–80

Industrial Workers of the World (IWW), 140, 163

International News Service, 154, 157

Jacobs, H. D. "Al," 154, 155

Jarrell, Clarence, 134

Jeffrey, W. Va., 109, 151–52
Johnson, Davenport, 143
Johnson, Hiram, 62–63
Jones, Mary (Mother Jones), 16; and fake telegram, 78–79; and Sid Hatfield's death, 74–75; speeches of, 16–18, 19, 35; as subject of injunctions, 36
Justice, Martin, 36, 60

Kackley, Charles M., 58
Keeney, Frank, 4, 9, 16, 29, 36, 65, 130; ballpark speech of, 86–89; and Bandholz, 98; jailing of, 165–66; and Mother Jones, 78; relations of to Sid Hatfield, 67, 75; rumors concerning, 63
Kelly, Charley, 20
Kelly's Creek, W. Va., 4, 108
Kemp, Eli, 124
Kentucky, 58
Kentucky National Guard, 30, 53
Kenyon, William S., 64
Kermit, W. Va., 39
Kirkpatrick, Jim, 68–70
Kitchin, Henry, 124
Koontz, Arthur, 34

Laurel City, W. Va., 4
Lavinder, A. D., 57–58
Lawson, Captain, 137
Lens Creek, W. Va., 3–9, 76, 77–78
Lewis, John L., 13–14, 26, 36, 60–61, 156
Lick Creek tent colony. *See* Tent colonies, Lick Creek
Little Coal River, 75, 82, 86. *See also* Big Coal River; Spruce Fork
Lively, Charlie, 9; as Baldwin-Felts spy, 33; later life of, 166–67; at Senate hearing, 64–65; and Sid Hatfield's murder, 68–71, 74; at trial, 45–46, 47; and UMWA, 50–51
Logan, W. Va., 81, 86, 103, 116–17, 125, 153, 163

Logan Banner, 83, 90
Logan County, W. Va., 81, 83–85, 90–91, 107
Longacre, W. Va., 4, 108
Lynn Company Store, 58–59

McCorkle, W. A., 112, 131
McCoy, J. C., 48, 52
McCoys (family), 10. *See also* Hatfields and McCoys
McDowell, John, 22, 44
McDowell County, W. Va., 29–30, 60, 69, 114–15
McGuire (no first name), 78
McKellar, Senator, 65–66
McMillion, William, 58–59
Madison, W. Va., 86, 87–89, 91–92, 96, 149
Marcum, John S., 42, 47–48
Marfork, W. Va., 4
Marmet, W. Va., 76–77
Martial law, 53–54, 56, 112–13, 120, 130–31, 156
Martin, C. A., 151, 160–61
Matewan, W. Va., 12–13; Battle of, 19–24, 25–26; and battle trial, 42–49, 50–51; defendants from, 30, 42–44, 166, 174; federal troops in, 39; and Three Days Battle, 51–52
Medley, Charles A., 94–96
Mifflin, W. Va., 106
Milliken, L. F., 122, 124, 127, 128
Mill Creek, W. Va., 117, 119, 125
Miner, Valentine S., 144
Miners: background of, 6; guerilla warfare tactics among, 30, 38, 51–54; as immigrants, xvii, 11, 104; strikes by, 14, 29, 35, 166
Miners' army: appearance of, 3, 134; on Big Coal River, 79, 86; bombing of, 126, 139–40, 146, 163, 181; casualties of, 78, 124, 133, 134; character of, 100; commandeering of vehicles by, 79–80, 95, 108–09, 126–27, 132,

Miners' army (*cont.*)
153; discipline of, xvii–xviii, 8, 134; food service of, 132, 136; formation of, 3–9, 120, 179; indictment of, 165; and lack of leadership, xviii, 5, 135–36; at Lens Creek, 76–77; relation of to federal troops, 147; strength of, 130; surrender by, 160–64; veterans among, xviii, 3; "victory" of, 164
Mine wars, xi, 165–66
Mingo County, W. Va., 3–9, 14, 53; martial law in, 56–63; and militia, 55–56, 115; miners jailed in, 164; violence in, 38–39, 50–53
Mitchell, Billy, xviii, 94, 142, 145, 146, 181. *See also* Air service
Mohawk, W. Va., 30, 32, 66–67
Montcoal, W. Va., 4
Montgomery, Samuel B., 34, 66–67, 73–74
Mooney, Fred, 58, 65, 75, 78, 86–89, 130, 165–66
Mooresburg, Tenn., 144
Morgan, Ephraim, 34, 46, 60–61, 74; and Bandholz, 86, 130, 131; and calls for volunteers, 116; and establishment of National Guard, 117; and federal troops, 53, 84, 111, 112, 131; and martial law, 56; and police, 102
Morris, Mildred, 154, 157
Morrison, William M., 105, 106
Morrow, Governor, 53
Mullins, Bob, 23, 26
Mullins, W.H.B., 109, 130
Munsey, Dee, 5, 75, 135
Munsie, Jim, 123–24
Murray, Philip, 60–61, 131

Nation, The, 9
National Guard. *See* Kentucky National Guard; West Virginia National Guard
News reporters, 7, 9; and freedom of the press, 156–59; in Mingo

News reporters (*cont.*)
County, 39–40; and Sid Hatfield, 61–62; stories of, 162; at trial, 43, 48
New York Herald, 154
New York Times, 40, 61, 62, 115, 140
New York Tribune, 154
New York World, 39
Nineteenth Infantry Regiment, 39–41, 84, 113, 137, 148–53
Nolan, W. Va., 58
Norfolk & Western Railroad, 10

Ostfriesland, 94

Page, Ben, 35, 36, 44
Paint Creek, W. Va., 98, 101, 107
Passwords, 80, 88, 92, 117, 123–24, 162
Petry, Bill, 82, 130, 131
Petry, Chris, 77–78
Peytona, W. Va., 86, 87
Philadelphia Inquirer, 157
Philadelphia Public Ledger, 43
Pinson, C. C., 56, 61
Pocahontas Coalfield, 36
Pond Creek mines, 35, 37–38
Porter, A. C., 111–12, 120
Powell, E. O., 23, 47
Prisoners: of Chafin's army, 140–41; of miners' army, 109–10, 126, 141; of state police, 104, 105

Racine, W. Va., 79, 87, 99
Railroads, xiii, 130, 148–53. *See also* Miners' army, commandeering of vehicles by; Norfolk & Western Railroad
Raleigh County, W. Va., 108
Reade, George W., 54
Red Jacket, W. Va., 18
Red Jacket Coal Co., 36
Refugees, 106, 107, 111–12, 161
Reporters. *See* News reporters

Reynolds, Ed, 77, 79–80, 91, 133, 135
Roanoke, Va., 142–44
Roanoke Times, 143–44
Roberts, James, 133
Roderfield, W. Va., 68

Sanders, Joseph J., 42, 48, 51
Savage, Joe W., 116–17, 138–39, 162
Senate investigation, 62–63, 64–67
Shanks, David, 137
Sharples, W. Va., 86, 102–05, 106–10, 152
Shuttleworth, C. A., 153
Sizemore, Jerry, 138–39
Slavin, Lant, 55
Smart, Charles T., 151–52
Sovereign, W. Va., 106
Sparkes, Boyden, 154–55, 157–59
Speck, Harry L., 145
Spruce Fork, 82, 86, 92–93. *See also* Big Coal River; Little Coal River
State police. *See* West Virginia State Police
Staton, Harry C., 51–52
Stone Mountain Coal Company, 19–20, 52
Stoner, Rex K., 142–43
Strikes. *See* Miners, strikes by
Strother, James French, 67
Sullivan, Jessie V., 99
Sutherland, Senator, 112
Sutphin, Emory, 133

Tent colonies, 28, 39–41, 166; at Lick Creek, 36, 40, 59–60, 62–63; raids on, 59–60
Testerman, C. C., 13, 15; as cited in trial, 45–46, 48; death of, 19–24; funeral of, 26. *See also* Testerman, Jessie
Testerman, Jessie, 27; at Battle of Matewan, 24; at funeral, 72–74; relations of with Sid Hatfield, 28, 30, 50, 67; at Sid's murder, 68–71; at trial, 42, 48

Thacker, W. Va., 32, 38, 68
Thompson, C. F., 53–54, 84–85; and Bandholz, 86, 98–101, 131; at Blair, 120–22; and federal troops, 149, 153
Thompson, "Red," 127, 135
Three Days Battle, 51–53, 55
Thurmond, Walter R., 125
Tinsley, Tot, 23, 26
Trains. *See* Railroads
Treason, 136, 165, 166
Trial, Matewan battle. *See* Matewan, and battle trial
Tug River Valley, W. Va., 10, 14, 28, 166
Twenty-sixth Infantry, 113, 137, 149, 161

UMW Journal, 50, 74
United Mine Workers of America (UMWA), Charleston office of, 25, 74; injunctions of, 36–38, 39; and lawsuits, 36–37, 166; and Lively, 51; in Mingo County, 15, 28–29, 32; origin of, xii–xiv, 12; Williamson office of, 60. *See also* Lewis, John L.
United Press International, 154, 157

Van Fleet, C. J., 68–69
Vaughan, Manley, 58
Vinson, Z. T., 65
Vulcan, W. Va., 68

Waddill, Edmund, Jr., 37–38
Wade, W. B., 109
Wainwright, J. Mayhew, 91
Waldron, C. W., 134–35
Walker, Henry, 7
War Eagle Coal Company, 58
Weeks, John W., 53, 54, 85, 91; and martial law, 111–12; optimism of, 156
Welch, W. Va., 66–69
West Virginia legislature, 31, 51, 112

West Virginia National Guard, 7,
51, 84, 112, 117–18
West Virginia State Police, 7, 26, 38–
39, 84; and Chafin's army, 125;
and reporters, 155; at Sharples,
102–05; size of, 51
West Virginia Supreme Court of
Appeals, 36–37
Wharncliff, W. Va., 68
Wheeling Intelligencer, 67, 74
White, "Bad Lewis," 92, 102, 135; and
commandeering of train, 95–96;
as custodian of prisoners, 110, 126
White, Jim, 133
White, Oscar, 140
Whitesville, W. Va., 5, 77, 109
Whitt, Dan, 52

Wilburn, John, 123, 165
Wilburn, John E., 122–24, 135, 165
Wilder, Ike, 56
Wiley, William M., 107, 136
Williams, Art, 22–23, 45
Williams, G. C., 132
Williamson, W. Va., 18, 28, 29, 37,
39, 55–56, 60–61
Wilson, John J., 148–53
Wilson, Woodrow, 26
Wobblies. *See* Industrial Workers of
the World
Woodsill, Samuel, 148

Yates, John, 38
"Yaller Dog" contracts, 14, 36
Young, Howard, 141